W9-BCF-793

05934

HILLYER
In pursuit of poetry

In Pursuit of Poetry

Books by Robert Hillyer

Poetry

Eight Harvard Poets
Sonnets and Other Lyrics
The Five Books of Youth
Alchemy
The Hills Give Promise
The Halt in the Garden
The Seventh Hill
The Gates of the Compass
Collected Verse of Robert Hillyer
A Letter to Robert Frost and Others
In Time of Mistrust
Pattern of a Day
Poems for Music
The Death of Captain Nemo
The Suburb by the Sea
The Relic and Other Poems

Drama

The Engagement Ring
The Masquerade

Fiction

The Happy Episode
Riverhead
My Heart for Hostage

Translations

A Book of Danish Verse
The Coming Forth by Day

General

First Principles of Verse
In Pursuit of Poetry

IN
PURSUIT
OF
POETRY

Robert Hillyer

McGraw-Hill Book Company, Inc.
NEW YORK   TORONTO   LONDON

IN PURSUIT OF POETRY

TO MY WIFE
without whose patient collaboration this book would
not have come into existence

Foreword

Poetry attempts to seize thoughts and emotions from the flow of time and shape them into something more lasting and beautiful than they were in the ordinary course of human experience. Observation and memory play equal parts in the selection of the thought and emotion, while the imagination, working at fiery intensity, selects one element to be expressed and burns away all irrelevant material that clings to it. At the same time, the poet is starting to frame the theme in words, heightening and condensing them, and setting them to a recurrent rhythm, a repetition of emphasis, such as we find at the basis of all natural things, the rotation of the planets, the ebb and flow of the sea, the turning of the seasons, the beat of our own hearts. The Universe has a vast rhythm of its own, to which the poet's ear is like a shell echoing the waves of the sea.

The feeling that man has lost his bright destiny in the confusion of the material world is the inspiring disappointment that spurs on creative temperaments to recapture at least the semblance of perfection. Epic or lyric, love sonnet or folk song, ballad or satire, all poetry seeks to establish the importance of each moment in the experience and growth of mankind. When we speak of the literature of an age or a country we instinctively mean its poetry; comparatively little prose survives beyond its generation. Poetry is the essence; prose the accident.

The ideal reader of poetry would be familiar with the poetry of the past as well as the present, and he would know something about the technique of the art. He cannot hope to develop taste from a few selections or from many works from a single period, especially his own. He should also know something of the technique of verse, which is as delicate and elaborate as orchestration. Music, to which poetry is allied, has a double set of artists, the composers and the interpreters. It takes a trained performer to change the black dots that the composer provides into the sounds that he intended the audience to hear. But poetry looks deceptively easy. Instead of black dots we see English words, and therefore it would seem that reading it would require no special skill. But it does. In classical and mediaeval times there were trained speakers and chanters of verse. Every Elizabethan was accomplished in singing the lyric verse of his time.

The reader is forewarned that the language of poetry is condensed and that he must listen for the overtones or suggestions as well as the literal meaning. He should then be able to understand the lines unless the poet is willfully obscure. But since poetry is an art primarily for the ear rather than the eye, he may have trouble with the metrics and rhythms. Hence, although there is no occasion for him to learn metrics in detail, he should be able to study the text with some understanding of its manifold structure, to school himself to observe the different lengths of the vowels, the pauses that correspond to rests in music, and the varying strength of accents, or stresses.

It is my intention to discuss and explain many such phenomena. I shall then trace the history and principles of the various metrical and stanzaic forms that have developed in our language through the centuries. Lastly, from my own point of view and indulging myself freely in my own preferences and prejudices, I shall give a brief critical account of important poets and poetical movements from Chaucer to the present.

Acknowledgments

Mr. A. S. Burack and The Writer Company for passages from my *First Principles of Verse,* a handbook for poets

President Stewart H. Smith of Marshall College for passages from my Scott Lecture No. 1, delivered at that institution

Mr. Howard Nemerov for passages from his *Mirrors and Windows* and *The Salt Garden*

Mr. E. E. Cummings and Harcourt, Brace and Company for passages from his *Poems 1923–1954*

The Clarendon Press, Oxford, for passages from *The Poetical Works of Robert Bridges*

Mrs. James Stephens and The Macmillan Company of London and The Macmillan Company of New York for a poem from the *Collected Poems of James Stephens*

The Trustees of the Hardy Estate and The Macmillan Company of London and The Macmillan Company of New York for passages from the *Collected Poems of Thomas Hardy*

The Devin-Adair Company for passages from the *Collected Poems of Oliver St. John Gogarty*

Mr. Ralph Hodgson, Macmillan Company, Ltd., and St. Martin's Press, Inc., for a passage from Mr. Hodgson's new book, *The Skylark and Other Poems*

Charles Scribner's Sons for "As in the Midst of Battle there is Room" from *Poems* by George Santayana

Charles Scribner's Sons for passages from *A Swimmer in the Air* copyright 1957 by Howard Moss and used by permission of Charles Scribner's Sons, and a passage from "Cry from Montauk" by Howard Moss, first published in *The New Yorker* (copyright 1948 by Howard Moss) and reprinted from *The Toy Fair* by Howard Moss with the permission of Charles Scribner's Sons

Contents

Foreword   vii

PART I   *The Magic of Words*   I

PART II *The Elements of Verse*   31
    Meter and Rhythm   31
    Metrical Irregularities   34
    The Length of Lines   38
    Adornments   38
    How to Read Verse Aloud   41
    Stanza Forms   52
    The Ode   77
    Blank Verse   80
    Some French Forms   83
    The Sonnet   88
    The Kinds of Poetry   114

PART III *A Brief Survey of the Background
of Poetry in English*   119

PART IV *Poetry in the Twentieth Century*   172
    Some Recommended Reading   219
    Index   223

In Pursuit of Poetry

PART I *The Magic of Words*

I have called this book *In Pursuit of Poetry* to indicate that the essential spirit of poetry is always on the wing and indefinable. No one can communicate the exact effect of a poem any more than a poet can describe the exact moment when the idea for a poem swung into his mind. "How do you write a poem? Is it a sudden inspiration or do you sit down and say to yourself that you're going to write a poem?" How many times I have been asked that question in almost precisely those words. There is no answer, of course. Every poem has its own method of coming to birth, sometimes by long labor, and occasionally by a quick impulse so overmastering that the result is a kind of divine dictation. The same variety of mood applies to the reception of a poem by a reader.

Music, dancing, and poetry are the oldest of the arts and came into being before the dawn of history, moving to the recurrent rhythms of Nature itself. The most ancient poems that survive from Egypt, China, and the Old Testament speak to us clearly from the heart of our remotest forerunners. In the words of Walter Savage Landor:

> Past ruin'd Ilion Helen lives,
>   Alcestis rises from the shades;
> Verse calls them forth; 'tis verse that gives
>   Immortal youth to mortal maids.

Poetry is the one unbroken thread between us and the past; from vanished cities and civilizations this common utterance links us with the heroism and piety, the loves and festivals—all that has gone before, unchanged and ever renewed.

So long as men can breathe, or eyes can see,
So long lives this, and this gives life to thee.

"With this key," says Wordsworth, "Shakespeare unlock'd his heart."
We might say of poetry in general, "With this key Mankind unlock'd
his heart." The reader responds with his *memory*, in which are experiences and emotions similar to those expressed in the poem, and
with his *imagination*, which is stimulated by rhythm and phrasing.

A good poem can be read again and again and still hold something
in reserve for the next reading. The Greek philosopher Heraclitus
observed, "One cannot step twice into the same river." The water
of the river has changed, we have changed, the seasons have changed;
everything is in flux. With each new reading of a poem life has
flowed past us, the landscape around us is different, and we are never
twice in exactly the same mood. Also, memories of former readings
add their special gloss of associations to the printed text. Harold
Nicolson, in one of his reminiscent sketches, describes how, during
his last year at school, the Master recited a passage from Virgil to a
group of boys sitting on the lawn in the summer evening. "The warm
sun was slanting through the pine trees. The soft and solemn hexameters rolled on." The passage was from the sixth book of the
Aeneid, that touching and beautiful conversation between Aeneas
and his father in the Underworld. In later years, Nicolson could not
detach the beauty of the lines from the enchantment of the summer
evening long past, and they were woven into the memory of his
boyhood. Such associations are common with all of us. The trouble
today is that we do not give these associations a chance to form.
There is so little reading of poetry nowadays. One reason for the
decline of appreciation is the fact that poetry is so seldom read in
family groups any more, or among teachers and pupils as a recreation
rather than as an assignment. And then, of course, so few people
know how to read aloud.

In the mingling of music and sense with our own response at the
heightened moment that art provides, we pass through the poetic
experience never twice the same. Since human emotions remain the
same through the centuries, a lyric from the remotest past speaks
to us with a present voice, and the years between seem to dissolve.
"A homesick shepherd, I wade into the river to watch the fishes who
come swimming from the north where my country lies." There

speaks the Egyptian exile. And again, from ancient Egypt, "There was never anyone, who, having departed, was able to carry away his possessions with him."

Homesickness in its various forms is a pervasive element of our life and of our art, and exemplifies that concentration of the moment which is at the heart of poetry. We are always searching for a country we have never seen and loves we have never known.

> Forlorn! the very word is like a bell
> To toll me back from thee to my sole self!

says Keats at the end of his *Ode to a Nightingale*. Where had he been whence he did not want to return to the actualities of life? Somewhere in a forest beyond the world "through verdurous glooms and winding mossy ways," opened to him by the song of the nightingale. And even his faery lands brought him at last to the margin of "perilous seas forlorn." But for a moment he had been beyond the bounds of everyday, and he affirmed in his ode the existence of another world governed by fancy and imagination.

With the current of time we see everything flowing away, and we begin to understand that in the ephemeral quality of our world lies its dearest charm. Mankind is born to discontent, divine discontent, as it is often called. If his dreams were translated into reality, then he would push forward yet farther into another dream.

The modern Danish poet, winner of the Nobel prize, Johannes V. Jensen, in his poem on Christopher Columbus, made the point that as soon as Columbus discovered his western world, his dream was destroyed. I have translated one of the stanzas thus:

> For when he discovers the saving isle,
>   his visions flee.
> A new world is wedged between his soul and
>   the ultimate sea.
> And turning back, embracing the ocean,
> He bears in his heart, forever burning,
> The burden of the wandering billows,
>   the freight of eternal yearning.

It is not the tragedy of life that youth passes, that flowers fade, that the seasons fold away into autumn; tragedy lies in the failure to live the present to the full, to seize on the beauty of life as it passes.

As Walter Pater says, in the famous sentence in his *Renaissance,* "To burn always with this hard, gemlike flame, to maintain this ecstasy, is success in life."

> He who bends to himself a joy
> Doth the winged life destroy;
> But he who kisses the joy as it flies
> Lives in eternity's sunrise.

So writes William Blake. And Horace, in one of his best-loved odes: *Carpe diem, quam minimum credula postero:* "Seize on the day; there is little trust to be put in the future." This mood is so frequent in poetry that we may well call it the theme of *carpe diem.* An ancient Egyptian advises

> Enjoy yourself more than you have ever done.

There is Shakespeare's

> What is love? 'tis not hereafter;
> Present mirth hath present laughter;
>   What's to come is still unsure:
> In delay there lies no plenty;
> Then come kiss me, sweet and twenty,
>   Youth's a stuff will not endure.

There is Herrick's

> Gather ye rosebuds while ye may,
> Old Time is still a-flying.

And Robert Frost's

> Earth's the right place for love:
> I don't know where it's likely to go better.

And there are hundreds of other examples. But *carpe diem* has an undertone of melancholy; the present is passing, passing swiftly. The Egyptians handed around a skull among the banquet guests to make them appreciate their good luck in being alive.

The homesickness which we find in a large body of romantic poetry, for the Eden that lies behind us and the gardens of the Hesperides that lie before, we might call evocative poetry. Sometimes, at its most extreme, it depends on music and imagery alone, and this we might call *incantational* poetry. At the opposite extreme, there is the poetry of statement, wit, and epigram, as in the couplets of Alexander Pope.

Let us take examples of the two extremes, incantational and epigrammatic poetry. First, the incantational, Coleridge's *Kubla Khan:*

> In Xanadu did Kubla Khan
> A stately pleasure-dome decree:
> Where Alph, the sacred river, ran
> Through caverns measureless to man
>> Down to a sunless sea.
> So twice five miles of fertile ground
> With walls and towers were girdled round:
> And here were gardens bright with sinuous rills,
> Where blossomed many an incense-bearing tree;
> And here were forests ancient as the hills,
> Enfolding sunny spots of greenery....

At the opposite extreme, take the following passage from Pope's *Essay on Criticism,* wherein the neatness of the phrasing is wedded to the strict heroic (that is to say, classical) couplet:

> True Wit is Nature to advantage dress'd,
> What oft was thought, but ne'er so well express'd;
> Something whose truth convinced at sight we find,
> That gives us back the image of our mind.
> As shades more sweetly recommend the light,
> So modest plainness sets off sprightly wit....

We should not wish poetry to be confined to Coleridge's suggestive incantation or Pope's exquisite statement; these are the opposite bounds of poetry, and between lie numberless gradations of song and epigram. In passing, we note the existence of many an incantational passage in Dryden, the neoclassic poet, such as this:

> All, all of a piece throughout,
> Thy chase had a Beast in view,
> Thy wars brought nothing about,
> Thy lovers were all untrue.
> 'Tis well an old age is out,
> And time to begin a new.

Thus poetry may move not only through the supernatural evocations of Coleridge and the old ballads that inspired him, not only in Shelley's vision of the bright Athens that shall arise when the golden years return, but also in the commonest objects we see around us, touched to a momentary glory by the poet's attention. According to an old fragment, "Love and the street stones will light their hidden lamps for you; when you see the light you are on the path home." Or, as Wordsworth remarks in *The Prelude:*

> Not like a temple rich with pomp and gold
> But a mere mountain chapel that protects
> Its simple worshippers from sun and shower.
> Of these, said I, shall be my song; of these,
> If future years mature me for the task,
> Will I recall the praises, making verse
> Deal boldly with substantial things. . . .

Later in the century, Walt Whitman bade his Muse migrate from Greece and Ionia and take her place "Smiling and pleas'd, with palpable intent to stay . . . install'd amid the kitchen-ware!"

Robert Frost's poetry often illustrates the transmutation of familiar events and landscapes into symbols of man and his drama on the stage of time. This revelation of the eternal in the familiar is one of the most important aspects of poetry. Emily Dickinson expresses this idea with consummate skill:

> Eden is that old-fashioned house
> We dwell in every day,
> Without suspecting our abode
> Until we drive away.
> How fair, on looking back, the day
> We sauntered from the door,
> Unconscious our returning
> Discover it no more.

Every subject in the world is open to poetic treatment, and by its very nature poetry exalts everything it touches upon. If a sordid effect be conveyed by a poem, there has been a grave mistake somewhere; or if a platitude remain a platitude when expressed in verse, we cannot call that poetry. The poet's task is to raise a mortal to the skies or draw an angel down (to borrow Dryden's phrasing). He presents his material intensely, in concentrated and heightened form. The true poetic temperament is that faculty that feels the most ordinary events of life as something wonderful and interesting, the most ordinary routine of life as something beautiful and significant. It may be that the poet's nerves are strung tighter, that his imagination is more active than others'. Without losing sight of reality, the poet observes it with a greater excitement than others do. In like manner, he uses the same words as everybody else, but in rarer and more suggestive combinations. To invoke metaphor: the poet is the stained-glass window that transmits sunlight just as ordinary windows do, but colors it as it passes through. And the poet should rest content with that; no man is great enough to be both the window and the sunlight. And no man should be so perverse as to be merely a distorting glass.

Unfortunately, many poets of our time do function as a distorting glass, and the resultant obscurity and queerness have alienated the general reader from poetry. The ambition to be "original" (in the false sense) has induced many versifiers to adopt strange diction and bizarre forms. The modernist who regards his own thoughts as too vast to be "trammeled" by traditional forms has much to prove. As Robert Frost has often remarked, "Free verse is playing tennis with the net down." Or we might say that it is a river the banks of which are removed so that it spreads out without restraint into a marsh. If every writer is to be a law unto himself, criticism, and even the expression of opinion, is superfluous.

Free verse, the metaphysical style, the struggle between convention and innovation—such phenomena are by no means new. The controversy between the Ancients and the Moderns, which so enlivened the first decades of this century, has one of its monuments in Swift's *Battle of the Books* and goes back at least as far as Aristophanes' attacks on Euripides. The contrived phrasing and fancy diction favored by some contemporary poets have their counterparts not only in the Euphuists of Elizabeth's time, but well over a thousand years earlier among the groups of poetasters and grammarians who quipped and punned in the portico of the great library at Alexandria.

Gibbon's account of the poets of tenth-century Constantinople applies with almost painful accuracy to the obscurantist writings of our own day: "In every page our taste and reason are wounded by the choice of gigantic and obsolete words, a stiff and intricate phraseology, the discord of images, the childish play of false or unseasonable ornament, and the painful attempt to elevate themselves, to astonish the reader, and to involve a trivial meaning in the smoke of obscurity and exaggeration ... their poetry is sinking below the flatness and insipidity of prose ... they forgot even the rules of prosody." Thus, at different periods through the centuries, the desire to be strikingly original has distorted or abandoned the technique of verse.

If poetry is the soul, the techinque of verse (which will be dealt with more explicitly later) is the body. As John Donne says,

> Love's mysteries in souls do grow,
> And yet the body is his book.

In general, it may be said that the good poet loses himself in the theme he is contemplating and the discipline for its expression. This escape from self in the creation of a work of art is the greatest joy that life can afford the poet; the triumph over the obstacles of expression produces an excitement in which, delighted with some sounding line or expert turn of phrase, the reader may share.

> I love all beauteous things,
>   I seek and adore them;
> God hath no better praise,
> And man in his hasty days
>   Is honoured for them.
>
> I too will something make
>   And joy in the making;
> Altho' tomorrow it seem
> Like the empty words of a dream
>   Remembered on waking.

In these lines Robert Bridges celebrates the pleasures of creation. A poet, according to the Greek root of the word, is a *maker*.

Intricate though verse seems, it is a more natural form of expression than prose. Verse means a turning, and since the turn must come full circle on itself, we speak of it as a repeating, or recurrent, rhythm, just as in music. Prose rhythm is non-recurrent; hence, verse is more natural because it is closer to the rhythms of the universe—and note that *universe* means a concerted turning. We walk, we breathe, our hearts beat in recurrence; the sun and moon, the stars in their courses, the changing seasons—all these are recurrent: we are metrical creatures in a metrical universe. That is why, in every literature, great poetry precedes great prose, sometimes, as in Greece, by centuries.

In verse the smallest recurrent unit is the metrical foot; the next largest is the line length, and the largest of all is the stanza (sometimes called the strophe). In much of our poetry a set rhyme-scheme, repeated from stanza to stanza, adds another strong recurrent effect. Sometimes we find the repetition of a line or part of a line, and this we call a refrain. It is usually found in the folk ballad, in song poetry, and in the so-called French forms, such as the ballade or rondeau.

One measure of a poet's skill lies in his manipulation of the various shades of diction. Some words are prosaic, or "flat" and have no extra significance beyond their literal meaning as in the dictionary. But a large proportion of the words in any language imply emotions or ideas quite apart from their literal meanings. These implications we call suggestions or overtones and much of the effect of poetry resides in them. They cannot be transferred from one language into another; that is why no poetry in translation can wholly re-create the effect of the original.

Let us take a compound without overtones, a flat word: *lampshade*. Although it is flat, it is composed of two words that have strong overtones. Consider all the secondary meanings implied by the word *lamp,* by the word *shade*. To go further, take the word *rose*. I would venture a guess that nine times out of ten when a poet uses this word he means not the common or garden variety of rose, but that metaphorical flower that suggests love or passion or the ephemeral quality of earthly desire, or, as the *rosa sine spina,* the Queen of Heaven herself. Or consider the word *cross*. It has lost its basic meaning of the instrument for the execution of criminals and become the symbol of a religion. History and myth have made many objects and proper names take on symbolic overtones, such as the Crown, the hammer-and-sickle, the Grail, Sir Galahad, Helen of Troy, and so forth. Many birds and beasts have become symbolic, the eagle, the serpent, the lamb, the dove, among others. Poets are always creating new symbols by the context of their poetry, and thus Masefield chooses the Norwegian lemmings, that periodically, for no known reason, rush westward and fling themselves into the sea, as the symbol of Mankind's journey toward the unknown. He uses the words *westward* and *drown* with increasing significance to enhance the parallel:

> Once in a hundred years the Lemmings come
> Westward, in search of food over the snow,
> Westward, until the salt sea drowns them dumb,
> Westward, till all are drowned, those Lemmings go.
>
> Once, it is thought, there was a westward land,
> (Now drowned) where there was food for those starved things,
> And memory of the place has burnt its brand
> In the little brains of all the Lemming Kings.
>
> Perhaps, long since, there was a land beyond,
> Westward from death, some city, some calm place,
> Where one could taste God's quiet and be fond
> With the little beauty of a human face;
>
> But now the land is drowned, yet still we press
> Westward, in search, to death, to nothingness.

In the last six lines of the poem, the animals have been transformed into human beings, who still press on toward death though their faith in the afterlife has long since been drowned. Many flowers, such as the rose and the lily, have long been touched with symbolism, and again, the poets often invest some less celebrated bloom with added meaning, as in the first stanza of William Blake's *Sunflower*:

> Ah, Sunflower, weary of time,
>   That countest the steps of the sun;
> Seeking after that sweet golden clime,
>   Where the traveller's journey is done....

The botanical fact that the sunflower turns all day following the course of the sun is used as a symbol of the human soul aspiring toward eternity.

Such examples of symbolic overtones could be multiplied indefinitely. Dante Gabriel Rossetti, whose painter's eye makes his poems especially graphic, reversed the process of symbol-making, and noted how the human memory, failing to retain even a great grief, preserved only the visual image of the flower without any overtones of emotion:

The wind flapp'd loose, the wind was still
Shaken out dead from tree and hill:
I had walk'd on at the wind's will,—
I sat now, for the wind was still.

Between my knees my forehead was,—
My lips, drawn in, said not Alas!
My hair was over in the grass,
My naked ears heard the day pass.

My eyes, wide open, had the run
Of some ten weeds to fix upon;
Among these few, out of the sun,
The woodspurge flower'd, three cups in one.

From perfect grief there need not be
Wisdom or even memory:
One thing then learnt remains to me,—
The woodspurge has a cup of three.

Many symbols, and abstract words as well, have become trite through overuse. These, and other hackneyed or distorted expressions, make up what is commonly called "poetic diction," and good poets avoid them. However, in reading the old poets, remember that many words that have become stale in our time were fresh in theirs.

We must also take into account the symbolic or figurative diction of the "metaphysical" style, which Donne made popular in the first half of the seventeenth century, and which, owing to the Donne revival in the first half of this century, became one of the most fashionable mannerisms of contemporary poetry. "Metaphysical" is a misleading term for this kind of writing; it was the unfortunate choice of Dr. Johnson, who did better, however, in his description of the style as one in which "the most heterogeneous ideas are yoked by violence together; nature and art are ransacked for illustrations, comparisons, and allusions; their learning instructs, their subtlety surprises; but the reader commonly thinks his improvement dearly bought, and though he sometimes admires, is seldom pleased." Here is an example from Donne's *Hymn to God my God, in my Sickness:*

Whilst my physicians in their love are grown
Cosmographers, and I their map, who lie

> Flat on this bed, that by them may be shown
> That this is my south-west discovery . . .

and so on, tediously. "Ingenious" or "fantastic" would be a better
term for this sort of thing than metaphysical, but Dr. Johnson's
term is now so generally accepted that it is too late to suggest a
change.

The *music* of words cannot be analyzed. It is possible to note
combinations of vowels or consonants and various metrical effects,
but the whole sound of poetry is too complex and composed of too
many elements to be explained. It is like the melodic sense of the
composer, a gift of the sensuous imagination. A mere delight in
sonorous sound does not necessarily indicate the working of a poetic
ear; there must sometimes be abrupt and jagged effects as well as
smooth cadences—each in its proper place. Browning sometimes errs
at one extreme, and Poe at the other.

All of us have experienced emotions too vague to be set in a definite
verbal formula, but which have suggested phrases or a sentence. Or
sometimes in a dream verses occur to us that seem heavenly utterance
(though they probably are not).

Most of the moods and emotions that find expression in all but
the most epigrammatic or satirical poetry are of the nature of dreams.
Just as a dream may be so vividly real that it clings to us after we
awaken, so the mood of the poet in creation isolates him in a world
of the imagination and phrase-making that excludes every other
impulse. It is essential that he yield completely to this, even though
he run a spiritual risk, for if he hold back, if he stint his inspiration,
either through caution or the knowledge that it is lunchtime and he
is hungry, he will not be the single-toned lyre that nature intended.
The many conspicuous social failures among artists of all sorts does
not mean that they are less responsible than other men, but that they
have taken more than the usual risks and strains of living and have
not always come through unscathed. Shelley's invocation, "Make me
thy lyre even as the forest is," is not mere rhetoric, it is a call to glory
—and perhaps disaster.

When the mood leaves off, revision begins. The poet cannot, like
the man in the dream, leave the mood to dictate the final form as well
as the content of the poem. Once in a great while a poem is produced
in this way by a genius with whom technical excellence is instinctive.

The supreme poem of unedited mood and picture is, of course, Coleridge's *Kubla Khan*. The music is perfect, the images enchanting, and we ask no more of the poem than that it possess us with its literally meaningless incantation even as the original mood possessed the poet. There are other fragments of the same sort, such as Hamlet's haunting quatrain:

> Why, let the stricken deer go weep,
> The hart ungallèd play;
> For some must watch, while some must sleep:
> So runs the world away.

Here there is no "message," but anyone with an ear for the music of words will not fail to catch the weary melancholy of the lines.

The Three Critical Questions. There are three questions to be asked about a poem—or, indeed, any work of art: (1) What is the author's intention? (2) Has he succeeded in it? (3) Was the intention worth while in the first place?

Many modern critics shirk the asking and answering of these three questions, especially the third one; hence, much that passes for criticism today is mere impressionism.

The first question does justice to the author, and assures a careful reading with a view to establishing the ideas and emotions that he wished to express. If, after conscientious reading, we cannot answer the first question at all, then we conclude that the author is willfully obscure, incomprehensible. There is a good deal of poetry today that shuns all intelligible communication, and its acceptance or rejection will depend on the reader's individual indulgence in mystification. But most poets intend to communicate, and be they as simple as Wordsworth or as complex as Browning, their purpose in writing should be accurately determined.

The second question has to do with the standards of the medium in which the author expresses himself. These standards are impersonal; they are the result of all the technical developments that have gone before. These will be explained in chapters yet to come.

The third question, "Was the intention worth while?" returns to the ideas and emotions of the poem, this time measuring them, not by the author's individual purpose, but by the general standards of human experience and aspiration. It is difficult but important not to let our own prejudices intrude here.

Let us return to the first question and determine the intention of two poems, one which has a moral, the other which only seems to have one: Oliver Wendell Holmes's *The Chambered Nautilus* and Keats's *Ode on a Grecian Urn*.

The Chambered Nautilus

This is the ship of pearl, which, poets feign,
　　Sails the unshadowed main,—
　　The venturous bark that flings
On the sweet summer wind its purpled wings
In gulfs enchanted, where the Siren sings,
　　And coral reefs lie bare,
Where the cold sea-maids rise to sun their streaming hair.

Its webs of living gauze no more unfurl;
　　Wrecked is the ship of pearl!
　　And every chambered cell,
Where its dim dreaming life was wont to dwell,
As the frail tenant shaped his growing shell,
　　Before thee lies revealed,—
Its irised ceiling rent, its sunless crypt unsealed!

Year after year beheld the silent toil
　　That spread his lustrous coil;
　　Still, as the spiral grew,
He left the past year's dwelling for the new,
Stole with soft step its shining archway through,
　　Built up its idle door,
Stretched in his last-found home, and knew the old no more.

Thanks for the heavenly message brought by thee,
　　Child of the wandering sea,
　　Cast from her lap, forlorn!
From thy dead lips a clearer note is born
Than ever Triton blew from wreathèd horn!
　　While on mine ear it rings,
Through the deep caves of thought I hear a voice that sings:—

Build thee more stately mansions, O my soul,
　　As the swift seasons roll!
　　Leave thy low-vaulted past!
Let each new temple, nobler than the last,

Shut thee from heaven with a dome more vast,
    Till thou at length art free,
Leaving thine outgrown shell by life's unresting sea!

This is definitely a poem with a "moral," and very good of its kind. The entire description leads up to the climax "Thanks for the heavenly message brought by thee." That clinches the intention.

Now take Keats's *Ode on a Grecian Urn,* the last two lines of which seem to summarize a moral:

I

Thou still unravish'd bride of quietness,
    Thou foster-child of silence and slow time,
Sylvan historian, who canst thus express
    A flowery tale more sweetly than our rhyme:
What leaf-fring'd legend haunts about thy shape
    Of deities or mortals, or of both,
        In Tempe or the dales of Arcady?
What men or gods are these? What maidens loth?
What mad pursuit? What struggle to escape?
    What pipes and timbrels? What wild ecstasy?

II

Heard melodies are sweet, but those unheard
    Are sweeter; therefore, ye soft pipes, play on;
Not to the sensual ear, but, more endear'd,
    Pipe to the spirit ditties of no tone:
Fair youth, beneath the trees, thou canst not leave
    Thy song, nor ever can those trees be bare;
        Bold Lover, never, never canst thou kiss,
Though winning near the goal—yet, do not grieve;
    She cannot fade, though thou hast not thy bliss,
        For ever wilt thou love, and she be fair!

III

Ah, happy, happy boughs! that cannot shed
    Your leaves, nor ever bid the Spring adieu;
And, happy melodist, unwearied,
    For ever piping songs for ever new;

More happy love! more happy, happy love!
  For ever warm and still to be enjoy'd,
    For ever panting, and for ever young;
All breathing human passion far above,
  That leaves a heart high-sorrowful and cloy'd,
    A burning forehead, and a parching tongue.

IV

Who are these coming to the sacrifice?
  To what green altar, O mysterious priest,
Lead'st thou that heifer lowing at the skies,
  And all her silken flanks with garlands drest?
What little town by river or sea shore,
  Or mountain-built with peaceful citadel,
    Is emptied of its folk, this pious morn?
And, little town, thy streets for evermore
  Will silent be; and not a soul to tell
    Why thou art desolate, can e'er return.

V

O Attic shape! Fair attitude! with brede
  Of marble men and maidens overwrought,
With forest branches and the trodden weed;
  Thou, silent form, dost tease us out of thought
As doth eternity: Cold Pastoral!
  When old age shall this generation waste,
    Thou shalt remain, in midst of other woe
Than ours, a friend to man, to whom thou say'st,
  'Beauty is truth, truth beauty,'—that is all
    Ye know on earth, and all ye need to know.

Unlike Holmes's poem, this does not move to its "moral" as a climax, and some critics have objected to the last two lines as moving away from the main meaning. That meaning is, of course, a celebration of emotions, sensations, and forms that hang suspended and unconsummated through eternity, freed from the withering of time. The artist who wrought the urn captured the mortal beauty, halted it, and made it immortal. Keats's ode is the artist's tribute to art.

These two poems are both in the rhetorical style, and we accept the heightened diction, so far from the talk of everyday, because that was the idiom that the poet considered most appropriate for the expression of his idea.

The question of style belongs to the field of rhetoric, but I shall speak of it here because it has a relation to the first critical question: we must recognize the stylistic intention of the poet. In general, there are two kinds of style, the *rhetorical,* heightened and dignified, and the *conversational,* informal and familiar. Dryden says of his *Annus Mirabilis,* "I wanted not only height of fancy, but dignity of words to set if off." On the other hand, Wordsworth aimed for "a selection of language really used by men." Each has its dangers as well as its virtues; the first may become bombastic, the second, prosaic. Shakespeare, Milton, and the second generation of Romantic poets often used high rhetoric effectively; Chaucer, Skelton, Donne, Pope, Browning, and Robinson, the conversational style. Robert Frost's poetry seldom departs from the conversational style.

Most poets use both styles and sometimes combine them in a single poem. Take, for example, Andrew Marvell's splendid *To His Coy Mistress:*

> Had we but world enough, and time,
> This coyness, Lady, were no crime.
> We would sit down, and think which way
> To walk and pass our long love's day.
> Thou by the Indian Ganges' side
> Shouldst rubies find: I by the tide
> Of Humber would complain. I would
> Love you ten years before the Flood,
> And you should, if you please, refuse
> Till the conversion of the Jews.
> My vegetable love should grow
> Vaster than empires, and more slow;
> An hundred years should go to praise
> Thine eyes, and on thy forehead gaze;
> Two hundred to adore each breast,
> But thirty thousand to the rest;
> An age at least to every part,
> And the last age should show your heart.
> For, Lady, you deserve this state,

Nor would I love at lower rate.
　　But at my back I always hear
Time's wingèd chariot hurrying near;
And yonder all before us lie
Deserts of vast eternity.
Thy beauty shall no more be found,
Nor in thy marble vault shall sound
My echoing song: then worms shall try
That long preserved virginity;
And your quaint honour turn to dust,
And into ashes all my lust:
The grave's a fine and private place,
But none, I think, do there embrace.
　　Now therefore, while the youthful hue
Sits on thy skin like morning dew,
And while thy willing soul transpires
At every pore with instant fires,
Now let us sport us while we may,
And now, like amorous birds of prey,
Rather at once our time devour,
Than languish in his slow-chapt power.
Let us roll all our strength and all
Our sweetness up into one ball;
And tear our pleasures with rough strife
Thorough the iron gates of life:
Thus, though we cannot make our sun
Stand still, yet we will make him run.

The diction of most of this poem is conversational, even, at times, playful, but the climax, beginning "But at my back I always hear" is high rhetoric. With what artistry does the poet lead us back to the more familiar idiom, until he can say, with almost colloquial lightness,

The grave's a fine and private place
But none, I think, do there embrace.

When we have established the intention of the poet, we can proceed to the second question, concerning its success. This involves meter, rhyming, rhythm, figures of speech, verbal felicity. Often he must be judged by the rules for a set form. Or perhaps he has broken them intentionally to gain a desired effect. In that case, we must decide whether or not the experiment was justified by the results. For example, Pope comdemned the use of ten monosyllables in a five-stress iambic line, making fun of the practice by writing one himself:

> And ten low words oft creep in one dull line.

Yet take this sonnet of Michael Drayton's, one of the finest we have:

> Since there's no help, come let us kiss and part;
> Nay, I have done, you get no more of me,
> And I am glad, yea glad with all my heart
> That thus so cleanly I myself can free;
> Shake hands forever, cancel all our vows,
> And when we meet at any time again,
> Be it not seen in either of our brows
> That we one jot of former love retain.
> Now at the last gasp of Love's latest breath,
> When, his pulse failing, Passion speechless lies,
> When Faith is kneeling by his bed of death,
> And Innocence is closing up his eyes,
> > Now if thou wouldst, when all have given him over,
> > From death to life thou might'st him yet recover.

The first three lines are entirely monosyllabic, and monosyllables predominate in the rest of the poem. This is a triumph of the conversational style. There are many poets who never broke a rule and never composed a memorable line; scarcely any great poet has been rule-perfect—perhaps we should say, *no* great poet. Rules resulted from the gradual accumulation of poetical experience, they are guides to the most efficient means of expression. This discussion, however, should not lead us to the conclusion that the breaking of rules is a virtue in itself!

There are many other elements that must be considered in connection with the second question, and I must refer the reader to the later section of this book in which technical matters are more specifically explained.

The third question requires broad thinking in a field where subjective limitations are inevitable. Was the author's intention worth while? I suppose a good intention would be to communicate a stirring narrative, an original and important idea, or a reminiscent emotion to as many sensitive readers as possible, for a poet who desires to express only his personal idiosyncrasies (and there are many such) is no poet at all but an exhibitionist. All art, in spite of many modern tendencies to the contrary, is more or less enduring as its intention is more or less communal, granted that the receptive community is the intelligent and responsive part of the general population. That is a minority and always has been. The audience for verse is like a pyramid, the influence of critics increasing as we approach the tapering point at the top.

At the bottom of the pyramid is the unguided and sometimes uneducated part of the audience that loves rhymed platitudes and only occasionally, as it were by chance, deviates into appreciation of some solitary masterpiece. Rhymesters like Edgar Guest are the laureates of the many, who will vindicate their choice with almost passionate conviction against the claims of what they would call "high-brow" poetry. Once when Robert Frost was lecturing in Detroit, he made some jesting reference to Edgar Guest, forgetting that Detroit was his home town. At the end of the lecture an indignant dowager swept up to the platform. "What kind of car do you drive?" she asked belligerently. "A Ford," said Frost. *"Mr. Guest,"* said she, "drives a *Cadillac."*

One solitary masterpiece often known to such people is Gray's *Elegy Written in a Country Churchyard.* Almost from the moment of its publication, this great poem captured the eager many and the discriminating few (with the exception of Dr. Johnson, whose prejudice against Gray was natural, almost prophetic, in view of the fact that in Gray's work were many buds that were to be among the flowers of romanticism a few decades later). Another popular masterpiece is Edward FitzGerald's *Rubaiyat,* but we can not put this in a class with the Elegy. It is quotable and at times magnificent, but the phrasing is almost too glib to be true, and much of its charm is in the exotic background, which convinces only for the moment, like stage scenery.

Just a little higher on the pyramid is the audience that loves the bad poems of good poets and hence does those poets a good deal of harm. The most conspicuous victim in our own times of such lethal enthusiasm is Edna Millay. Her popularity among people who chose all the wrong things—the Bohemian (or Greenwich Village) pieces, especially that nauseating little bit beginning, "My candle burns at both ends," and some of the more absurd poems of passion, that might well have dragged her into oblivion along with Elinor Glynn and Ella Wheeler Wilcox—such popularity made conventional reviewers who aspired to be taken for critics afraid to risk their reputations by praising her. The fact is that she was, when freed of affectation and propaganda, a very fine poet, and nowhere more so than in the posthumous volume *Mine the Harvest*.

Before I ascend to the next step of the pyramid, the reader will, I hope, grant me a little digression. I have just spoken of Edna Millay as occasionally a "very fine" poet. There is an almost insurmountable difficulty in assigning poets to their relative places by means of adjectives. If we speak of a "great" poet, we are putting him in a very small company, and the word is often misapplied. Yet if we speak of a "good" poet, which ought to mean just what it says, nevertheless, we seem to be damning him with faint praise. Then there is the difficulty with the words "major" and "minor." Theoretically, a major poet should be one who, like Shakespeare, deals with major themes in substantial bulk, and a minor poet should be one who deals with minor themes within a small scope. Excellence may, again theoretically, be attributed to a minor as well as a major poet: Herrick is as good in his way as Shakespeare in his. But this distinction has, unfortunately, been lost, and if I should speak of Herrick as a minor poet, the reader would conclude that I meant second-rate. There is no solution for these adjectival problems, which I call to the reader's attention for his guidance in reading reviews and criticisms, including my own.

And now we may ascend to the next step of the pyramid. Here we find an audience of wide yet discriminating interest in poetry. These readers have, or desire to have, more information on the subject in order to enlarge the scope for their appreciation and give them more confidence in their own judgments. To this enlightened minority I address this book, and I need not describe it further.

At the apex of the pyramid is the small group of the elite, critics as well as poets. One of the most common foibles of mankind is the desire to be counted among the elite. Every member of the human race is a snob of one sort or another. Virgil's *Aeneid* presented the Emperor Augustus with princely Trojan ancestors, and Layamon's

Brut d'Angleterre did no less for the kings of England. In our own country every kind of organization exists for the veneration and display of ancestry, and more coats of arms adorn our hallways than ever the College of Heralds acknowledged. An ancestor of my own, writing shortly after the American Revolution, tells how itinerant peddlers went through New England selling coats of arms to the same men who, not a decade before, had been firing their flintlocks at the aristocracy they came to emulate.

It is not strange that the literary elite (and they have certain social overtones as well) should pour their influence down the pyramid and, in our time, set fashions in both poetry and criticism that have puzzled some, converted others, and, in any case, scared off so many readers who might have enjoyed poetry, that never before in history has the audience been so small or so uncertain of its own taste. This situation will be discussed more at length in my conclusion.

It is difficult to describe the ideal reader of poetry, because poetry itself is undefinable. It is like electricity, which is beyond analysis though we still continue to light our lamps. It is like life itself, which remains a mystery, although, by the accumulation of experience we may learn to live well and wisely. So it is with the judgment of poetry: the continued familiarity with it develops an audience capable of an instinctive choice of the best.

The Development of Poetic Style

In the twentieth century there have been a number of revolutions in poetry that will go down in literary history, though some of the exemplars of them may not. For example, the "imagism" of Amy Lowell is an item that history will have to record, but her own writings are a lifeless heap of labored and synthetic decorations. The audience that she attracted by her personal vigor and keenness has fallen away, and it is not likely that she will gain a new one. Many fashionable poets have suffered the same fate. No poet of his time was more popular than Abraham Cowley, who survives in literary history but is seldom read. Within thirty years his works were neglected, and in 1737 Pope could write, "Who now reads Cowley?" —a cruel but not inappropriate question.

With so many schools and experiments as we have at present, we are forced to go back and consider which qualities in poetry remain true amid changes of taste, and which are merely passing phenomena. As a background for conclusions, let us look into the history of our poetry and consider the evolution of form and content, both in this passage and in chapters to come.

Anglo-Saxon verse was written in lines of four accents with a pause dividing the line into two halves. Each accent had an indeterminate number of weak syllables grouped around it. There was no rhyme, but alliteration, similar stressed consonant sounds, adorned the verse. Some two centuries before Chaucer, our verse began shifting its emphasis from the alliterative patterns of the Anglo-Saxons to the rhymed pattern of the Continent. The transitional poem, partly alliterated and partly rhymed, was Layamon's *Brut,* c. 1225. That was the first evolution into the rhymed and metered verse that we know.

Such changes do not necessarily involve discarding what has gone before. We still use alliteration, though not in a fixed scheme, and some of the syllabic freedom of Anglo-Saxon verse remains, though with a good deal more restraint, so that we have many irregularities that would be impossible in formal French verse. The meters that we know today, many of them established in the writings of Geoffrey Chaucer, supplanted the somewhat limited technique of ancient times, yet absorbed some of its principles.

Such evolution is like a natural growth, a survival of the fittest. Elements that aid or enrich expression are retained; the rest discarded.

The next experiment was a failure, yet influenced our verse. English verse, as we know, is measured by accents, classic verse by long and short syllables, or time meter.* Read the following line with as little accent or stress as possible and emphasizing the difference between the long and short syllables, and you will get some idea of a metric based on equal time units:

Golden the dreams from her childhood, bright on the lawn and the peachbough.

It is impossible to maintain this effect in our verse, for English is basically an accentual language. Some of the early Elizabethans did not agree, and attempted to substitute time meter for accent meter.

* Accentual meter is sometimes called *qualitative* verse; time meter, *quantitative* verse, but I have abandoned these terms as confusing and awkward.

Richard Stanyhurst tried it in his translation of the *Aeneid*, with comical results. I quote for the amusement of the reader this description of Dido dying on her funeral pyre:

> Thrice did she endeavor to mount and rest on her elbow;
> Thrice to her bed sliding she quails, with whirligig eyesight
> Up to the sky staring, with belling screechcry she roareth,
> When she the desired sunbeams with faint eye receiveth.

Incited by an academic pedant named Gabriel Harvey, poets as capable as Spenser and Sidney made tentative experiments in classical time units. The Elizabethan public became greatly interested. When Queen Elizabeth visited a grammar school and asked the children what they would like her to talk about, they requested an example of the classic hexameter in English, to which the Queen replied, extemporizing:

> Persius a crab-staff, bawdy Martial, Ovid a fine wag.

The hexameter is faulty, but the wonder is that it was requested or produced at all. In what school would our children demand a hexameter and what President would be able to accommodate them?

The musician-poet Thomas Campion brought matters to a head with his pamphlet, *Observations in the Art of English Poesie* (1602), in which he not only discarded rhyme and accentual meter but provided examples of the classic forms transferred to English verse. This essay was answered by the gentle poet Samuel Daniel, in his *Defence of Rhyme* (1603), in which he wondered that a poet of such commendable rhymes as Campion should attack rhyme. Out of all this controversy, with its scores of attempts in time meter, just one poem, a superb poem, survives, Campion's *Rose-cheeked Laura:*

> Rose-cheeked Laura, come;
> Sing thou smoothly with thy beauty's
> Silent music, either other
> Sweetly gracing.
>
> Lovely forms do flow
> From consent divinely framèd:
> Heav'n is music, and thy beauty's
> Birth is heavenly.

These dull notes we sing
Discords need for helps to grace them;
Only beauty purely loving
    Knows no discord;

But still moves delight,
Like clear springs renewed by flowing,
Ever perfect, ever in them-
    Selves eternal.

Blank verse as the vehicle for drama was one of the most important developments in the Age of Elizabeth. I have described elsewhere its invention in the Earl of Surrey's translation of Virgil, its transformation in Marlowe's mighty line into a medium of such strength that it served as the foundation of Shakespeare's dramatic verse. Shakespeare's flexible technique not only evolved within itself but absorbed variations from other playwrights, notably, in his later plays, from Fletcher. Fletcher made extensive use of what is sometimes called the "monosyllabic feminine ending"; that is, unlike the normal feminine ending, like "feather," where the weak syllable is part of the last word, it employs two monosyllabic words: thus, from Fletcher's *The Wild-goose Chase:*

And I'll be short; I'll tell you because I love you,

and from Shakespeare's *Henry the Eighth:*

She shall be lov'd and fear'd; her own shall bless her.

On no other evidence than the prevalence of these endings in *Henry the Eighth,* some foolish scholars have assigned the play, or at least part of it, to Fletcher. This is nonsense; the play is Shakespeare's throughout. The most annoying aspect of that wrong attribution is that Shakespeare's beautiful song in *Henry the Eighth,* "Orpheus with his lute," is in many anthologies assigned to Fletcher, or to Shakespeare with a question mark.

Elizabethan dramatic blank verse established the form in a series of important works which have extended down to our own day in much of the work of E. A. Robinson and Robert Frost.

The next swing of the pendulum in English verse was John Donne's deliberate roughening of meter, distributing his accents with wild freedom so that in many of his lines we have an unexpected jar when an accent pounds a syllable where the meter does not demand it, or a feeling of surprised emptiness where an accent is missing from its accustomed place. Ben Jonson remarked to William Drummond of Hawthornden that "Donne for not keeping of accent deserved hanging" and that "Donne himself for not being understood would perish." This prophesy nearly came true, for after his death Donne was almost entirely forgotten until his revival in the 1920s, since when he has been overpraised. His influence on modern English and American poetry has been enormous under the aegis of T. S. Eliot.

In the mid seventeenth century, Edmund Waller revolted against the looseness and roughness of Donne and his followers and imposed on English verse the tight, closed five-stress couplet, commonly called the Heroic Couplet, in which the verse is entirely smooth and each couplet has an independent syntax, never overflowing into any other. Waller's couplet, the vehicle for Dryden's long poems and the exclusive vehicle for Pope, ruled the eighteenth century, until once again the pendulum swung, and the Romantic poets overthrew it, and when they did write couplets, they delighted in opening them so that one would glide into another through whole paragraphs, as in Keats's *Endymion:*

> A thing of beauty is a joy for ever:
> Its loveliness increases; it will never
> Pass into nothingness; but still will keep
> A bower quiet for us and a sleep
> Full of sweet dreams, and health, and quiet breathing.
> Therefore, on every morrow, are we wreathing
> A flowery band to bind us to the earth,
> Spite of despondence, of the inhuman dearth
> Of noble natures, of the gloomy days,
> Of all the unhealthy and o'erdarkened ways
> Made for our searching. . . .

And so forth. Perhaps Keats overdid it. Revolutionaries always go to extremes.

A single poem of great significance in the development of our verse is Coleridge's *Christabel.* Whether this poem was merely symptomatic of Romantic freedom in general or directly influential on the work of other poets, we cannot know, but it embodied certain principles that are with us still. Coleridge noted that "the meter of Christabel is not, properly speaking, irregular, though it may seem so from its being founded on a new principle; namely, that of counting in each line the accents, not the syllables. Though the latter may vary from seven to twelve, yet in each line the accents will be found to be only four."

The verse easily absorbs these irregularities:

> The night is chill; the forest bare;
> Is it the wind that moaneth bleak?
> There is not wind enough in the air
> To move away the ringlet curl
> From the lovely lady's cheek—
> There is not wind enough to twirl
> The one red leaf, the last of its clan,
> That dances as often as dance it can,
> Hanging so light, and hanging so high,
> On the topmost twig that looks up at the sky.

It is not necessary to go into Coleridge's application of his principle and the fact that he did not always have the four accents and that the variety of the syllables ranged from four to thirteen. The two important points are that the principle was by no means "new" as Coleridge stated, and that from the time of the Romantic poets to the present day it has been accepted as one phase of poetic practice, especially in four-stress verse. Readers who have followed my exposition will easily recognize Coleridge's "new" principle as the fundamental rule in Anglo-Saxon verse. It was also used freely in Elizabethan song poetry. Modern poets avail themselves of this syllabic freedom, sometimes to excess. It is not, in general, applied to five-stress verse, though both Robert Bridges and his friend Gerard Manley Hopkins extended it to the pentameter (see pages 84 and 184).

The next revolt took place in America, and was, of course, Whitman's. I should not call Whitman's work free verse, however, but *dithyrambic* verse; that is, a basically metrical rhythm over which play extra syllables or long pauses where syllables are missing. The meter changes from one kind to another with the greatest freedom. When he is writing at his lyric best, his meter is most noticeable, as for example:

Out of the cradle endlessly rocking,
Out of the mocking bird's throat, the musical shuttle,
Out of the Ninth-month midnight,
Over the sterile sands and the fields beyond where the child leaving his bed wander'd alone, bareheaded, barefoot....

The accents here are muted, and the verse has almost the effect of classic dactylic meter. Again, we have a loose iambic effect in

When lilacs last in the dooryard bloom'd,
And the great star early droop'd in the western sky in the night,
I mourn'd, and yet shall mourn with ever-returning spring.

We do not find completely non-metrical verse until we come to the work of Stephen Crane, Carl Sandburg, and William Carlos Williams, to name only three of the best known out of a large crowd.

Today there are innumerable varieties of experience in verse, from the free and incomprehensible *Cantos* of Ezra Pound to the strict traditionalism—classicism, one might say—of Robert Frost.

Modes of thought change as well as forms of poetry and the two are inextricably bound together. The Elizabethans were pastoral, Platonic, and steeped in music. The school of Donne was obsessed with inner searching of the self, and thought in terms of symbols and fantastic metaphors. The eighteenth century made reason its guide and wit its idiom. Pope and his school had an aversion to wild nature; they preferred parks and formal gardens and the elegance of the strict heroic couplet. The Romantic poet looked to imagination rather than reason as his guide and loved the solitudes of forest and hill, where, amid untrammeled Nature, he could feel akin to cosmic forces and tune his soul to immensity. The great Victorians were concerned with ethical and philosophical matters, with the exception of Browning's dramatic monologues, which, like Chaucer's *Canterbury Tales,* but from a far different angle, sprang from a sheer delight in observing people and the human comedy.

With all these changes of form and content behind us, it is not surprising that modern poetry should abound in schools and innovators. In general, we have passed through our "metaphysical" period, and the influence of T. S. Eliot is on the decline. The trend now favors the elegance and precision of the eighteenth century.

In our quick and turbulent age, change will doubtless be more frequent than in the past, and the problem of the critic more complex. What roots should we look for to determine whether a poet is a living growth or a parasite without roots—like mistletoe, beloved by druids and young lovers but scarcely desired by the oak? How shall we distinguish between the fakirs and the prophets?

All that we can say is that the majority of the modern poets who give us satisfaction, such as Bridges, Frost, Robinson, Sassoon, Hodgson, and the great Irish school of Yeats, Stephens, and Gogarty, regard life, in spite of its dissonances, as essentially a harmony in which they are a part. They are at home in this world.

It is not true, as some critics contend, that attention to the past—both history and poetic tradition—dulls the perceptions to what is going on around one. In Robert Bridges' philosophical epic, *The Testament of Beauty,* the timelessness of the images is a delight. The poet gives us a picture of himself as he sits on his porch composing his "loose Alexandrines." As he writes, he sees an ouzel building her nest in the rafters. Or an aeroplane passes through the sky and into his poem. Or a steam thresher chatters in the field beyond. All these realistic and modern details he weaves into the timeless theme of his poem, which celebrates the gradual evolution of the spirit of man toward perfection.

We might say that all great poetry, of whatever age, has the power of moving on through the years, keeping pace with mankind through his ever-changing landscape. It is the second-rate, following the current vogue, that soon goes out of fashion. All great poetry is modern. "Chaucer's power of fascination is enduring," as Matthew Arnold noted. We can go back even farther than Chaucer and relive with the authors of antiquity the adventures, material and spiritual, which are with us in the flash and music of their lines.

Most of our great poets have added to their native tradition a knowledge of the ancients. A recent example of one so influenced is A. E. Housman. His work is the tragic song of the English countryside and its simple folk. His diction depends for its effect almost wholly on words of native stock. His forms, too, are basic, usually variations of the folk ballad. But reading on, having followed him through Shropshire and through folk poetry, we strike a deeper root, one that goes back to the Greeks, their restraint, polish, and exalted stoicism. It is not surprising to learn that Housman lived a double life, as poet and as Classical scholar.

Or take Robert Frost. He sprang into fame as the exponent of northern New England in the cadences of its own idiom. Reading carefully, we hear the controlled music of his conversational style. His realism is not photographic; it is symbolic of the relation between man and nature and God, and the redeeming companionship between man and man. Most of his poems are dialogues between two people in the poem or between the poet and his reader. When we seek the roots that sustain his poetry, we at first find the obvious one, that of New England and Emerson, and there is another going back through English literature to the work of George Crabbe, and yet another that goes back to Greek literature and thought.

Frost is an excellent Greek scholar, and the light of Athens is on his philosophy. Some years ago at an academic gathering a student was arguing in favor of the rootless kind of poetry then in vogue and against formal education for the poet. He cited Frost as a poet who had developed through his inborn talent without recourse to the past. By good fortune, a professor of Greek, who had formerly taught Frost at Harvard, was among those present. He took us up into his study and produced his old records. Opposite Frost's name, across the page, recitation after recitation, test after test, was an unbroken series of *A*s.

The deepest root of poetry penetrates so far that it loses itself in the entangled aspirations of mankind. A good poet is at home in his countryside and his world, and at one with the spirits and traditions of the past. These truths, however, are but aspects of the one truth that poetry is the highest expression of what is most natural to man in every phase of his life. The single idea of the poet is to create from disharmony, harmony; from formlessness, form, and to be glad in the work of his hands for its own sake, whether or not anyone will, in the future, remember his name.

Meter and Rhythm

The structure of poetry, like that of music, is based on repetition, or regular recurrence of stress. As I have said, the smallest unit of this regularly recurring accent, or stress, is the metrical foot. When we scan a line of verse aloud, we measure these metrical feet to determine the nature of the versification. In this case, we do not hear the rhythm of the phrasing. Meter is like the left hand of the pianist playing a regularly recurring beat; phrasing is like his right hand, weaving all sorts of irregularities over the beat.

Let us take one of Ben Jonson's best-known lyrics:

> Still to be neat, still to be drest,
> As you were going to a feast;
> Still to be powder'd, still perfumed:
> Lady, it is to be presumed,
> Though art's hid causes are not found,
> All is not sweet, all is not sound.

Let us now scan it according to strict meter:

> Still tó | be neát | still tó | be drést |
> As yóu | were gó | ing tó | a feást |
> Still tó | be pów | der'd stíll | per fúmed |
> La dý | it ís | to bé | pre súmed |
> Though árt's | hid cáu | ses aré | not fóund |
> All ís | not sweét | all ís | not sound |.

These are iambic feet, theoretically a weak syllable followed by a strong one. But assuredly we do not read the poem as we have scanned it. Reading it thus we get only its metrical, or syllabic, sense, not its rhythmical sense. Rhythm comes only when we read it for its meaning, with due regard for the variety in the length of syllables and the movements of the pause.

> Stíll to be neat | stíll to be drest |
> As you were going || to a feast |
> Stíll to be powder'd | still perfumed |
> Lády || it is to be presumed
> Though art's hid causes || are not found
> Áll is not sweet | all is not sound |.

All verse—and all music—is made up of both meter and phrasing, which are coexistent in the general rhythmical scheme. But though they exist together, it is the phrasing, or time rhythm, that we actually hear, not the metrical accent. Thus, we do not hear, "Still *to* be *neat,* still *to* be *drest,*" but "*still* to be *neat* (pause) *still* to be *drest.*" I must emphasize that the time units are not regularly recurrent and that they are composed of *duration*—the *length* or *shortness* of the syllables—and *pause,* that corresponds to the rest in music.

Here we have the paradox of accent, or stress. English verse is indubitably based on a *theoretical* (or metrical) pattern of regularly recurrent accent. An iambic pentameter, we say, is a five-foot (or five-stress) line; each foot containing an unaccented, followed by an accented, syllable. It would be difficult to hear many such lines in the whole range of English verse, for our verse is based on recurrent accent as an iceberg is based on the larger part that is submerged and invisible. But take away that submerged part, and the iceberg would tip over. Thus we have the paradoxical fact that variations in phrasing are effective *only* because they *are* variations over a fixed system of accents.

Let us examine, then, the various kinds of metrical feet according to the relation between the strong and weak syllables.

Feet of two syllables we may call two-part meter, and there are three kinds, including the *iambic,* which is the prevailing metrical unit in the largest proportion of English verse. The two-part feet are these:

Iambic, the strong syllable following a weak one: de líght.

Trochaic, strong followed by weak: splén did.

Spondaic, two evenly balanced syllables: salt foam. It should be added that the spondee is found only here and there as one or two spondees may be used to vary a line of some other meter. Milton's line beginning with three spondees is famous, and the reader will easily understand why the foot must be used sparingly:

Rocks, Caves, | Lakes, Fens, | Bogs, Dens, | and shádes | of déath.

When we come to the three- and four-part feet, we find a wild syllabic irregularity. Also, one kind of three- or four-part verse may easily slide into feet of another kind. With this warning, I give the basic scansion for these feet:

Dactylic, a strong syllable followed by two weak ones: splén did ly

Amphibrachic, a strong syllable between two weak ones:

de líght ful

Anapestic, a strong syllable preceded by two weak ones:

in ter twíne

The dactylic foot is a falling meter, the anapest, rising.

The four-part meters are even more undisciplined than the three-part, and again I shall limit my comment to the normal meters, reserving my discussion of irregularities to a separate section, which the reader may study or omit as he pleases. There are four kinds of four-part verse. These are called *paeons,* and are designated according to the placing of the strong accent:

First paeon, with the accent on the first syllable:

Nót ed is a | Scótch man for his | pár si mo ny |.

Second paeon, with the accent on the second syllable:

In Pá ra dise | the án gels sing | de líght ful ly |.

Third paeon, with the accent on the third syllable:

In the twí light | we were dréam ing | on the móun tain |.

Fourth paeon, with the accent on the fourth syllable:

> Out of the óak | af ter the storm | flut tered a bírd |.

Metrical Irregularities

It is desirable, but not absolutely necessary, for a reader in pursuit of poetry to recognize the various irregularities the poets have employed. In practice, the chapter on How to Read Verse Aloud provides what is needed in order to hear the cadences that play over the basic meters and give the ultimate audible effect. If, however, the reader is interested in prosody, he should be informed of the various irregularities that are found in the meter itself. These I will treat briefly.

By far the greater part of English poetry employs the iambic measure. The iambic fits our language. The five-stress iambic line —iambic pentameter—is long enough to include in its scope many subtle variations and shadings without departing from the normal measure, so it accepts fewer irregularities than does the shorter line, the four-stress iambic. The long poems in English are mostly in iambic pentameter, as are the plays of Shakespeare and later dramatic works such as the plays of Tennyson and the "masques" of Robert Frost. Rhymed or unrhymed, the form usually exhibits only five obvious irregularities:

The trisyllabic foot: Two-part meter in five-stress verse is fairly regular in assigning two syllables to each foot, but an extra syllable is sometimes added:

> And tróu | ble deaf héav | en with | my boót | less críes |.

The feminine ending, where an extra weak syllable occurs in the last foot of the line:

> Thus háve | I hád | thee as | a dréam | doth flát ter |
> In sleép | a kíng | but wák | ing no | such mát ter |.

The transferred accent, where positions of the weak and strong accents are reversed, as here in the first foot:

> Múch have | I tra | velled in | the realms | of góld |.

This device is so common at the beginning of a line that it would scarcely be noticed. Less common is the transferred accent in the body of the line:

> When féll | the dárk | bríng ing | its beá | con stárs |.

The spondee, consisting of two strong syllables:

> The hórse | men róde | bright shod | with flý | ing spárks |.

The hovering accent or *light spondee:*

> The rúde | fore fa | thers óf | the hám | let sleép |.

This is called the hovering accent because the accent seems equally distributed between halves. They are usually long syllables about evenly balanced, as *fore* and *fa*.

Four-stress iambic verse will accept any number of irregularities, slipping into trochaic, or even three-part measures, and back again without the slightest difficulty. Longer iambic lines than the pentameter can scarcely be varied at all.

Iambic lines of any length may sometimes start without the first weak syllable. These are called *beheaded* or *acephalous* lines, and are found less frequently in five-stress lines than in shorter ones. Here is a normal iambic line:

> The shádows deépen ón the láwn at dúsk;

we behead it and produce

> Shádows deépen ón the láwn at dúsk.

Trochaic lines of any length may sometimes end without the last weak syllable. These are called *truncated* or *catalectic* lines. Here is a normal trochaic line:

> Shádows deépen ón the láwn at twílight,

and submitting it to truncation, or catalexis, we produce exactly the same line as the beheaded iambic:

> Shádows deépen ón the láwn at dúsk.

With the exception of the long dactylic hexameters (six-foot lines) which we find occasionally, as in Longfellow's *Evangeline,* the three-part meters behave with wild irregularity. These feet would become monotonous without constant variation. Therefore, although the three-part rhythm continues to throb underneath, a minority of the feet carry out the syllabic arrangement. Usually they are something like this:

> Kíng of the | góld en | ís lands |
> Lórd of the | fár thermost | stránd |
> Oút of our | vál leys and | hígh lands |
> We rál ly | to yóur | com mánd |.

The first foot is a dactyl, the second two feet are trochees; in the second line the first two feet are dactyls, and the third foot is one long, strong syllable, substituting for three syllables; in the third line the first two feet are normal dactyls followed by a trochee; the fourth line consists of an amphibrach and two iambs. This is a mild example; the interested reader can try his powers of analysis on the three-part poems of Swinburne. For instance:

> And the hígh | gods toók | in hánd
> Fíre and the | fál ling of | teárs |,
> And a méa | sure of slíd | ing sánd |
> From ún der | the feét | of the yeárs |.

Line 1: anapest, iamb, iamb; line 2: dactyl, dactyl, one-syllable foot; line 3: anapest, anapest, iamb; line 4: amphibrach, iamb, anapest.

If the three-part rhythms are wildly irregular, the four-part are tumultuous. They are most frequently found without their full quota of syllables, pauses and long vowel sounds compensating for the blanks. One paeon moves easily into another, and all four may be found in a single poem. Furthermore they may easily slip back into the iambs and trochees from which they came. The first and third paeons are merely two trochaic feet with one stress canceled; thus our example of the first paeon could theoretically be scanned thus:

> Nó ted | ís a | Scótch man | fór his | pár si | món y |.

Likewise, each second and fourth paeon consists, theoretically, of two iambic feet with one stress canceled:

in Pá | ra díse | the án | gels síng | de líght | ful lý |.

Of course, we should not wish to read it that way.

The opening of Walter de la Mare's "The Listeners" is a good example of the paeon in action:

Is there ány | body thére? | said the Tráveller |

Knócking on the | moon lít | dóor |

And his hórse | in the sílence | champed the grásses |

Of the fórest's | férny | flóor. |

And a bírd | flew up óut | of the túrret |

Abóve | the Tráveller's | héad: |

And he smóte | upon the dóor | again a sécond time |

Is there ány | body thére? | he sáid.

Without analyzing this in detail, I will merely point out that the last paeon in the seventh line has collected two extra syllables besides its own four.

Of course the paeons seem and are elaborate in structure, but they are often found in the simplest as well as the most complex verse. They are found in folk poetry and in nursery rhymes. Consider "Sing a song of sixpence"—a first paeon followed by a spondee, and roughly paeonic throughout the following lines of the poem. Gerard Manley Hopkins averred that his verse was based on the first paeon, and, of course, his prosody is of the most complex.

With the mention of Hopkins' name, we are coming too close to the border of the pathless swamp of advanced prosody, where many a controversialist has miserably left his bones. What I have said so far is fairly basic and acceptable to all; beyond this, contending theories thicken, and I shall go no farther.

And, as I said, all this material, though it may be of interest to the reader and should not be omitted, is not indispensable in the pursuit of poetry.

The Length of Lines

The second longest unit of recurrence is the line. Lines are of differing length, but most of our poetry is in lines of five or four feet. I prefer to use the terms four-stress, six-stress, and so forth to indicate the length of the lines, but there is a terminology long established that the reader should know, for he may well encounter it in other discussions. I have used the iambic foot in my examples:

Monometer (one foot): I know.

Dimeter (two feet): I know a road.

Trimeter (three feet): I know a road that leads.

Tetrameter (four feet): Iambic tetrameter is often called an *octosyllabic* line: I know a road that leads me back.

Pentameter (five feet): I know a road that leads me back to hills.

Hexameter (six feet). Iambic hexameter is called an *Alexandrine:* I know a road that leads me back to hills I loved.

Heptameter (seven feet). Iambic heptameter is called a *septenary:* I know a road that leads me back to hills I loved to climb.

Octameter (eight feet): I know a road that leads me back to hills I loved to climb at dawn.

If we add a line with a similar terminal rhyme sound, we produce the smallest stanzaic unit, the couplet:

I know a road that leads me back to hills I loved to climb at dawn
Where stands a ruined house with gardens overgrown and weedy lawn.

Adornments

The three adornments of English verse are alliteration, assonance, and rhyme.

Alliteration is the repetition of a stressed consonant sound. In Anglo-Saxon (now usually called Old English) verse, alliteration played the same part that rhyme does in modern verse: it was a fixed and expected enrichment of the lines. Each line was composed of four stresses divided by a pause into two equal halves. The alliteration was fixed on the third stress and was echoed on the first stress, the second stress, or both:

To a wandering *tr*ibe	*tr*iumph comes seldom,
*Sw*iftly they must flee	*sw*allowed in dust-clouds,
Their *h*orses' *h*oofs	*h*ammering in the distance.

The fourth stress was left without alliteration.

The effect of this old form is occasionally found in modern verse, notably in passages in T. S. Eliot's *Murder in the Cathedral,* but as a rule alliteration is used sparingly and in no regular pattern. Note the *l* and *p* sounds in this passage from Tennyson's *Lotos Eaters:*

> ...ah, why
> Should life all labour be?
> Let us alone. Time driveth onward fast,
> And in a little while our lips are dumb.
> Let us alone. What is it that will last?
> All things are taken from us, and become
> Portions and parcels of the dreadful Past.

The *p* alliteration in the last line strikes us as being too heavy. There is not nearly so much of it as of the *l* sound, but *l* is a much lighter consonant, and the alliterations are more scattered. Swinburne's alliterations are sometimes excessive:

> For winter's rains and ruins are over,
> And all the seasons of snows and sins....
>
> O sweet stray sister, O shifting swallow,
> The heart's division divideth us....

Swinburne was quite aware of this flaw in his own work and wrote a parody of it, beginning

From the depth of the dreamy decline of the dawn through a notable
  nimbus of nebulous moonshine,
Pallid and pink as the palm of the flag-flower that flickers with fear of
  the flies as they float,
Are they looks of our lovers that lustrously lean from a marvel of mystic
  miraculous moonshine,
These we feel in the blood of our blushes that thicken and threaten with
  throbs through the throat? ...

Assonance was the chief adornment of Old French poetry. It consists of a repetition of similar vowel sounds. Until modern times it was used without any set pattern in English verse, though there are single lines where the poet has evidently enjoyed placing it symmetrically. Consider the *a, u,* and short *i* sounds in the opening line of Coleridge's *Kubla Khan:*

In Xanadu did Kubla Khan,

or the short *i* and *o* sounds, together with the repetition of the complete syllable *mel* is Shakespeare's

Philomel with melody.

Contemporary poets, Archibald Macleish and W. H. Auden, for example, sometimes use assonance in place of rhyme. It has become a kind of fad.

Rhyme probably originated in the Orient. Classical verse does not employ it, but we begin to find it in the Latin hymns of the early Church. From there it passed into the mediaeval lyrics of the troubadours and into English about the year 1200. Rhyme is a repetition of the final sound of a word with differing introductory sounds; thus *t ime* and *cl ime;* or, in two-syllable or "feminine" endings: *f eather* and *w eather.* Besides such normal rhymes, we have imperfect rhymes, where there is a slight change in the vowel sound: *s ent* and *t int* or *s imple* and *t emple.* Identical rhymes, in which two words with different spelling but pronounced the same, are customary in French poetry but not considered good form in English: *r eign* and *r ain,* for example, or *w ither* and *wh ither.* False rhyme has up to this time been considered taboo; in false rhyme the terminal consonant sound is only approximated: *t ime* and *l ine,* or *m ember* and *t ender.* Although on my ear false rhyme has the effect of dissonance, many of the more consciously up-to-date poets seem to delight in it; oftentimes they will introduce it where a normal rhyme would be much more natural, as though they were perversely avoiding the rhyme sound. For example, they will take a singular, such as *thong* and rhyme it with a plural, such as *songs,* for no purpose, as far as I can tell, but to sour the rhyme.

John Milton was one of the great self-justifiers of history. When Parliament refused permission to license his pamphlet on divorce, he countered with *Areopagitica: A Speech for the Liberty of Un-licensed Printing,* which concerned a specific grievance of the author himself but has been acclaimed by succeeding generations as a great blow for the freedom of the press. And so it was with Milton's rhyming. Never very much at ease in rhyme, he decided that "It is no necessary adjunct or true ornament of poem or good verse ... but the invention of a barbarous age to set off wretched matter and lame meter." In actual practice, most poets seem to have agreed with Oscar Wilde that rhyme is "the one string we have added to the Greek lyre." We can say three things for it: that it has been in the language long enough so that it is per-fectly natural, that it enriches the harmonies of purely lyrical poetry, and that it makes verse easier to remember by heart. It remains, however, an adornment, and is not essential to poetry, as is demonstrated by the great body of our poetry that is written in blank verse.

How to Read Verse Aloud

The reader who thinks he does not care for poetry may not be hearing it at all. I have noted that music, the sister art of poetry, needs two sets of artists for its effect, the composers and the interpreters, or performers. Chopin needs his concert pianist, Bee-thoven his symphony orchestra with its conductor. Years of prac-ticing lie behind the performers who interpret music for us.

Luckily, no such exhaustive training is demanded of the reader of poetry, but there are a few principles to be observed, and some practice is necessary. For example, in speaking dramatic blank verse, some actors stress the meter too much and the effect is un-naturally rhetorical; some ignore it and the great rhythms are lost in an effect of prose.

Even with the following rules in mind, no two people will render poetry in the same way, and that is as it should be. There remains a wide margin of differing tempos, emphases, and pitch, as in music different conductors may vary in their interpretation of a symphony.

When we scan a line of verse aloud to determine the funda-mental meter, we measure it out very much as a metronome clicks off the measures of music. That is the skeleton of our verse, the hidden framework that makes it hold its shape and prevents it from disintegrating into free verse. For example, here is the metrical skeleton of the fine water dirge from *The Tempest*:

> Full fá thom fíve thy fá ther líes
> Óf his bónes are có ral máde
> Thóse are péarls that wére his éyes:
> Nó thing óf him thát doth fáde
> Bút doth súf fer á sea-chánge
> Ín to sóme thing rích and stránge. . . .

The first line is a regular four-stress iambic line, the others have dropped off the first, weak syllable (beheaded, or acephalous, iambics). It is obvious that we would not read this line according to this accentual scheme. There is another rhythm playing over it, the *non-recurrent* rhythm, supported by the accentual meter, but covering it over. This is the *time rhythm*. It consists of *duration,* the interplay between short and long syllables, and *pause,* which corresponds to the rest in music. Taking these elements into account, we read Shakespeare's lyric thus:

> Full fáthom fíve | thy fáther líes
> Of his bónes || are coral máde
> Thóse are péarls || that wére his éyes:
> Nóthing of him || that doth fáde
> Bút doth súffer | a sea-chánge
> Into sómething rích | and stránge.

(I have marked the long pauses ||, and the short ones |.) The first three lines, with the long vowel sounds at the end of each second and fourth foot, divide into two cadences each, thus giving a kind of rocking rhythm to the verse, like the waves of the sea. The other three lines are read closer to the accentual meter, though the rocking rhythm still subtly controls them. In the foot "sea-change" the two syllables are evenly balanced; a full accent does not descend on either of them but seems to hover between them. As I have said, the effect is called *hovering accent* (a term so poetical that a former student of mine christened his sailboat the

Hovering Accent). That foot may perhaps more conveniently be called the English *light spondee*.

As we scan meter, the iambic pentameter is a five-foot line, each foot composed of an unaccented syllable followed by an accented syllable. Read aloud, almost no lines conform to that pattern. Take, for example, a moderately regular line, the one that opens Keats's *On First Looking into Chapman's Homer:*

Much have I tra vell'd in the realms of gold.

Much and *tra* receive full stresses, but *much* is metrically in the wrong half of the foot; it is a "transferred accent." *Realms* and *gold* have weaker accents because the vowel sounds are long, and it would be jarring to hit them with a full stress. *In* cannot be accented at all. Thus we have an iambic pentameter with two primary accents, two weak accents, and one foot that contains no accent at all. Why, then, is such a line acceptable to the ear?

The line is firm because the *time rhythm* with its ever-changing units gives balance to the line as a whole. *Duration* depends on the varying length of the syllables and is usually controlled by the vowel sounds. Although long duration usually depends on long vowels, in a few words like *strength,* in which the consonants, too, draw out the sound, we find not only a full stress but a long duration as well. But usually the duration shrinks where the accent is strong, as in *much,* and expands where the accent is weak, as in *realms.* The third foot in Keats's line, *vell'd in,* has neither stress nor time-value, and, with the word *the,* is merely an introduction to the long syllable *realms. Realms* and *gold,* long syllables, compensate for the missing stress. Thus we have a constant interplay between stress and time, *strength* and *length,* which, in spite of irregularities in parts of the line, brings the entire line into rhythmical balance at the end.

With due apologies to Keats, let us rewrite his line, substituting short syllables for his long ones: "Much have I travell'd in the infinite." "In the infinite," having neither strong accents nor long vowels, destroys the rhythm. The line drops to pieces. Keats's original line should be read thus:

Múch have I trável'd || in the r̄ealms of ḡold.

It is essential that the reader observe these varying lengths and also the pauses with his most alert attention. In learning to read verse, it is a good thing to overobserve them for practice. Also, acceleration is just as important as retard. Short syllables should be hurried or the long cannot fulfill their contrasting function. Take Housman's line:

The fleet foot | on the síll of shade.

It is as necessary to hurry over the quick syllables *on the* as to draw out the long ones, *fleet, foot,* and *shade.* The only accent, and that not a strong one, falls on the word *sill.*

A more striking example is Robert Bridges' iambic pentameter (with a trisyllabic effect in the third foot):

Ah | soon || when Wínter has all our vales opprést

The very long durations *ah* and *soon,* with their attendant pauses, *are equal in time to the nine syllables that follow.* It is apparent how divergent are the underlying meters and actual rhythms of English verse.

At this point the reader is doubtless wondering what he should do about the metrical stress. We have agreed that beneath the ever-changing contours of the time rhythm, a regular, though hidden, metrical pattern sustains the verse like a skeleton. Metrical verse will always provide an accentual syllabic analysis. Such a chart might be compared to an X-ray picture of the bony structure beneath the flesh. Milton's

Hail hó ly Líght off spring of Heáv'n first bórn

actually reads

Hail holy Light || offspring of Heáv'n first born.

In Shakespeare's

A géntler heárt | did never sway in coúrt

the bone structure is nearer the surface; we might call it a thin line. For the sake of variety, poets often place contrasting fat and thin lines in sequence. To solve the problem stated at the beginning of this paragraph, we may say that in the speaking of verse the reader can disregard metrical stress entirely, provided he read naturally so that the accents fall where they would in lively conversation. In reading aloud, accent takes care of itself, and it is almost impossible not to put an accent where one truly belongs.

Pitch is a much vaguer subject, because the raising or lowering of the voice varies with each individual. A relative of mine used to start every sentence at the top of the scale, slide to the bottom about two-thirds of the way through, and, at the end, slide halfway up again. Someone who did not know English would have thought him to be in a state of perpetual worry. For the most part, we Americans do not avail ourselves of changing pitch. Unconsciously we avoid it as an affectation and lose half the effectiveness of our native tongue in one long monotone of drone, drawl, or growl. The effect is flat and blurred, especially since we run our syllables and words together, like a piece of prose without any punctuation. We ought to let every syllable come out round and full like a golden bubble! But we don't. The result is hard on poetry. The American voice is, in general, far richer than the English. Leaving out Cockney—and that super-Cockney, the "Oxford accent"—we mistakenly accord superiority to the English *voice,* whereas actually it is the flexible *pitch* that makes the Englishman's talk so much more articulate than ours. Pitch is to our language as gesticulation is to the French, its expressiveness, its emphasis, and its point. The Elizabethans doubtless spoke the language up and down through its whole gamut, and echoes of that eloquence linger in the talk of Irishmen today. *Without sliding pitch the reading of verse cannot be effective.* Strangely enough, in contradiction to their natural speech, the Irish poets I have heard, Yeats, AE, and James Stephens chanted their verse in two alternating tones, and the result was extremely monotonous. I cannot suggest any formula for pitch. Everyone feels the shape of phrases differently and will set the pitch according to his own interpretation of the lines. In moments of excitement we Americans vary our pitch, and any good poem should arouse excitement enough to limber up the vocal cords.

Enjambment is the overflow of one line into another, a syntactical structure that continues beyond the end of one line into the next, or even, as especially with Milton, through whole passages. Lines that do not overflow into the next we call *end-stopped*. Here is a passage from Christopher Marlowe's end-stopped blank verse:

Was this the face that launched a thousand ships,
And burnt the topless towers of Ilium?
Sweet Helen, make me immortal with a kiss.
Her lips suck forth my soul; see where it flies!—
Come, Helen, come, give me my soul again.
Here will I dwell, for Heaven is in these lips,
And all is dross that is not Helena. . . .
Oh, thou art fairer than the evening air
Clad in the beauty of a thousand stars;
Brighter art thou than flaming Jupiter,
When he appeared to hapless Semele;
More lovely than the monarch of the sky
In wanton Arethusa's azured arms:
And none but thou shalt be my paramour!

Shakespeare used enjambment freely, sometimes more and some-times less than in the following passage, which is characteristic:

The barge she sat in, like a burnish'd throne,
Burned on the water; the poop was beaten gold,
Purple the sails, and so perfumed that
The winds were love-sick with them; the oars were silver,
Which to the tune of flutes kept stroke, and made
The water which they beat to follow faster,
As amorous of their strokes. For her own person,
It beggar'd all description; she did lie
In her pavilion,—cloth-of-gold of tissue,—
O'er-picturing that Venus where we see
The fancy outwork nature. . . .

Milton's verse is written with so much enjambment that it often gives the effect of great paragraphs. This result was probably owing to the influence of classical verse, in which Milton was well steeped. In the classics lines run over into each other through longer units even than in Milton's verse. Here is a typical passage from *Paradise Lost*:

For should Man finally be lost, should Man
Thy creature late so lov'd, thy youngest son
Fall circumvented thus by fraud, though joynd
With his own folly? that be from thee far,

That far be from thee, Father, who art judge
Of all things made, and judgest only right.
Or shall the Adversarie thus obtain
His end, and frustrate thine, shall he fulfill
His malice, and thy goodness bring to naught,
Or proud return though to his heavier doom,
Yet with revenge accomplish't and to Hell
Draw after him the whole race of mankind,
By him corrupted? ...

John Donne's enjambments are so extreme that he sometimes divides
the syllables of a single word between two lines:

Gracious loves all as one, and thinks that so
As women do in divers countries go
In divers habits, yet are still one kind,
So doth, so is Religion; and this blind-
ness too much light breeds....

And that kind of enjambment, I should say, is going too far.

A more pleasing use of the device may be found in such lines as
these by Andrew Marvell:

Thou by the Indian Ganges' side
Shouldst rubies find: I by the tide
Of Humber would complain. I would
Love you ten years before the Flood,
And you should, if you please, refuse
Till the conversion of the Jews.

There are two wrong ways and one right way of treating this
frequently found device. One wrong way is to pause at the end of
every line and thus sacrifice the sense to the verse. Some Shakespearean actors do this. The second wrong way is to read the verse as
though it were prose, thus blotting out the division of the verses
entirely. Most Shakespearean actors do this. A sentence leaps from
line to line ignoring metrical boundaries—and how shall we preserve
the integrity of the individual lines without placing pauses where
they do not naturally occur? Or, on the other hand, how shall we
preserve the normal syntax without melting the lines together in a
formless mass?

The dilemma actually does not exist. All poets, consciously or instinctively, have indicated the method to be employed in reading enjambments. Nearly always a line that runs over into the next one is terminated by a long vowel that can be extended a little. Here, then, is the rule for reading enjambments: draw out the last syllable of the first line; then, *without pause or change of pitch,* launch into the second line. Thus:

→
Thou by the Indian Ganges' side
←   →
Shouldst rubies find: I by the tide
←   →
Of Humber would complain. I would
←
Love you ten years before the Flood,
→
And you should, if you please, refuse
←
Till the conversion of the Jews.

At this point let us summarize a few principles for the reading of verse before we start on more complicated matters:

1. Read out in a full but unstrained voice.

2. Do not dramatize the poem.

3. Do not chant it. (But chanting is better than reading it like prose.)

4. Stress only the syllables that would be stressed in lively conversation; indeed, let stress take care of itself.

5. Make clear the difference in duration between short and long syllables: read the short ones quickly and the long ones slowly.

6. Observe all pauses extravagantly. Silence can never make a mistake.

7. Vary the pitch eagerly.

8. When lines overflow into each other, draw out the last syllable of the overflowing line, and, without pause or change of pitch, collide with the first syllable of the line that follows.

These eight principles would be valueless without the ninth, which governs them all. The ninth is, quite literally, the heart of the matter, for its steady pulse sends life through all the veins of English verse. My discovery of it was a happy accident. For years I had been vaguely conscious of swaying back and forth in time to the verse

I was reading. I was a human metronome. A poem of great syllabic irregularity, Walter de la Mare's *Listeners,* seemed to demand an explanation of this weaving that evened out lines and parts of lines of very disproportionate length.

> "Is there anybody there?" said the Traveller,
> Knocking on the moonlit door.

Both these paeonic lines have three metrical feet. The lines are metrically of the same value, but the first line has twelve syllables, the second has seven. Both of them divide into two equal time units, and these units are equal in the two lines and all that follow them in the poem, in spite of the wide discrepancy in the number of syllables:

> Is there anybody there? | said the Traveller,
>
> Knocking on the moon lit door.

Continuing my experiment, I discovered the cardinal principle, the prime movement, of our verse. *All lines in English verse, more than one foot in length, divide into two equal time units. These units cut across feet, accent, syllables, and may even split a single long syllable. More often than not, there is no actual pause between them.* Theoretically, the best way to read English verse would be to a metronome. Practically, there are various accelerations and retards that change the tempo but never disorganize the equality of the two halves of a single line.

There is a natural instinct, perhaps because verse was originally sung, to divide lines into two equal parts. Greek and Latin verse and the French classical Alexandrine have middle pauses called *medial caesuras,* that are part of the basic meter. Our own division into two equal time units may well be an echo from the Anglo-Saxon verse of our remote ancestors. This verse, like those already mentioned, had medial caesuras, but unlike those, accommodated, on each side of the pause, a widely varying number of syllables. It is not surprising that such a survival should remain from the roots of our language any more than that a large proportion of our words are derived from the Anglo-Saxon. There are lines in many recent poets, notably Meredith and Swinburne, which would fit Anglo-Saxon metrics perfectly:

Bórn without síster | bórn without bróther
—Swinburne

Shall the birds in vain then | valentine their sweethearts
—Meredith

In T. S. Eliot's *Murder in the Cathedral* are several passages in the old Anglo-Saxon versification—two heavy stresses on each side of a pause with an indeterminate number of syllables in each half of the line.

The reason the double metronomic rhythm does not become monotonous is that the number of syllables within the two units constantly varies, along with the durations and the position of the pauses:

The l o n e c o u c h | of his everlasting sleep.
—Shelley

In this line, three syllables balance against seven.

A good many consonants, such as *n, m, l,* and *ng,* have echoes that fill out a unit:

Wake for the sun | has scáttered into flight.
—Fitzgerald

Note how the two long syllables *Wake* and *flight* balance the two ends of the line.

When two identical consonants collide at the end of one word and the beginning of another, we are forced to give a short pause to avoid running the two words together:

While she lies || sleeping

Sometimes, as I have said, the units divide in the middle of a word, as in the first of these two lines:

Whére in her Mediterrán | ean mirror gazing
Old Asia's dreamy face | wrínkleth to a wéstward smile.
—Robert Bridges

Now let us chart an entire poem according to these principles. I have chosen one of my own for the experiment, not knowing what effect the analysis might have on the ghosts of my great predecessors:

Night Piece

There is always the sound of falling water here
By day, blended with birdsong and windy leaves
By night, the only sound, || steady and clear
Through the darkness and half- heard through sleepers' dreams.
Here in the mottled shadow of glades, the deer
Unstartled, waits || until the walker is near,
Then with a silent bound, || without effort is gone,
And the sound of falling wa ter goes on and on.

These are not stars reflected in the lake,
They are shadows of stars that were there aeons ago;
When you walk by these waters at night, you must forsake
All you have known of time; || you are timeless, alone,
The mystery almost revealed like the breath you take
In the summer dawn || before the world is awake,
Or the last breath || when the spirit beyond recalling
Goes forth to the sound of water forever falling.

Swift as deer, || half-thoughts in the summer mind
Flash with their hints of happiness and are gone;
In the dark waters || of ourselves we find
No stars but shadows of stars which memory lost
Dark are the waters under the bridge we crossed,
And the sound of their falling knows neither end nor start.
Frail are your stars, || deep are your waters, mind;
And the sound of falling water troubles my heart.

In these twenty-four lines I have indicated where they fold back on
themselves in the second unit of the rhythm, and it will be noted
that in only nine does the turning back of the pendulum coincide
with a pause.

Try reading the following poem, William Cory's beautiful adapta-
tion from the Greek Anthology, swaying back and forth in time to the
double rhythm of each line, and indicate where you found the line
folding back on itself:

They told me, Heraclitus, they told me you were dead,
They brought me bitter news to hear and bitter tears to shed.

I wept as I remember'd how often you and I
Had tired the sun with talking and sent him down the sky.

And now that thou art lying, my dear old Carian guest,
A handful of grey ashes, long, long ago at rest,
Still are thy pleasant voices, thy nightingales, awake;
For Death, he taketh all away, but them he cannot take.

To my ears, the lines double back thus: line 1 after "Heraclitus"; line 2 squarely on the word "to" between "news" and "hear"; line 3 after "remember'd"; line 4 after "talking"; line 5 after "lying"; line 6 after "ashes"; line 7 after "voices". In line 8, there are two possibilities, depending on how you read it. According to my reading, with a long pause after "Death," the line turns back on the word "all," but it would be quite possible (though perhaps less rhythmically subtle) to swing back after the word "away."

Now try some other poems.

Stanza Forms

The *stanza* is the largest unit of metrical recurrence.

The two oldest stanzaic forms in the language are the *four-stress couplet,* which was often employed by Chaucer and other courtly poets, and the *ballad stanza,* which was the popular measure of the folk ballad.

Chaucer's *Book of the Duchess* and *House of Fame* are in four-stress couplets. What we learn from these early poems is that this couplet, even in the hands of a master like Chaucer, becomes monotonous in a long poem. The present poet laureate, John Masefield, used the form for two of his long narratives, *Reynard the Fox* and *Right Royal,* and though he varies the form every way possible, even falling into three-part meter (anapests, dactyls, and amphibrachs) for long passages, the verse inevitably becomes tiresome. The longest successful poems in the four-stress couplet are Milton's *L'Allegro* and *Il Penseroso* (and my ear finds them monotonous and wooden).

But for short lyrical works this couplet is one of the most singing forms in the language. Take, for example, Marlowe's pastoral, *The Passionate Shepherd to His Love:*

> Come live with me and be my love,
> And we will all the pleasures prove

That hills and valleys, dales and fields,
Woods, or steepy mountain yields.

And we will sit upon the rocks,
Seeing the shepherds feed their flocks
By shallow rivers, to whose falls
Melodious birds sing madrigals.

And I will make thee beds of roses,
And a thousand fragrant posies,
A cap of flowers, and a kirtle
Embroider'd all with leaves of myrtle.

A gown made of the finest wool,
Which from our pretty lambs we pull,
Fair-linèd slippers for the cold,
With buckles of the purest gold.

A belt of straw and ivy buds,
With coral clasps and amber studs,
And if these pleasures may thee move,
Come live with me, and be my love.

The shepherd swains shall dance and sing
For thy delight each May-morning.
If these delights thy mind may move,
Then live with me and be my love.

Marlowe was a frequent guest of Sir Walter Ralegh's at his
house in Sherborne in Dorsetshire, where Ralegh maintained a kind
of minor court for writers and scientists. We may imagine that
Marlowe, having finished his exquisite pastoral, made haste to show
it to Ralegh, who, being a realist, regarded it with a somewhat cynical
eye. At any rate, he produced a poem in answer to Marlowe's, using
the same form:

The Nymph's Reply to the Shepherd

If all the world and love were young,
And truth in every shepherd's tongue,
These pretty pleasures might me move
To live with thee and be thy love.

But time drives flocks from field to fold,
When rivers rage and rocks grow cold,
And Philomel becometh dumb,
The rest complains of cares to come.

The flowers do fade, and wanton fields,
To wayward winter reckoning yields,
A honey tongue, a heart of gall,
Is fancy's spring, but sorrow's fall.

Thy gowns, thy shoes, thy beds of roses,
Thy cap, thy kirtle, and thy posies,
Soon break, soon wither, soon forgotten:
In folly ripe, in reason rotten.

Thy belt of straw and ivy buds,
Thy coral clasps and amber studs,
All these in me no means can move,
To come to thee, and be thy love.

But could youth last, and love still breed,
Had joys no date, nor age no need,
Then these delights my mind might move,
To live with thee and be thy love.

Then came John Donne, who was inspired by the first lines of these poems to write a variation on the theme. But Donne's imagination, fanciful and sometimes grotesque, swung off on a tangent of its own, and produced a marvelously "conceited" poem in the best "metaphysical" style:

The Bait

Come live with me, and be my love,
And we will some new pleasures prove
Of golden sands, and crystal brooks,
With silken lines, and silver hooks.

There will the river whispering run
Warm'd by thy eyes, more then the Sun.
And there the enamor'd fish will stay,
Begging themselves they may betray.

When thou wilt swim in that live bath,
Each fish, which every channel hath,
Will amorously to thee swim,
Gladder to catch thee, than thou him.

If thou, to be so seen, be'st loath,
By Sun, or Moon, thou dark'nest both,
And if my self have leave to see,
I need not their light, having thee.

Let others freeze with angling reeds,
And cut their legs, with shells and weeds,
Or treacherously poor fish beset,
With strangling snare, or windowy net;

Let coarse bold hands, from slimy nest
The bedded fish in banks out-wrest,
Or curious traitors, sleavesilk flies
Bewitch poor fishes wand'ring eyes.

For thee, thou needst no such deceit,
For thou thy self art thine own bait;
That fish that is not catch'd thereby,
Alas, is wiser far than I.

A stanza form is determined by the line lengths and the rhyme-scheme, both of which must be correspondingly the same in every stanza. The *ballad stanza* is an ancient folk measure exactly fitted to the singing breath. Recite the following septenary:

There lived a wife at Usher's Well and a worthy wife was she.

It filled one breath precisely, didn't it?—thus indicating that the septenary is a natural line for singing. The ballads were sung in the hall of a castle by a minstrel, or by lonely women at their household tasks, or by groups of workmen or artisans singing at their work, work which, in the days of the handicrafts, was rhythmical and served as an accompaniment to the singing. Weaving, sawing, hauling on ropes—all such occupations were well adapted to solo and chorus. The sailors' ballads, or sea chanties, sung by sailors as they hauled at the lines of a sailing vessel, lasted well into this century until sail finally vanished from the sea. The ballads were doubtless composed by some gifted leader, but they were changed and modified by the crowd and by one generation after another, who sang them without ever thinking of putting them down on paper. When Sir Walter Scott was collecting ballads in the Highlands of Scotland, one old woman assured him that if he wrote them down they would not be ballads any more. There is some truth in this observation, for ballads belong in the oral tradition. Some of them were set down in Elizabethan times, and Sir Philip Sidney was deeply moved by the ballad *Chevy Chase* (though being a good Renaissance man, he thought it would have been much better if the Greek poet Pindar had written it!). It was not until the "Gothic" antiquarianism of the eighteenth century, however, that ballads were treated with respect and a good many of them published in 1765 by Thomas Percy in his *Reliques of Ancient English Poetry*. The book was immensely popular and eventually, with the Romantic poets, swung the ballad into serious literature, with such works as Coleridge's *Rime of the Ancient Mariner* and Keats's *La Belle Dame sans Merci*.

Many ballads had *refrains,* where even the shiest member of the company could add his voice to the general roar:

> There were twa sisters sat in a bower;
> *Binnorie, O Binnorie!*
> There came a knight to be their wooer,
> *By the bonny milldams of Binnorie.*

Though the normal form of the ballad is the *septenary,* there are dozens that exhibit variations on the form, such as introducing two-foot lines or lengthening the stanza to four four-foot lines. Ballads are not usually printed as septenaries, but are broken up into alternating line lengths of four and three stresses, thus:

> There lived a wife at Usher's Well,
>   And a wealthy wife was she;
> She had three stout and stalwart sons,
>   And sent them o'er the sea.
>
> They hadna been a week from her,
>   A week but barely ane,
> When word came to the carline wife
>   That her three sons were gane.

They hadna been a week from her,
    A week but barely three,
When word came to the carline wife
    That her sons she'd never see.

"I wish the wind may never cease,
    Nor fashes in the flood,
Till my three sons come hame to me
    In earthly flesh and blood!"

It fell about the Martinmas,
    When nights are lang and mirk,
The carline wife's three sons came hame,
    And their hats were o' the birk.

It neither grew in syke nor ditch,
    Nor yet in ony sheugh;
But at the gates o' Paradise
    That birk grew fair eneugh.

"Blow up the fire, my maidens!
    Bring water from the well!
For a' my house shall feast this night,
    Since my three sons are well."

And she has made to them a bed,
    She's made it large and wide;
And she's ta'en her mantle her about,
    Sat down at the bedside.

Up then crew the red, red cock,
    And up and crew the gray;
The eldest to the youngest said,
    " 'Tis time we were away."

The cock he hadna crawed but once,
    And clapped his wings at a',
When the youngest to the eldest said,
    "Brother, we must awa'."

"The cock doth craw, the day doth daw,
    The channerin' worm doth chide;

Gin we be missed out o' our place,
A sair pain we maun bide."

"Lie still, lie still but a little wee while,
Lie still but if we may;
Gin my mother should miss us when she wakes,
She'll go mad ere it be day."

"Fare ye weel, my mother dear!
Fareweel to barn and byre!
And fare ye weel, the bonny lass
That kindles my mother's fire."

The dialect here, as in most of the ballads, is Anglo-Scottish, for the ballads were composed in the northern part of England and the southern part of Scotland; hence, they are often called Border Ballads. Their themes are many: ghost stories, as in *The Wife of Usher's Well;* tales of fairyland, especially of the mortal who falls into the power of the Queen of the Fairies, as in the famous *Thomas the Rhymer,* or *Tam Lin;* battle poems, like *Chevy Chase;* tales of the court, like *Sir Patrick Spens* (a great sea poem) or *The Three Maries;* domestic situations, usually humorous, like *The Old Cloak* and *Get up and Bar the Door;* love stories, and tales of Robin Hood.

The ballad stanza is not confined to ballad material. It is often used in lyrics, such as Herrick's

Bid me to live, and I will live
Thy Protestant to be;
Or bid me love, and I will give
A loving heart to thee. . . .

Nearly all poets have used the stanza somewhere, and it is especially conspicuous in Emily Dickinson's work. It is the *common meter* of the Hymnal:

O God our help in ages past,
Our hope for years to come,
Our shelter from the stormy blast,
And our eternal home.
—Isaac Watts

It is doubtless the hymn book that influenced Emily Dickinson in her choice of this and other stanzas. The ballad stanza is also a favorite of A. E. Housman:

> And wish my friend as sound a sleep
> As lads I did not know,
> That shepherded the moonlit sheep
> A hundred years ago.

It will be noted that in *The Wife of Usher's Well* only the second and fourth lines rhymed, the first and third being left without rhyme. This is the common practice of the folk ballad. But when the stanza enters consciously literary poetry, as in the passages from Herrick, Watts, and Housman, all the lines are rhymed alternately, *abab*.

The *four-stress quatrain* (known to the Hymnal as *long meter*) is also one of the basic stanzas. A good example is George Herbert's beautiful Easter poem:

> I got me flowers to straw Thy way,
> I got me boughs off many a tree;
> But Thou wast up by break of day,
> And brought'st Thy sweets along with Thee.
>
> Yet though my flowers be lost, they say
> A heart can never come too late;
> Teach it to sing Thy praise this day,
> And then this day my life shall date.

Or, for a modern example, take Robert Frost's *The Aim Was Song:*

> Before man came to blow it right
> The wind once blew itself untaught,
> And did its loudest day and night
> In any rough place where it caught.
>
> Man came to tell it what was wrong:
> It hadn't found the place to blow;
> It blew too hard—the aim was song!
> And listen—how it ought to go.
>
> He took a little in his mouth,
> And held it long enough for north

To be converted into south,
  And then by measure blew it forth.

By measure. It was word and note,
  The wind the wind had meant to be—
A little through the lips and throat.
  The aim was song—the wind could see.

The *In Memoriam stanza,* as its name indicates, is the stanza form of Tennyson's great elegy. Tennyson did not invent it; it is found in versions of the psalms by the seventeenth-century poet George Sandys and elsewhere, and it is the rhyme scheme, though the meter is different, of Shakespeare's *Phoenix and the Turtle.* It is occasionally found today. Here are three stanzas from *In Memoriam:*

Love is and was my Lord and King,
  And in his presence I attend
  To hear the tidings of my friend
Which every hour his couriers bring.

Love is and was my King and Lord,
  And will be, tho' as yet I keep
  Within his court on earth, and sleep
Encompass'd by his faithful guard,

And hear at times a sentinel
  Who moves about from place to place
  And whispers to the world of space,
In the deep night, that all is well.

The rhyme-scheme, *abba,* is the same as in the first four lines of the Petrarchan sonnet, and it may well be that that was the origin of Tennyson's stanza. Oscar Wilde, in his poem *The Sphinx,* combined two lines into one long one, *octameter,* thus making two of the rhymes internal:

False Sphinx! False Sphinx! By reedy Styx old Charon leaning on his oar
Waits for my coin. Go thou before, and leave me to my crucifix,
Whose pallid burden, sick with pain, watches the world with wearied
    eyes,
And weeps for every soul that dies, and weeps for every soul in vain.

One of the most interesting and important forms in the language is the *five-stress couplet.* It is the perfect vehicle for a single epigram:

No *Spring,* nor *Summer* Beauty hath such grace
As I have seen in one *Autumnal* face.
                              —JOHN DONNE, *The Autumnal*
To work a wonder, God would have her shown
At once a bud, and yet a rose full-blown.
                              —ROBERT HERRICK, *On the Virgin Mary*
My soul, sit thou a patient looker-on,
Judge not the play before the play is done:
Her plot hath many changes; every day
Speaks a new scene; the last act crowns the play.
                              —FRANCIS QUARLES

There are two kinds of five-stress iambic couplet, the *"open"* couplet, where one couplet flows into another through a series of enjambments, and the *"closed"* couplet, usually called the heroic (classical) couplet, where every couplet is a single unit of syntax, and there is no overflow from one into another.

We find the open five-stress couplet in Chaucer's Prologue to the *Canterbury Tales* and in many of the tales themselves:

> Bifel that in that seson on a day,
> In Southwerk at the Tabard as I lay
> Redy to wenden on my pylgrimage
> To Caunterbury with ful devout corage,
> At nyght was come into that hostelrye
> Wel nyne and twenty in a compaignye,
> Of sondry folk, by aventure yfalle
> In felaweshipe, and pilgrimes were they alle,
> That toward Caunterbury wolden ryde.
> The chambres and the stables weren wyde. ...

Marlowe's couplets in *Hero and Leander* are less open than Chaucer's. We have already seen Marlowe as the master of end-stopped verse in a passage from *Dr. Faustus.*

The man who originated the closed or "heroic" couplet was Edmund Waller in the mid seventeenth century. Pope called the verse before Waller's time "that former savagery." Repelled by the loose verse of Donne and his followers, Waller turned to French models, substituting for the closed Alexandrine couplet of French classic verse the closed five-stress couplet in English. The revolution that he brought about established that form as the only serious vehicle for a century and a half. Immensely popular in his own time, he later won high praise from Voltaire, who maintained that polished versification in English was invented by Waller, and, in his own country, from Dryden, who said that "the excellence and dignity of rhyme were never fully known till Mr. Waller taught it; he first made writing easily an art, first showed us to conclude the sense, most commonly, in distichs, which in the verse of those before him runs on for so many lines together, that the reader is out of breath to overtake it." Strange are the caprices of fame! Today, Waller is generally known for only two exquisite lyrics, *On a Girdle* and *Go, Lovely Rose*. But the heroic couplet, as he established it, flows like a great tide through the poetry of Dryden, Pope, Samuel Johnson, Goldsmith, Crabbe, and even as far as Byron's *English Bards and Scotch Reviewers.*

With what delight did the young John Keats overthrow the heroic couplet! That Bastille of English versification fell before him. Using the open, overflowing couplet in *Sleep and Poetry,* he not only attacked the couplet of Pope, but went back further and paid his respects to the seventeenth-century French critic Boileau, whom he held accountable for the entire trend:

> . . . a schism
> Nurtured by foppery and barbarism
> Made great Apollo blush for this his land.
> Men were thought wise who did not understand
> His glories: with a puling infant's force
> They sway'd about upon a rocking-horse
> And thought it Pegasus . . . no, they went about
> Holding a poor decrepit standard out,
> Marked with most flimsy mottoes, and in large
> The name of one Boileau!

In *Endymion* young Keats almost too deliberately pulls his meaning through couplet after couplet, and the effect is breathless:

> Nor do we merely feel these essences
> For one short hour; no, even as the trees
> That whisper round a temple become soon
> Dear as the temple's self, so does the moon

The passion poesy, glories infinite,
Haunt us till they become a cheering light
Unto our souls, and bound to us so fast,
That, whether there be shine, or gloom o'ercast,
They always must be with us, or we die.

    Therefore 'tis with full happiness that I
Will trace the story of Endymion.
The very music of the name has gone, . . .

It is with some relief that we turn back to Pope:

Now, they who reach Parnassus' lofty crown,
Employ their pains to spurn some others down;
And while self-love each jealous writer rules,
Contending wits become the sport of fools:
And still the worst with most regret commend,
And each ill Author is as bad a Friend.
To what base ends, and by what abject ways,
Are mortals urged thro' sacred lust of praise!
Ah, ne'er so dire a thirst of glory boast,
Nor in the Critic let the Man be lost!
Good-nature and good-sense must ever join;
To err is human, to forgive, divine.

Today the five-stress couplet is standard with all metrical poets.
It is conspicuously to be found in John Masefield's *King Cole* and
some of his other works. No one bothers now about the strife between the open and closed couplet; poets follow their ear and use
both. The advantage lies with the heroic couplet, as the following
poems, the first by E. A. Robinson, the second by Robert Frost, show:

The Prodigal Son

You are not merry, brother. Why not laugh,
As I do, and acclaim the fatted calf?
For, unless ways are changing here at home,
You might not have it if I had not come.
And were I not a thing for you and me
To execrate in anguish, you would be
As indigent a stranger to surprise,
I fear, as I was once, and as unwise.

Brother, believe as I do, it is best
For you that I'm again in the old nest—
Draggled, I grant you, but your brother still,
Full of good wine, good viands, and good will.
You will thank God, some day, that I returned,
And may be singing for what you have learned,
Some other day; and one day you may find
Yourself a little nearer to mankind.
And having hated me till you are tired,
You will begin to see, as if inspired,
It was fate's way of educating us.
Remembering then when you were venomous,
You will be glad enough that I am gone,
But you will know more of what's going on;
For you will see more of what makes it go,
And in more ways than are for you to know.
We are so different when we are dead,
That you, alive, may weep for what you said;
And I, the ghost of one you could not save,
May find you planting lentils on my grave.

The majority of the couplets in Robinson's poems are closed, and
in Robert Frost's *The Tuft of Flowers* they are printed as separate
stanzas:

I went to turn the grass once after one
Who mowed it in the dew before the sun.

The dew was gone that made his blade so keen
Before I came to view the leveled scene.

I looked for him behind an isle of trees;
I listened for his whetstone on the breeze.

But he had gone his way, the grass all mown,
And I must be, as he had been,—alone,

"As all must be," I said within my heart,
"Whether they work together or apart."

But as I said it, swift there passed me by
On noiseless wing a bewildered butterfly,

Seeking with memories grown dim o'er night
Some resting flower of yesterday's delight.

And once I marked his flight go round and round,
As where some flower lay withering on the ground.

And then he flew as far as eye could see,
And then on tremulous wing came back to me.

I thought of questions that have no reply,
And would have turned to toss the grass to dry;

But he turned first, and led my eye to look
At a tall tuft of flowers beside a brook,

A leaping tongue of bloom the scythe had spared
Beside a reedy brook the scythe had bared.

I left my place to know them by their name,
Finding them butterfly-weed when I came.

The mower in the dew had loved them thus,
By leaving them to flourish, not for us,

Nor yet to draw one thought of ours to him,
But from sheer morning gladness at the brim.

The butterfly and I had lit upon,
Nevertheless, a message from the dawn,

That made me hear the wakening birds around,
And hear his long scythe whispering to the ground,

And feel a spirit kindred to my own;
So that henceforth I worked no more alone;

But glad with him, I worked as with his aid,
And weary, sought at noon with him the shade;

And dreaming, as it were, held brotherly speech
With one whose thought I had not hoped to reach.

"Men work together," I told him from the heart,
"Whether they work together or apart."

The *heroic quatrain,* consisting of four iambic pentameters rhymed
alternately, *abab,* was probably derived from the first quatrain of

the English, or Shakespearean, sonnet. We first find it in Sir John Davies' *Nosce Teipsum* (Know thyself) (1599), a fine metaphysical poem in the true sense of the term, dealing with human knowledge and the soul of man. Some nimble scholar ought to reprint this old poem and without riddling it with footnotes. Here are a few stanzas:

> I know my Soul hath power to know all things,
> Yet is she blind and ignorant in all;
> I know I am one of Nature's little kings,
> Yet to the least and vilest things am thrall!
>
> I know my Life's a pain and but a span;
> I know my sense is mocked in everything:
> And to conclude, I know myself a Man;
> Which is a proud, and yet a wretched thing! ...
>
> Even so the Soul, which in this earthly mould,
> The Spirit of God doth secretly infuse;
> Because at first She doth the earth behold,
> And only this material world She views! ...
>
> Yet, under Heaven, She cannot light on aught
> That with her heavenly nature doth agree:
> She cannot rest! She cannot fix her thought!
> She cannot in this world contented be!

Dryden used the form for his *Annus Mirabilis, or, The Year of Wonders, 1666,* an overlong poem on the naval war with the Dutch and the great fire of London. Of his stanza form, Dryden says, "I have chosen to write my poem in quatrains, or stanzas of four in alternate rhyme, because I have ever judged them more noble, and of greater dignity, both for the sound and number, than any other verse in use amongst us." The nobility and dignity of this stanza have caused it to be termed the English elegiac stanza, partly because the finest poem in this form, Thomas Gray's *Elegy Written in a Country Churchyard,* comes to mind when we speak of it. The *Elegy,* universally admired, has inspired readers as diverse as General Wolfe and Bernard Berenson. No wonder!:

> Beneath those rugged elms, that yew-tree's shade,
>   Where heaves the turf in many a mould'ring heap,
> Each in his narrow cell for ever laid,
>   The rude Forefathers of the hamlet sleep.

Let not Ambition mock their useful toil,
 Their homely joys and destiny obscure;
Nor Grandeur hear with a disdainful smile
 The short and simple annals of the poor.

Far from the madding crowd's ignoble strife,
 Their sober wishes never learn'd to stray;
Along the cool sequester'd vale of life
 They kept the noiseless tenor of their way.

Here is an up-to-the-minute example of the form by Howard
Nemerov. His heroic quatrains appeared in *The New Yorker* for
12 December 1959.

Elegy for a Nature Poet

It was in October, a favorite season,
He went for his last walk. The covered bridge,
Most natural of all the works of reason,
Received him, let him go. Along the hedge

He rattled his stick; observed the blackening bushes
In his familiar field; thought he espied
Late meadow larks; considered picking rushes
For a dry arrangement; returned home, and died

Of a catarrh caught in the autumn rains
And let go on uncared for. He was too rapt
In contemplation to recall that brains
Like his should not be kept too long uncapped

In the wet and cold weather. While we mourned,
We thought of his imprudence, and how Nature,
Whom he'd done so much for, had finally turned
Against her creature.

His gift was daily his delight, he peeled
The landscape back to show it was a story;
Any old bird or burning bush revealed
At his hands just another allegory.

Nothing too great, nothing too trivial
For him; from mountain range or humble vermin

He could extract the hidden parable—
If need be, crack the stone to get the sermon.

And now, poor man, he's gone. Without his name
The field reverts to wilderness again,
The rocks are silent, woods don't seem the same.
Demoralized small birds will fly insane.

Rude Nature, whom he loved to idealize
And would have wed, pretends she never heard
His voice at all, as, taken by surprise
At last, he goes to her without a word.

You will note that, as is the custom with many of the younger
contemporary poets, Mr. Nemerov uses the form freely, introducing
two strong trisyllabic feet in line 5, and cutting off the final line of
the fourth stanza after the second foot, to give an effect of climax.
The "elegy" has a slightly satiric tone, which does not, however,
destroy the underlying pathos. This is a successful example of the
polyphonic emotional quality striven for by many modern poets
and seldom as successfully as in these lines.

Three stanza forms that have an honorable tradition behind them
but are seldom to be found in modern poetry are the *rime royal,* the
Spenserian stanza, and the *ottava rima.*

Rime royal is a seven-line stanza in iambic pentameter rhymed
ababbcc. It was a favorite with Chaucer, who used it in *The
Parlement of Foules,* in *Troilus and Criseyde,* and in *The Man of
Law's Tale* and *The Prioress's Tale* from *The Canterbury Tales.*
King James I of Scotland, while sailing to France, was captured by
English sailors in 1406 and remained a prisoner in England until
1424, and during those eighteen years he built up a fine reputation
as a poet. One of his favorite stanzas was the one we call the rime
royal in honor of its royal practitioner. Many early poets found this
stanza to their taste, including John Skelton and Sir Thomas Wyatt.
It is the stanza of Shakespeare's *Rape of Lucrece.* It was employed
by Edmund Spenser, Michael Drayton, and Samuel Daniel. After
that it disappeared, to be revived by the nineteenth-century poet William Morris in his *Earthly Paradise.* It would have slipped away
again, had it not been that John Masefield, disciple of Chaucer, chose
it as the form for three of his long narrative poems, *The Daffodil*

Fields, The Widow in the Bye Street, and his masterpiece, *Dauber.*
Here is the old stanza under full sail again in a passage from *Dauber:*

> Darkness came down—half darkness—in a whirl;
> The sky went out, the waters disappeared.
> He felt a shocking pressure of blowing hurl
> The ship upon her side. The darkness speared
> At her with wind; she staggered, she careered;
> Then down she lay. The Dauber felt her go,
> He saw her yard tilt downwards. Then the snow
>
> Whirled all about—dense, multitudinous, cold—
> Mixed with the wind's one devilish thrust and shriek,
> Which whiffled out men's tears, defeated, took hold,
> Flattening the flying drift against the cheek.
> The yards buckled and bent, man could not speak.
> The ship lay on her broadside; the wind's sound
> Had devilish malice at having got her downed.
>
> How long the gale had blown he could not tell,
> Only the world had changed, his life had died.
> A moment now was everlasting hell.
> Nature an onslaught from the weather side,
> A withering rush of death, a frost that cried,
> Shrieked, till he withered at the heart; a hail
> Plastered his oilskins with an icy mail. . . .

Two or three years ago, I published a short poem in rime royal
in *The New Yorker,* confident that this was the first example of it
to be published in America. Then, by one of those inspirations of
memory that are so few and far between, I remembered the Negro
poet, my friend and student, the late Countee Cullen. He was enrolled
in the course in versification that I gave for many years at Harvard.
In that course, I had the students practice writing in all the different
forms of English verse. In Cullen's third book, *Copper Sun,* he
published his exercises. Since he was a good poet, they were well
worth preserving. He included them in a section called "At Cambridge" which, "with grateful appreciation," he dedicated to me.
There they all are, ballad stanzas, heroic couplets, four-stress couplets,
blank verse, Spenserian stanzas—he must have liked the Spenserian
stanza, for he wrote an extra poem in it—and rime royal:

To Lovers of Earth: Fair Warning

Give over to high things the fervent thought
You waste on Earth; let down the righteous bar
Against a wayward peace too dearly bought
Upon this pale and passion-frozen star.
Sweethearts and friends, are they not loyal? Far
More fickle, false, perverse, far more unkind
Is Earth to those who gave her heart and mind.

And you whose lusty youth her snares intrigue,
Who glory in her seas, swear by her clouds,
With Age, man's foe, Earth ever is in league.
Time resurrects her even while he crowds
Your bloom to dust, and lengthens out your shrouds
A day's length or a year's; she will be young
When your last cracked and quivering note is sung.

She will remain the Earth, sufficient still,
Though you are gone and with you that rare loss
That vanishes with your bewildered will.
And there shall flame no red, indignant cross
For you, no quick white scar of wrath emboss
The sky, no blood drip from a wounded moon,
And not a single star chime out of tune.

As far as I know, the first rime royals in America were Countee
Cullen's. The young poets of today are searching out old forms
eagerly, and it may be that some of them will follow Masefield's
example and write a masterwork in rime royal, but somehow I doubt
it; that extra line just before the couplet is difficult to tame.

The Spenserian stanza evolved out of Chaucer's *Monk's Tale.*
Chaucer took the interlocking rhyme scheme of the eight-line *ballade*
stanza from France, *ababbcbc,* thus:

Although that Nero were as vicius
As any feend that lith ful lowe adoun,
Yet he, as telleth us Swetonius,
This wydè world hadde in subjeccioun
Both est and west, south and septemtrioun.
Of rubies, saphires, and of peerless white

Were all his clothès brouded up and doun;
For he in gemmès greetly gan delite.

Edmund Spenser, Chaucer's most inspired disciple, added a six-foot
line to the *Monk's Tale* stanza and gave us his nine-line form:

The whiles some one did chaunt this lovely lay:
Ah! see, whoso fair thing doest fain to see,
In springing flowers the image of thy day.
Ah! see the Virgin Rose, how sweetly she
Doth first peep forth with bashful modesty,
That fairer seems the less ye see her may.
Lo! see soon after how more bold and free
Her barèd bosom she doth broad display;
Lo! see soon after how she fades and falls away.
                                                   —*The Faerie Queene*

The stanza floated two long poems of faded merit during the eight-
eenth century, Shenstone's *The Schoolmistress* and Thomson's *The
Castle of Indolence,* and came to great glory with the Romantic
poets. We find four major Romantic poems in the Spenserian stanza:
Robert Burns's *The Cotter's Saturday Night,* Lord Byron's *Childe
Harold's Pilgrimage,* Keats's *Eve of St. Agnes,* and Shelley's *Adonais.*
These works are too long for quotation. The opening stanza of
The Eve of St. Agnes and a stanza from *Adonais* will suffice to show
how flexibly the form adapted itself to the more modern idiom:

St. Agnes' Eve—Ah, bitter chill it was!
The owl, for all his feathers, was a-cold;
The hare limped trembling through the frozen grass,
And silent was the flock in woolly fold;
Numb were the Beadsman's fingers, while he told
His rosary, and while his frosted breath,
Like pious incense from a censer old,
Seem'd taking flight for heaven, without a death,
Past the sweet Virgin's picture, while his prayer he saith.

And from *Adonais:*

The One remains, the many change and pass;
Heaven's light forever shines, earth's shadows fly;
Life, like a dome of many-coloured glass,

Stains the white radiance of Eternity,
Until Death tramples it to fragments.—Die,
If thou wouldst be with them that thou dost seek!
Follow where all is fled! Rome's azure sky,
Flowers, ruins, statues, music, words, are weak
The glory they transfuse with fitting truth to speak.

Here is the strange phenomenon: except for the opening stanzas of Tennyson's *Lotos Eaters,* the Spenserian stanza vanished with the Romantic poets. I have tried it, because in the nature of my job of teaching as well as my art as poet, I have had to try everything; but the form did not come naturally; it seemed laborious and a bit heavy. The times have speeded up, our rhythms are faster than those of our forebears, and the long stanza culminating in its alexandrine belongs to an age of ampler measures than ours, like the prose of the King James Bible. We can still appreciate such beauties, but we cannot create them, and, if we tried, the effect would probably seem archaic.

Although the eight-line stanza, the ottava rima, rhyming *ababab cc,* is found in the poems of Wyatt and the Elizabethans, it is best known in Byron's *Don Juan.* That Satanic combination of slapstick, wit, mock-heroic, serious poetry, and wild, Hudibrastic rhyming, is an enduring *tour de force.* With what gusto does Byron belabor the older generation of Romantic poets:

> All are not moralists, like Southey, when
> He prated to the world of "Pantisocracy";
> Or Wordsworth unexcised, unhired, who then
> Season'd his pedlar poems with democracy;
> Or Coleridge, long before his flighty pen
> Let to the *Morning Post* its aristocracy;
> While he and Southey, following the same path,
> Espoused two partners (milliners of Bath).

Canto III, xciii

What a snob Byron was! Though he was a revolutionary, you may be sure that he would still have been *Lord* Byron in any ideal commonwealth he might imagine. Shelley was well born, too, an acceptable friend for Lord Byron, although Shelley was no snob. In fact, Shelley, who, in spite of a somewhat conscientiously irregular life, was at heart a puritan, was often shocked and repelled by Byron's way of life, with which he was in close contact in Italy. Continuing on the subject of the older romanticists, Byron remarks:

> Such names at present cut a convict figure,
> The very Botany Bay in moral geography;
> Their loyal treason, renegado rigour,
> Are good manure for their more bare biography.
> Wordsworth's last quarto, by the way, is bigger
> Than any since the birthday of typography;
> A drowsy frowzy poem, call'd the *Excursion*,
> Writ in a manner which is my aversion.
>
> Canto III, xciv

One of his most amusing thrusts is in the last ottava rima of canto I:

> "Go, little book, from this my solitude!
> I cast thee on the waters—go thy ways!
> And if, as I believe, thy vein be good,
> The world will find thee after many days."
> When Southey's read and Wordsworth understood,
> I can't help putting in my claim to praise—
> The first four rhymes are Southey's, every line:
> For God's sake, reader! take them not for mine!

On the subject of Keats he is kindly but condescending:

> John Keats, who was kill'd off by one critique,
> Just as he really promised something great,
> If not intelligible, without Greek
> Contrived to talk about the gods of late,
> Much as they might have been supposed to speak.
> Poor fellow! His was an untoward fate;
> 'Tis strange the mind, that very fiery particle,
> Should let itself be snuffed out by an article.
>
> Canto XI, lix

Poets who possess the classical languages fluently are prone to feel somewhat superior to their less learned fellows. We are reminded of Ben Jonson, self-educated to a magnificent pedantry, saying of Shakespeare,

> For though thou hadst small Latin and less Greek,
> From thence to honour thee I would not seek.

The fact is that the large majority of well-known poets in our literature have been well versed in Latin and Greek and show some influence from the classics.

The passages I have so far quoted from the poem are among the hundreds of digressions from the main story of Don Juan, his wanderings and loves. Byron's best genius is shown in the way he can change suddenly from wit to serious poetry that is truly moving, such as this stanza:

> Ave Maria! blessèd be the hour!
> The time, the clime, the spot, where I so oft
> Have felt that moment in its fullest power
> Sink o'er the earth so beautiful and soft,
> While swung the deep bell in the distant tower,
> Or the faint dying day-hymn stole aloft,
> And not a breath crept through the rosy air,
> And yet the forest leaves seem'd stirr'd with prayer.
>
> Canto III, cii

I have used the ottava rima in occasional verses, and find it flexible and easy. It is surely nervous and speedy enough for our times, and I should not be surprised to see a revival of it.

Another importation from Italy is the *terza rima,* the interlocking rhyme-scheme of Dante's *Divine Comedy, a b a, b c b, c d c,* etc., until the end, *d e d, e.* It is not often found, but two poems, at least, Shelley's sweeping *Ode to the West Wind* and Robert Bridges' exquisite *London Snow,* make it worthy of mention. Shelley's great ode is familiar to all my readers, and I shall quote only one stanza, the climax of the poem. You will note that Shelley ties up his final rhyme with a couplet, rather than a single line. Also, the fact that the stanzas are fourteen lines long (*quatorzains*) gives them the effect of irregular sonnets:

> Make me thy lyre, even as the forest is:
>   What if my leaves are falling like its own?
> The tumult of thy mighty harmonies

Will take from both a deep autumnal tone,
Sweet though in sadness. Be thou, Spirit fierce,
  My spirit! Be thou me, impetuous one!

Drive my dead thoughts over the universe,
  Like wither'd leaves to quicken a new birth;
And, by the incantation of this verse,

  Scatter, as from an unextinguish'd hearth,
Ashes and sparks, my words among mankind!
  Be through my lips to unawaken'd earth

The trumpet of a prophesy! O Wind,
If Winter comes, can Spring be far behind?

How different, yet, in its way, equally successful, is Bridges' *London Snow*:

When men were all asleep the snow came flying,
In large white flakes falling on the city brown,
Stealthily and perpetually settling and loosely lying,
  Hushing the latest traffic of the drowsy town;
Deadening, muffling, stifling its murmurs failing;
Lazily and incessantly floating down and down;
  Silently sifting and veiling road, roof and railing;
Hiding difference, making unevenness even,
Into angles and crevices softly drifting and sailing.
  All night it fell, and when full inches seven
It lay in the depth of its uncompacted lightness,
The clouds blew off from a high and frosty heaven;
  And all woke earlier for the unaccustomed brightness
Of the winter dawning, the strange unheavenly glare:
The eye marveled—marveled at the dazzling whiteness;
  The ear hearkened to the stillness of the solemn air;
No sound of wheel rumbling nor of foot falling,
And the busy morning cries came thin and spare.
  Then boys I heard, as they went to school, calling;
They gathered up the crystal manna to freeze
Their tongues with tasting, their hands with snow-balling;
  Or rioted in a drift, plunging up to the knees;
Or peering up from under the white-mossed wonder,

"O look at the trees!" they cried. "O look at the trees!"
  With lessened load, a few carts creak and blunder,
Following along the white deserted way,
A country company long dispersed asunder:
  When now already the sun, in pale display
Standing by Paul's high dome, spread forth below
His sparkling beams, and awoke the stir of the day.

  For now doors open, and war is waged with the snow;
And trains of somber men, past tale of number,
Tread long brown paths, as toward their toil they go:
  But even for them awhile no cares encumber
Their minds diverted; the daily word is unspoken,
The daily thoughts of labor and sorrow slumber
At the sight of the beauty that greets them, for
    the charm they have broken.

Bridges was one of the greatest technicians in the history of English poetry. Note the boldness with which he departs from the ten-syllable iambic pentameter. The first line is regular, with a feminine ending, but throughout the poem there are many trisyllabic feet, and in the last line of seventeen syllables the meter moves over into three-part, anapestic, rhythm. All these fluttering extra syllables falling across the main iambic meter give just the effect he intended —of falling snow.

Another frequently found stanza is the six-line combination of a quatrain with a couplet, which is found in various line-lengths, usually four or five feet. Here is the last stanza of Shakespeare's 199-stanza poem, *Venus and Adonis,* in which the form is used with five feet:

  Thus weary of the world, away she hies,
  And yokes her silver doves; by whose swift aid
  Their mistress, mounted, through the empty skies
  In her light chariot quickly is conveyed,
    Holding her course to Paphos, where their queen
    Means to immure herself and not be seen.

Poets delight, especially in lyric poetry, in inventing stanza forms of their own: they explore new combinations of rhyme and line length, each listening for his particular music in what he contrives.

A manuscript of Shelley's gives the bare metrical chart of the poem that finally turned out to be

Threnos

O World! O Life! O Time!
On whose last steps I climb,
   Trembling at that where I had stood before;
When shall return the glory of your prime?
   No more—Oh never more.

Out of the day and night
A joy has taken flight:
   Fresh spring, and summer, and winter hoar
Move my faint heart with grief, but with delight
   No more—Oh never more.

Here we have a stanza with line lengths 3, 3, 5, 5, 3, and a rhyme-scheme: *aabab,* and I suppose that there is no other poem with exactly the same structure. There are hundreds of such unique stanza forms in the work of our poets.

The Ode

Ode is one of the most indefinite terms in English verse. Almost any poem of substantial length and elevated tone may be called an ode. Yet an analysis of the various works in this class reveals three distinct types: the *stanzaic ode,* the *Pindaric ode,* and the *irregular ode.*

The *stanzaic ode* was originally an attempt in English to approximate the effect of the stanzaic odes of Horace. It is a series of strophes in similar form. Here are a few stanzas, describing the murder of King Charles I, from Andrew Marvell's *Horatian Ode upon Cromwell's Return from Ireland:*

That thence the royal actor borne
The tragic scaffold might adorn,
   While round the armèd bands
   Did clap their bloody hands.

He nothing common did, or mean,
Upon that memorable scene,
   But with his keener eye
   The axe's edge did try;

> Nor called the gods with vulgar spite
> To vindicate his helpless right,
> But bowed his comely head
> Down, as upon a bed.

I hate to say it, Marvell being one of my favorites, but this is dreadful poetry. He was much happier in the simple four-stress couplet.

William Collins' *Ode to Evening* gets its effects without the aid of rhyme, one with Thomas Campion's *Rose-cheeked Laura, Come* and Tennyson's lyrics from *The Princess,* in a group of short poems so melodious that the absence of rhyme is scarcely noted. Here are three stanzas from Collins' ode:

> For when thy folding-star arising shows
> His paly circlet, at his warning lamp
>   The fragrant hours, and elves
>   Who slept in buds the day,
>
> And many a nymph who wreathes her brows with sedge,
> And sheds the freshening dew, and, lovelier still,
>   The pensive pleasures sweet,
>   Prepare thy shadowy car;
>
> Then lead, calm votaress, where some sheety lake
> Cheers the lone heath, or some time-hallowed pile,
>   Or upland fallows grey
>   Reflect its last cool gleam.

The stanzaic ode, however, soon emerged from the influence of Horace as its strophes became longer and more complicated. The triumphs in this form are Shelley's *Ode to the West Wind* and John Keats's *On Melancholy, Autumn, On a Grecian Urn,* and *To a Nightingale.* These golden poems are too familiar to need quotation here.

The *Pindaric ode* is an attempt to reproduce in English the effect of the choric ode of the Greek poet Pindar. The form is complicated. It is tripartite, consisting of a strophe and an antistrophe (two stanzas identical in form) and an epode (a third stanza differing in form from the other two). These three stanzas form a triad that may be repeated any number of times, all the strophes and antistrophes throughout the poem matching and all the epodes corresponding in like manner. The Pindaric ode is too complex for general use. The only three examples I know of that actually hold to the form are Ben Jonson's *Ode to the Immortal Memory and Friendship of that Noble Pair, Sir Lucius Carey and Sir H. Morrison*, and two magnificent Pindaric odes, in strict classic form, Thomas Gray's *Progress of Poesy* and *The Bard*.

We are not done with Pindar. The seventeenth-century poet Abraham Cowley produced what he called "Pindaric" odes, but they were not Pindaric at all. Cowley failed to notice the strict triad construction and wrote poems of irregular strophes in which repetition played no part. Dryden followed suit with his *Alexander's Feast* and his *Song for St. Cecilia's Day*. It was a happy mistake, and opened a whole new vista of form, the poet having full license to vary his line lengths as he chose and place rhymes in no set scheme but anywhere where they were convenient and musical. It should be noted that Milton anticipated this irregular form in his *Lycidas*. Thanks to such works as Wordsworth's *Ode on the Intimations of Immortality from Recollections of Early Childhood* and Coleridge's *Dejection, an Ode,* this irregular false Pindaric is sometimes called the Romantic Ode.

I have invented the term *modulated verse* for informal poems or short ones in this irregular style. Edwin Arlington Robinson's *Man Against the Sky* is in modulated verse. So is Matthew Arnold's *Dover Beach,* perhaps the most justly famous example:

> The sea is calm to-night
> The tide is full, the moon lies fair
> Upon the straits;—on the French coast the light
> Gleams and is gone; the cliffs of England stand,
> Glimmering and vast, out in the tranquil bay.
> Come to the window, sweet is the night-air!
> Only, from the long line of spray
> Where the sea meets the moon-blanch'd land,
> Listen! you hear the grating roar
> Of pebbles which the waves draw back, and fling,
> At their return, up the high strand,
> Begin, and cease, and then again begin,
> With tremulous cadence slow, and bring
> The eternal note of sadness in. . . .

Blank Verse

If we include the drama, about three-quarters of our poetry in English is in *blank verse*. It is the instrument for Elizabethan drama, Milton's *Paradise Lost,* many of the long poems of Shelley and Keats, Wordsworth's *Michael, The Prelude, The Excursion;* Tennyson's *Idylls of the King* and *The Princess,* Browning's interminable *The Ring and the Book,* eighteen of Edwin Arlington Robinson's long narrative poems, many of Robert Frost's New England poems, and a host of other works by poets great and small. Blank verse relieves the poet from rhyme and at the same time imposes a strict discipline that can come only from the individual conscience, for the lack of rhyme and the conversational quality of blank verse are a temptation to garrulousness that is sometimes yielded to even by the best of poets. We recall King George III's remarks to Fanny Burney:

"Was there ever," cried he, "such stuff as great part of Shakespeare? only one must not say so! But what think you?—What?—Is there not sad stuff?—What?—What?—What?"

"Yes indeed," said Miss Burney, "I think so, sir, though mixed with such excellences, that——"

"Oh!" cried he, laughing good-humouredly, "I know it is not to be said! but it's true. Only it's Shakespeare, and nobody dare abuse him."

We will not agree with King George, that the great part of Shakespeare is "sad stuff," but some of the early plays could be dropped without loss to his reputation.

Thanks to his varied dramatic masterpieces and the *Sonnets,* Shakespeare's reputation is forever secure, but on the subject of Milton's *Paradise Lost* I shall always remain a heretic. Even Dr. Johnson admitted that it is one of the books which the reader admires and lays down, and forgets to take up again. "No one ever wished it longer than it is. Its perusal is a duty rather than a pleasure." On the other hand, *Paradise Lost* has been the inspiration of many a poet since Milton's time, and it is so generally applauded that I should perhaps ascribe my own lack of affection for it to a deficiency on my part. Most modern students, I have noticed, read it with avidity.

There is a tendency today to confuse *blank* verse with *free* verse, so it might be well at this point to emphasize the fact that the term applies to unrhymed iambic pentameter and to nothing else. Though the absence of rhyme would seem to invite all sorts of irregularities and metrical looseness, most writers have used the form with syllabic regularity, ten syllables to the line, except for the trisyllabic feet and feminine endings common in any kind of verse.

It was Henry Howard, Earl of Surrey, co-originator of the sonnet in English, who introduced blank verse into England with his translation of the second and fourth books of Virgil's *Aeneid*, published in 1557. Surrey, who had traveled in Italy and was well acquainted with Italian literature, as is shown by his translations from Petrarch, was probably familiar with Trissino's rhymeless tragedy, *Sofonisba*. However, he may well have invented blank verse in order to approximate Virgil's rhymeless verse. Surrey's blank verse is crude; sometimes it seems as though his only intention was to get ten syllables in each line, letting the accent fall where it would, and many of his verses cannot be scanned according to modern standards.

Blank verse was the instrument for the first English tragedy, *Gorboduc* (1565), but the first great master of the form was Christopher Marlowe, who, as I have already pointed out, composed in "endstopped" lines. It is a tribute to his genius that this repetitious kind of verse seldom, in his hands, became monotonous. As Beethoven built on Mozart, so Shakespeare built on Marlowe. His early verse was largely end-stopped, as may be seen in this passage from *The Comedy of Errors:*

> Hapless Ægeon, whom the fates have mark'd
> To bear the extremity of dire mishap!
> Now, trust me, were it not against our laws,
> Against my oath, my crown, my dignity,
> Which princes, would they, may not disannul,
> My soul should sue as advocate for thee.
> But, though thou art adjudgèd to the death,
> And passèd sentence may not be recall'd
> But to our honour's great disparagement,
> Yet will I favour thee in what I can. . . .

The verse of *Othello*, written in Shakespeare's prime, is much more open:

> Think'st thou I'd make a life of jealousy,
> To follow still the changes of the moon

With fresh suspicions? No; to be once in doubt
Is once to be resolvèd: exchange me for a goat,
When I shall turn the business of my soul
To such exsufflicate and blown surmises,
Matching thy inference. 'Tis not to make me jealous
To say my wife is fair, feeds well, loves company,
Is free of speech, sings, plays, and dances well;
Where virtue is, these are more virtuous;
Nor from mine own weak merits will I draw
The smallest fear or doubt of her revolt;
For she had eyes, and chose me. No, Iago;
I'll see before I doubt. . . .

And in one of the last and most beautiful plays, *The Tempest,* the cadences are more flexible yet:

You do look, my son, in a movèd sort,
As if you were dismay'd: be cheerful, sir.
Our revels now are ended. These our actors,
As I foretold you, are all spirits, and
Are melted into air, into thin air:
And, like the baseless fabric of this vision,
The cloud-capp'd towers, the gorgeous palaces,
The solemn temples, the great globe itself,
Yes, all which it inherit, shall dissolve,
And, like this insubstantial pageant faded,
Leave not a rack behind. We are such stuff
As dreams are made on; and our little life
Is rounded with a sleep. . . .

Modern blank verse is best exemplified in the works of Edwin Arlington Robinson and Robert Frost. Frost's poems are dialogues; he is always talking to someone within the poem, as in *West-Running Brook* and *The Death of the Hired Man,* or to the reader, as in *Birches,* poems too well known to need quotation here. His style is easy and conversational, but the underlying metrics are firm. Of Robinson's dozen or so narrative poems, the Arthurian *Tristram* is certainly the best and was widely read at the time of its publication. For some reason, Robinson, who is admittedly one of the three or four greatest American poets, is today largely ignored and almost forgotten. In this hurried age, it is better for a poet to stay alive if he wishes to maintain his hold on the public interest; if he dies, he will slip from the general consciousness, and though we may speak of him as immortal, we open his books no more.

Robinson's greatest masterpiece, *Amaranth,* partly satirical and partly philosophical, was passed over even at the time of its publication and received scant justice at the hands of reviewers. It is a study of misfit characters, all of them in the wrong profession or self-deceived that they are artists. It is a dark poem, but shot through with the best of Robinson's wry wit. The opening scene is in a shadowy Bohemian tavern that has the atmosphere of a nightmare. Here he introduces his various characters, one after the other, all the misfits of the modern world:

> ... The slight one
> Who sits erect, impervious and secure,
> Is Pink the poet. He cuts and sets his words
> With an exotic skill so scintillating
> That no two proselytes who worship them
> Are mystified in the same way exactly.
> All who believe themselves at one with him
> Will have a private and personal Pink,
> And their unshared interpretation of him—
> Which makes him universal for the few,
> And may be all he wants. ...

Possibly this and similar passages not complimentary to the advance guard in the arts account for the unsympathetic reception of *Amaranth* by the critics. At any rate, I recommend it highly to the reader as one of the neglected masterpieces of our time.

Some French Forms

Though the so-called French forms have not inspired many important poems in English, they exercise a certain charm. We have not so many similar rhyme sounds as there are in Italian or in French, so in such forms as the *ballade* (not to be confused with the ballad) or the *villanelle,* the poet in English must often strain for a rhyme. Dante boasted that the exigencies of his *terza rima* never forced him to alter the sense of what he had to say, but in English we have only two memorable poems in that form, Shelley's *Ode to the West Wind* and Bridges' *London Snow,* both of which have been quoted from. There is a line up to which the difficulty of the medium is a challenge and an inspiration; beyond that, no artistry can avail to conceal the labor involved. *Ars celare artem,* art should conceal art, says Horace, and that becomes impossible when the form is too intricate. The Petrarchan sonnet has been with us so long and can claim so many excellent poems in English, that it falls safely on the right side of the line between art and mere artistry.

With the ballade we are on more debatable ground. English has no poems in this manner to compare with those of François Villon. Graceful ballades we have, but nothing more. Swinburne has written some good ones, but he takes liberties with the form; Rossetti's translations from Villon are faulty and in no wise convey the splendor of the originals.

Though the ballade had many variations and was done to death even in France by too ingenious practitioners, the basic form has the following rhyme-scheme: three stanzas with interlocking rhyme, *ababbcbc,* terminating in an *envoi,* generally in the form of an apostrophic address to the "Prince," *bcbc.* The final line, identical in all four divisions, constitutes a *refrain.* The problem is complicated. There must be fourteen different *b* rhymes, six *a* rhymes, and eight *c* rhymes. Also, the refrain must always fall into place naturally and not have the effect of being tacked on. E. A. Robinson's *Ballade of Broken Flutes* is a good example:

> In dreams I crossed a barren land,
>   A land of ruin far away;
> Around me hung on every hand
>   A dreadful stillness of decay;
>   And silent, as in bleak dismay
> That song should thus forsaken be
>   On that forgotten ground there lay
> The broken flutes of Arcady.
>
> The forest that was all so grand
>   When pipes and tabors had their sway
> Stood leafless now, a ghostly band
>   Of skeletons in cold array.
>   A lonely surge of ancient spray
> Told of an unforgetful sea,

But iron blows had hushed for aye
The broken flutes of Arcady.

No more by summer breezes fanned,
   The place was desolate and gray;
But still my dream was to command
   New Life into that shrunken clay.
I tried it, and you scan today,
With uncommiserating glee,
   The songs of one who strove to play
The broken flutes of Arcady.

ENVOY
So, Rock, I join the common fray,
   To fight where Mammon may decree;
And leave, to crumble as they may,
   The broken flutes of Arcady.

It was the young Robinson, apprentice to his rhymes, and eager to
try all forms, who composed this ballade. It is about as good a poem
as we can find in that intricate scheme; even so, we note the padding
and extra adjectives for the sake of rhyme.

The ballade in English is more important as an influence than an
achievement. As we have noted, Chaucer took the eight-line stanza
for his *Monk's Tale,* from which Spenser derived the stanza bearing
his name. Ernest Dowson's best-known poem was evidently inspired by the ballade form. He took his title from Horace, *Non sum
qualis eram bonae sub regno Cynarae* (I am not what I was under
the sway of the kindly Cynara):

Last night, ah, yesternight, betwixt her lips and mine
There fell thy shadow, Cynara! thy breath was shed
Upon my soul between the kisses and the wine;
And I was desolate and sick of an old passion,
   Yea, I was desolate and bowed my head:
I have been faithful to thee, Cynara! in my fashion.

All night upon my heart I felt her warm heart beat,
Night-long within my arms in love and sleep she lay;
Surely the kisses of her bought red mouth were sweet;
But I was desolate and sick of an old passion,

When I awoke and found the dawn was gray;
I have been faithful to thee, Cynara! in my fashion.

I have forgot much, Cynara! gone with the wind,
Flung roses, roses, riotously with the throng,
Dancing, to put thy pale, lost lilies out of mind;
But I was desolate and sick of an old passion,
    Yea, all the time, because the dance was long:
I have been faithful to thee, Cynara! in my fashion.

I cried for madder music and for stronger wine,
But when the feast is finished and the lamps expire,
Then falls thy shadow, Cynara! the night is thine;
And I am desolate and sick of an old passion,
    Yea, hungry for the lips of my desire:
I have been faithful to thee, Cynara! in my fashion.

The poem is written in alexandrines, except for the fifth line, which has five feet. There is a double refrain in the fourth and sixth lines. The romantic agony of the poem has always made it a favorite with young people; in fact, the last phrase of the thirteenth line was taken as the title of a popular novel. In spite of its melodramatic quality and its tone of the 1890s, the poem still rings with a certain sincerity, and anyone familiar with Dowson's life knows with what anguish he penned the lines.

Dowson has also written some charming *villanelles,* a form which seldom displays more than an engaging charm. It is built on two rhyme sounds and the alternate introduction into three-line stanzas of two refrain lines that are combined at the end of the poem to make a double refrain. It may be in any line-length. Since this description is almost as intricate as the form itself, it will be better to quote a model. Robinson is the only poet I know of who has used the villanelle for a serious purpose. *The House on the Hill* is an unusually fine New England poem—and a good villanelle as well:

They are all gone away,
    The House is shut and still,
There is nothing more to say.

Through broken walls and gray
    The winds blow bleak and shrill:
They are all gone away.

> Nor is there one today
>> To speak them good or ill:
> There is nothing more to say.
>
> Why is it then we stray
>> Around the sunken sill?
> They are all gone away.
>
> And our poor fancy-play
>> For them is wasted skill:
> There is nothing more to say.
>
> There is ruin and decay
>> In the House on the Hill:
> They are all gone away,
> There is nothing more to say.

Repetition plays a large part in these old forms. They are at their best when every new repetition of a line or a phrase (as in Robinson's poem) conveys a fresh significance. In the *rondeau,* a fifteen-line form, we have again only two rhyme sounds, and a refrain consisting of the first half of the first line. As a rule, the rondeau is written in four-stress lines and has the following scheme: *aabba aab refrain aabba refrain.* The most famous rondeau of the century, correct in form as well as popular, is John McCrae's *In Flanders Fields:*

> In Flanders fields the poppies blow
> Between the crosses, row on row,
> That mark our place, and in the sky,
> The larks, still bravely singing, fly,
> Scarce heard amid the guns below.
>
> We are the dead; short days ago
> We lived, felt dawn, saw sunset glow,
> Loved and were loved, and now we lie
>> In Flanders fields.
>
> Take up our quarrel with the foe!
> To you from failing hands we throw
> The torch; be yours to hold it high!
> If ye break faith with us who die,

We shall not sleep, though poppies grow
In Flanders fields.

Slightest of all these French forms is the *triolet,* the small scope of which, as well as the intricate scheme, unfits it for serious employment. Here again, we find the double refrain. Of the eight lines, five are repetitions. First there are two lines (capital letters denote repetitions), then a line rhyming *a,* then a line rhyming *b,* then lines *A* and *B* repeated in double refrain and, if possible, with a new significance. Robert Bridges' *Triolet* is the mere plaything of a great poet:

> When first we met we did not guess
> That Love would prove so hard a master;
> Of more than common friendliness
> When first we met we did not guess.
> Who could foretell this sore distress,
> This irretrievable disaster
> When first we met?—We did not guess
> That Love would prove so hard a master.

It is astonishing that Bridges manages to say even that much in a triolet!

There are other French forms such as the *sestina* and the *rondel,* but they scarcely warrant the attention of the reader. Even with the ballade we are well over the line that separates art from labored artistry, and though such forms may serve as exercises for the young versifier, they have little to offer the reader.

The Sonnet

The main forms that I have taken up have developed through centuries and are the result of endless experiment. Their roots go as deep as the language's, and those that we still have with us are so natural that they might almost be cited as examples of Darwinian survival of the fittest. How foolish it is for the defenders of free verse to maintain that these metrical structures are not natural. Free verse has no roots at all, and is itself an unnatural departure from the ebb and flow of all things.

The sonnet would seem to be an arbitrary form; but, in tracing its history, I shall show how this form evolved through seven centuries to become the concisely eloquent stanza that it is. It is the most important single unit in our poetry, and has, from Elizabethan times to the present, engaged the best genius of all periods except the eighteenth century. Wordsworth's quietistic sonnet on the sonnet explains part of its attraction:

> Nuns fret not at their convent's narrow room;
> And hermits are contented with their cells;
> And students with their pensive citadels;
> Maids at the wheel, the weaver at his loom,
> Sit blithe and happy; bees that soar for bloom,
> High as the highest Peak of Furness-fells,
> Will murmur by the hour in foxglove bells:
> In truth the prison unto which we doom
> Ourselves, no prison is: and hence for me,
> In sundry moods, 'twas pastime to be bound
> Within the Sonnet's scanty plot of ground;
> Pleased if some Souls (for such there needs must be)
> Who have felt the weight of too much liberty,
> Should find brief solace there, as I have found.

The sonnet came to birth in Sicily at the court of that tremendous fellow, Frederick II (1194-1250), Holy Roman Emperor, King of Sicily, King of Jerusalem, etc., terror of popes and potentates, crusader and warrior, master of a harem of concubines, enlightened lawgiver, man of exquisite taste, student of philosophy, mathematics, architecture, literature, and patron of poets, who now, according to some accounts, sits in a cavern, with his beard grown into a granite table, whence he will emerge some day to rule his Empire again and bring in the golden age. Frederick's chancellor, Pietro della Vigna, is generally credited with the invention of the sonnet, but perhaps invention is the wrong word, for it doubtless evolved from Sicilian folk song. Giacomo da Lentino, Frederick's imperial notary, is another candidate for being "the onlie begetter" of this form.

At any rate, these early sonneteers rhymed the first eight lines, or octave, or octet, of the sonnet *ababab ab,* a scheme that was soon changed by Guittone d'Arezzo to *abba, abba,* as we find it in Dante, Petrarch, and in most of the "Italian" or "Petrarchan" sonnets thereafter. To the octave is added a six-line stanza called the sestet, and there are many rhyme-schemes for that, the most usual being *abc,*

abc and *aba, aba.* Petrarch sometimes concluded his sonnet with a couplet, for example, *acc, caa.* In recent years, George Santayana occasionally used a rhyme-scheme for his sestet that I do not remember seeing elsewhere: *ababba.*

English has not so many similar rhyme sounds as Italian, so it is natural that in Elizabethan England a new sonnet form developed in which only two rhymes of each sound were demanded. Hence we have the "English" or "Shakespearean" sonnet, consisting of three heroic quatrains followed by a heroic couplet: *abab, cdcd, efef, gg.* But even when we have these main schemes of the sonnet in mind, we must not be surprised to find many variations, as in the works of Sir Philip Sidney and Edmund Spenser.

"A sonnet is a moment's monument," says Rossetti, but it is much more than that. During the Renaissance it became one of the main viaducts of certain classic elements into Italy, then through France, and then into England, as the sonnet worked its way north. Emerson remarked that all English genius is tinged with Platonism (Emerson himself is soaked in it). Dante's *Vita Nuova,* which includes the first sonnet sequence in literature, celebrates his love for the celestial Beatrice, surely a Platonic lady, as the ideal of spiritual love. Petrarch (1304–1374), in devoting over three hundred sonnets to his Platonic lady, Laura, introduced the Platonic conception of ideal love to all Europe, and the subject took firm root in Elizabethan England, modified, as foreign influences are always modified in England, by English realism and humor. For over two centuries after his death the popularity and impact of Petrarch's sonnets were enormous both in France and England, and Laura was a name to conjure with when the poets strung their lutes to the theme of love. Thus the sonnet became an important messenger of the Renaissance of which the humanistic Petrarch was the first embodiment, as, in his love of wild nature and his hermitage at Vaucluse, he might be said to be the forerunner of the Romantics, five hundred years after. Speaking of the Romantics, Byron, who was no Platonist, loathed both Petrarch and the sonnet. "I never wrote but one sonnet before," he remarked, "and that was not in Earnest, & many years ago, as an exercise—& I will never write another. I detest Petrarch so much, that I would not be the man to have obtained his Laura, which the metaphysical, whining dotard never could." And in *Don Juan* he wrote:

> Think you if Laura had been Petrarch's wife
> He would have written sonnets all his life?

In that couplet he disposes of three of his detestations at once, Petrarch, the sonnet, and matrimony.

Leaving Byron to his cynicism, we return to sixteenth-century France, where the poet Clément Marot introduced the sonnet. It was taken up with enthusiasm by Philippe Desportes, and the group of poets known as the Pléiade, the most important members of which were Pierre de Ronsard and Joachim du Bellay. The sonnets of these men had a strong influence on the Elizabethans, and with them came another strand of classic influence, the *pastoral,* going back to the Greek poets Theocritus, Bion, and Moschus and the *Eclogues* of Virgil. The pastoral was the idyl of shepherds and shepherdesses, nymphs and the god Pan, living in an exquisite landscape of meadows, groves, and silver streams, where they tended their flocks and made love. Pastoral names, such as Phyllis and Corydon, Astrophel and Stella, became the usual nomenclature of Elizabethan sonnets and lyrics.

Before speaking of the sonnet in England, I should like to describe the thought-form of the sonnet, which is, in fact, more important than the rhyme-scheme, so important that both Spenser and Keats wrote sonnets in blank verse which are still recognizable as sonnets. All that follows is normal usage; many exceptions may be found, and in most of Milton's sonnets and many of Wordsworth's the divisions between the parts are not observed.

These divisions are one major and two minor, the major break being between the octave and the sestet. The two other breaks are usually observed, though sometimes no more than by a pause which a comma would indicate. The Italian sonnet divides thus: *abba | abba || cde | cde* (or *cdc'dcd*). The Italian sonnet, too, often has a monumental and sounding last line which, by its very rhetoric, sets it off as a single unit. This last line is important in the Italian form, and I shall give examples of it shortly. In the English sonnet, the breaks occur naturally between the quatrains and before the couplet: *abab | cdcd || efef | gg.* Instead of the sounding last line of the Italian sonnet, the terminal couplet of the English tends toward an epigrammatic illustration of what has gone before.

In one of these four divisions, the main idea of the sonnet will be found, as succinctly and straightforwardly stated as though it were prose. In the sixty-first sonnet of Michael Drayton's sequence, *Idea,* (note the Platonic title), which has already been quoted, the main theme of the poem is expressed right off in the first line: "Since there's no help, come let us kiss and part." Following that, the other three sections of the poem develop the theme by Variation 1, in which the lady is enjoined to keep their dead love secret, Variation 2, a little allegory, where Faith and Innocence keep watch by the death-bed of Love, and Variation 3, which is a climax:

> Now if thou wouldst, when all have given him over,
> From death to life thou might'st him yet recover,

which overthrows the entire idea of farewell with which the previous lines have been concerned. This surprise ending is typical of Drayton, and so are the awkward inversions in the last line, a "fault" that we find so often in his work that we come not only to excuse but to expect and almost to love it, as a kind of hallmark of one of the most beguiling poets in the language.

The eighty-seventh sonnet of Shakespeare's great sequence is also a farewell sonnet and carries its main idea in the first line:

> Farewell! thou art too dear for my possessing.

Shakespeare's final couplet does not turn its back on the previous meaning, as Drayton's does; rather, it sums it up:

> Thus have I had thee, as a dream doth flatter,
> In sleep a king, but, waking, no such matter.

Here is another of Shakespeare's sonnets, the eighteenth:

> Shall I compare thee to a summer's day?
> Thou art more lovely and more temperate:
> Rough winds do shake the darling buds of May,
> And summer's lease hath all too short a date:
> Sometimes too hot the eye of heaven shines,
> And often is his gold complexion dimm'd;
> And every fair from fair sometime declines,
> By chance or nature's changing course untrimm'd:
> But thy eternal summer shall not fade,

Nor lose possession of that fair thou owest;
Nor shall Death brag thou wander'st in his shade,
When in eternal lines to time thou growest;
　　So long as men can breathe, or eyes can see,
　　So long lives this, and this gives life to thee.

Two variations of the main theme, dealing with the uncertainty of mortal nature, precede the statement of it, which, therefore, comes out with the effect of a great climax: "But thy eternal summer shall not fade." The couplet again sums it up in epigrammatic form.

Incidentally, the idea of the poet's verses conferring immortality on the beloved is found in the classics and in nearly all the Elizabethan sonneteers. Drayton's phrasing of it is characteristically informal:

Thus shalt thou fly above the vulgar throng,
Still to survive in my immortal song.

I would say that there is little doubt that Shakespeare and Drayton were friends, and that the interplay between their sonnet sequences is the result of more than literary influence. The final edition of Drayton's *Idea* came out in 1619, after various editions going back to 1594, during the decade of sonnet sequences; in 1599 Francis Meres mentioned Shakespeare's "sugar'd sonnets among his friends," indicating that they had been passed around for some time in manuscript, as was the custom in those days, although they were not printed until 1609. Drayton was one of the company at the fatal dinner at the Mermaid Tavern, when Shakespeare, up from Stratford, ate and drank so much that he died of it. This was in 1616 if it be not legendary. Between them, Drayton and Shakespeare wrote the two most impolite sonnets to their ladies that have ever been penned. Here is Drayton's:

There's nothing grieves me but that age should haste,
That in my days I may not see thee old,
That where those two clear sparkling eyes are plac'd,
Only two loopholes then I might behold.
That lovely archèd ivory polish'd brow,
Defac'd with wrinkles that I might but see;
Thy dainty hair, so curl'd and crispèd now
Like grizzl'd moss upon some aged tree;
Thy cheek, now flush with roses, sunk and lean,

Thy lips, with age, as any wafer thin,
Thy pearly teeth out of thy head so clean
That when thou feed'st thy nose shall touch thy chin:
 These lines that now thou scorn'st, which should delight thee,
 Then would I make thee read but to despite thee.

Sonnet viii

Shakespeare's rude sonnet is even more uncomplimentary, for he does not look to the future, but scathingly analyzes the lady's present charms:

My mistress' eyes are nothing like the sun;
Coral is far more red than her lips' red:
If snow be white, why then her breasts are dun;
If hairs be wires, black wires grow on her head.
I have seen roses damask'd, red and white,
But no such roses see I in her cheeks;
And in some perfumes is there more delight
Than in the breath that from my mistress reeks.
I love to hear her speak, yet well I know
That music hath a far more pleasing sound:
I grant I never saw a goddess go,
My mistress, when she walks, treads on the ground:
 And yet, by heaven, I think my love as rare
 As any she belied with false compare.

Sonnet cxxx

In the course of the sonnet, he softens; besides, this is, perhaps, less an unfavorable account of "the dark lady" than a satire on the extravagant compliments to be found in so many of the Elizabethan sonnet sequences. Virgil's phrase, *incessu patuit dea* (the goddess was revealed by the way she walked) had been so taken up by Renaissance poets in writing of their loves that Shakespeare thought he might take a thrust at it: "My mistress, when she walks, treads on the ground." The main idea of Drayton's sonnet is expressed in the first line; in Shakespeare's, in the couplet.

When we turn to the Petrarchan sonnet, we find the same thought-structure with the addition of the high-sounding last line. Here is Keats's well-known sonnet, *On First Looking into Chapman's Homer:*

Much have I travell'd in the realms of gold,
And many goodly states and kingdoms seen;
Round many western islands have I been
Which bards in fealty to Apollo hold.
Oft of one wide expanse had I been told
That deep-brow'd Homer ruled as his demesne;
Yet did I never breathe its pure serene
Till I heard Chapman speak out loud and bold:
Then felt I like some watcher of the skies
When a new planet swims into his ken;
Or like stout Cortez when with eagle eyes
He star'd at the Pacific—and all his men
Look'd at each other with a wild surmise—
Silent, upon a peak in Darien.

Throughout the poem there are variations on the idea of discovery, which reaches a simple statement in "Till I heard Chapman speak out loud and bold." Pope's translation of Homer was standard in Keats's day, and his neat couplets vitiated all the power of the Greek epic. It is probable that Keats first knew his Homer through Pope, and when, on that autumn evening of 1815, he read, with his friend Cowden Clarke, Chapman's wild Elizabethan septenaries, the impact must have been tremendous.

In George Santayana's noble sequence—which should be better known than it is—we often find a combination of Petrarchan octave with Shakespearean sestet. This is not an uncommon practice, and, in spite of the howls of pedants, it is an effective and perfectly legitimate form. Here is one of Santayana's best:

As in the midst of battle there is room
For thoughts of love, and in foul sin for mirth;
As gossips whisper of a trinket's worth
Spied by the deathbed's flickering candle-gloom;
As in the crevices of Caesar's tomb
The sweet herbs flourish on a little earth,
So in this great disaster of our birth,
We may be happy and forget our doom.

For morning, with a ray of tenderest joy,
Gilding the iron heavens, hides the truth;

And evening gently woos us to employ
Our grief in idle catches. Such is youth,
Till from that summer's trance we wake, to find
Despair before us, vanity behind.

Sonnets, Second Series, xxv

The statement of the idea is in lines 7 and 8. The couplet rises to an epigrammatic climax, as we find in the Shakespearean form, together with a magnificently sounding last line, as in Petrarchan practice—a combination of two strengths.

The history of the sonnet in English is of absorbing interest and is still being made. The first sonnets were written by Sir Thomas Wyatt and Henry Howard, Earl of Surrey; this simple statement, which appears in all histories of English literature, seems to indicate that the two were close friends and were constantly in each other's company. Surrey was fifteen years younger than Wyatt. He does acknowledge Wyatt as his master in the writing of verse, and after Wyatt's death honored his friend's memory with an elegy. Both traveled in Italy and got to know Italian literature at first hand, becoming true Petrarchans. Both were courtiers and were blown hither and thither by the gusty changes of atmosphere at the court of Henry VIII. At one time, in 1543, Surrey rioted at night through sleeping London in company with Thomas Wyatt, Jr., and broke as many of the citizens' windows as he could. He was put in jail for this, and there composed his satire on London. Four years later he faced a graver charge—that of quartering his arms with those of Edward the Confessor. At this time, life under Henry VIII had become very uncertain, and Surrey was beheaded for high treason. He was twenty-nine at the time. Sir Thomas Wyatt had died in his bed of a fever, but he had trod near the brink of Henry's capricious patience many times, especially since he was believed to have been the lover of Anne Boleyn, Henry's second wife, before her marriage to the King. Luckily for him, Anne's stewardship of Henry's marriage bed was not very long, and by the time the rumor reached him, the King was beyond jealousy, for Anne was on her way to the scaffold.

We may regard Wyatt and Surrey as literary partners. Their works did not come out until after their death. Tottel's *Songs and Sonnets,* commonly called *Tottel's Miscellany,* came out in 1557, the year before Bloody Mary's death and the accession of Elizabeth to the throne. All the sonnets of these first sonneteers were influenced by Petrarch and some of them were direct translations.

The sonnets of Wyatt and Surrey were a false dawn; nothing more was heard of the sonnet for some years, and when it did reappear it was influenced not so much by Petrarch directly as indirectly through French writers. With the publication of Sir Philip Sidney's *Astrophel and Stella* in 1591, the dam burst, and everybody started writing sonnets and, usually, publishing them. There was probably some personal element in this, for Sir Philip had been the ideal of his age and vastly popular, but the sonnet form had a magic in itself that had already begun to work in the minds of a people who loved form for its own sake, and, always comparing themselves, in true Renaissance fashion, with their classic predecessors, delighted in a pattern so brief, so perfect in its brevity, and so challenging to emulation. Sonnet sequences poured from the presses: Sidney's *Astrophel*, 1591; Thomas Watson's *Tears of Fancy, or Love Disdained*, 1593; Barnaby Barnes's *Parthenophil and Parthenophe*, 1593; Thomas Lodge's *Phillis, Honoured with Pastoral Sonnets, Elegies, and Amorous Delights*, 1593; Giles Fletcher's *Licia or Poems of Love*, 1593; Samuel Daniel's *Delia*, 1594; the anonymous *Zepheria*, 1594; Edmund Spenser's *Amoretti*, 1595; Bartholomew Griffin's *Fidessa, More Chaste than Kind*, 1596; *Diella*, by R.L., Gentleman, 1596; William Smith's *Chloris, or the Complaint of the Passionate Despised Shepherd*, 1596; Robert Tofte's *Laura, The Toys of a Traveller, or the Feast of Fancy*, 1597; William Shakespeare's *Sonnets*, 1609, and Michael Drayton's *Idea*, 1619. (Of course, Shakespeare's sonnets had been in existence many years before their publication; and there had been several editions of Drayton's before the standard one of 1619; Drayton edited and reedited himself endlessly.)

As may be seen even from their titles, the greater number of Elizabethan sonnet sequences were conventional and artificial. However, it is too easy to assume, as some critics do, that the large majority were insincere. After all, everybody has been in love, and a young man in love or an older man reminiscent of being in love, might well take advantage of the rage to write sonnets and laboriously turn out a few in the current fashion, decked out with classical references, a pun or two, something from a French poet, probably Desportes, and as many "conceits" (ingenious figures of speech) as he could invent. The anonymous *Zepheria* is, I suppose, the worst of the sequences, as the following fragment from "Canzon 8" will demonstrate:

> Illuminating Lamps! Ye Orbs Crystallite!
> Transparent mirrolds! Globes divining beauty!
> How have I joyed to wanton in your light?
> Though was I slain by your artillery.

Lame as are the meter and rhyming, the lady whom they celebrate, the possessor of these extraordinary eyes, may have been flesh and blood. Thomas Watson, however, made no claim to originality and indicated the French, Italian, or classical source of each of his early poems, which we may therefore regard as scholarly exercises rather than the record of personal experience.

Sir Sidney Lee, who edited many of these sequences for *The English Garner,* seems to hate them and to regard their authors as thieves and plagiarists. With cold fury he points out the sources in Italian and French models, cites here a phrase and there a title stolen word for word, and seems to think, in the words of Arthur Symons, that "the Elizabethan poets were persons rather lacking in emotion and imagination, who translated and adapted the poems of French and Italian writers with great ability." The battle concerning the personal quality in the sonnets has gone on for some time and still rages. Even the great sonnet sequence of Shakespeare is involved. Wordsworth accepted the theory that "with this key" (of the sonnet) "Shakespeare unlock'd his heart," to which Robert Browning replied that if he did, "so much the less Shakespeare he." One could compile a thick volume of the arguments on this subject.

Out of the mass of sonnet writing, three fine sequences, Sidney's, Spenser's, and Daniel's, and two great sequences, Shakespeare's and Drayton's, emerge. I would say dogmatically that all these, except for portions of Daniel's, are autobiographical. Daniel's, heavily weighted with borrowings, seem to have been poems written for the occasion probably to two women whom he admired, one of whom had "golden" and one "sable" hair. It was golden in 1592 and changed to sable in 1601, probably indicating that he addressed the same sonnet to two different women at different times. The fact may not represent deep or faithful passion but it by no means rules out the possibility of autobiography! Daniel seems not to have been a passionate man in any case, but gentle, cultivated, and friendly. His

Delia is evenly poetical throughout, not rising to great heights but, in ten or twelve cases, producing sonnets of a quiet beauty:

> Care-charmer Sleep, son of the sable night,
> Brother to Death, in silent darkness born:
> Relieve my languish and restore the light,
> With dark forgetting of my care, return!
> And let the day be time enough to mourn
> The shipwreck of my ill-adventured youth:
> Let waking eyes suffice to wail their scorn
> Without the torment of the night's untruth.
> Cease, dreams, the images of day desires,
> To model forth the passions of the morrow;
> Never let rising sun approve you liars,
> To add more grief to aggravate my sorrow.
>   Still let me sleep, embracing clouds in vain,
>   And never wake to feel the day's disdain.
>
> Sonnet xlv

Sonnets XXXI through XXXV are arranged in a *corona;* that is, the first line of each sonnet is a repetition of the last line of the sonnet preceding it. Donne, in the first seven of his *Holy Sonnets* used the corona sequence. I know of no later use of this arrangement until *In Bohemia,* a corona of forty-nine sonnets (1922) by Katharine Lee Bates, professor of English at Wellesley College, who also wrote the words for *America the Beautiful.*

Edmund Spenser's *Amoretti* was addressed to Elizabeth Boyle, who became his wife. Being the work of a great poet, the eighty-eight sonnets are, naturally, of a high order, exalted, dignified, yet with many a charming personal touch:

> I joy to see how, in your drawen work,
> Yourself unto the bee ye do compare;
> And me unto the spider that doth lurk,
> In close await to catch her unaware.
> Right so yourself were caught in cunning snare
> Of a dear foe, and thrallèd to his love:
> In whose strait bands ye now captivèd are
> So firmly, that ye never may remove.
> But as your work is woven all above,

With woodbine flowers and fragrant eglantine:
So sweet your prison you in time shall prove,
With many dear delights bedeckèd fine.
    And all thenceforth eternal peace shall see,
    Between the spider and the gentle bee.

Sonnet lxxi

Every poet has his hallmark; one of Spenser's was a love for the interlocking rhyme, as we have seen in the Spenserian stanza. The sonnet, too, he changed to his liking, and his rhyme-scheme is different from all the rest: *abab, bcbc, cdcd, ee.*

Sir Philip Sidney was in love with Penelope Devereux, sister to that stupid and arrogant young man, Robert Devereux, who subsequently was made Earl of Essex, turned traitor, and was executed. All that lay in the far future when Penelope rejected Sidney's suit and married Lord Rich, whom the poet abuses in the twenty-fourth sonnet of *Astrophel and Stella:*

But that rich fool, who by blind fortune's lot
The richest gem of love and life enjoys;
And can with foul abuse such beauties blot,
Let him deprived of sweet but unfelt joys
Exiled for aye from those high treasures, which
(He knows not) grow in only folly rich.

Sidney's one hundred and eight sonnets are conversational, natural, and high-spirited, infused with youthful exuberance and, occasionally, youthful melancholy. Alone among the Elizabethans, he maintains the strict Petrarchan rhyme-scheme, except for occasional variation in the octave: *abab, abab.* In several instances, too, he employs the six-foot alexandrine, instead of the usual five-stress line. He opens his sequence thus:

Loving in truth and fain in verse my love to show,
That She, dear She! might take some pleasure in my pain,
Pleasure might cause her read, reading might make her know,
Knowledge might pity win, and pity grace obtain:
I sought fit words to paint the blackest face of woe,
Studying inventions fine, her wits to entertain;
Oft turning others' leaves, to see if thence would flow
Some fresh and fruitful showers upon my sunburnt brain:

But words came halting forth, wanting Invention's stay;
Invention, Nature's child, fled stepdame Study's blows;
And others' feet still seemed but strangers in my way.
Thus great with child to speak, and helpless in my throes;
Biting my truant pen, beating myself for spite:
"Fool," said my Muse to me, "look in thy heart, and write."

Charles Lamb says of Sidney's sonnets, "They are full, material, and circumstantiated. Time and place appropriates every one of them. It is not a fever of passion wasting itself upon a thin diet of dainty words, but a transcendant passion pervading and illuminating actions, pursuits, studies, feats of arms, the opinions of contemporaries, and his judgment of them."

The sixty-three sonnets that comprise Michael Drayton's *Idea* are in regular Shakespearean form. They abound in examples of that wrenched syntax that is one of his hallmarks and that, with all his revising and reediting, he never corrected. But they are wonderfully *alive*. Even when Drayton draws on the usual conceits and mythology, he seems to put his fist through them in exasperation. In Sonnet LIX the lover and Love exchange witticisms and proverbs, until, unable to support the badinage further, the poet closes with

And having thus a while each other thwarted,
Fools as we met, so fools again we parted.

Or, having worn out his patience with classical conceits,

I conjure thee by all that I have named
To make her love, or, Cupid, be thou damned.

Again, exasperation suffuses Sonnet XX.

An evil spirit, your beauty haunts me still ...
Thus am I still provok'd to every evil
By this good, wicked Spirit, sweet Angel-devil.

Then he is bothered by a young, "witless gallant" who begs Drayton to write just one sonnet for him so that he can present it to his lady. The poet obliges, writing as fast as his pen can trot, and not pausing even to blot the lines, so that the result was "much like his wit that was to use the same." The young gallant wins his mistress with Drayton's verses; she "doted on the dolt beyond all measure,"

> Yet by my troth this fool his love obtains,
> And I lose you for all my wit and pains.

The critics elicit three jeering sonnets, and Drayton himself apologizes for using the sonnet at all, so hackneyed had it become in his time. We do not know who Drayton's lady was. Some have surmised Anne Goodere, the daughter of his childhood patron, but I doubt it. After all, we know comparatively little of the day-to-day life of these mysterious Elizabethans. The poet could have had a dozen loves of whom we know nothing. All we do know is that one of them, nameless though she is, still flies, as the poet promised, "above the vulgar throng." Drayton's *Idea* is the most interesting sequence in the language except for Shakespeare's, to which, in lesser voice, it has many similarities. Even more than Drayton's, Shakespeare's sonnets are free from foreign influences.

There are one hundred and fifty-four sonnets by Shakespeare. The controversies and theories about them have been so numerous that a mere summary of such studies fills two fat volumes, in fine print, of the late Hyder Rollins's *Variorum* edition. Since that publication in 1944, other volumes have swelled the ranks, including Leslie Hotson's *Shakespeare's Sonnets Dated,* and George Elliott Sweet's *Shakespeare —The Mystery,* in which the authorship of the sonnets, along with all the rest of Shakespeare's work, is ascribed to Queen Elizabeth! As I wrote the author of this last, if we *must* have Shakespeare's writings assigned to someone else, I'd prefer the Queen to Bacon or Oxford as a candidate, but I am quite firm in my opinion that Shakespeare wrote his own poetry.

The sonnet sequence is an autobiographical account of Sacred and Profane Love, a favorite subject in the Renaissance. The Platonic lover is a friend, a young man of great beauty and high birth. His identity is hinted at in the dedication: "TO THE ONLIE BEGETTER OF THESE INSUING SONNETS MR. W. H. ALL HAPPINESSE AND THAT ETERNITIE PROMISED BY OUR EVER-LIVING POET WISHETH THE WELL-WISHING ADVENTURER IN SETTING FORTH. T. T." T.T. was the printer, Thomas Thorpe. Scores of tomes and articles have poured forth concerning the identity of "Mr. W. H." and one highly ingenious short story by Oscar Wilde, *The Portrait of Mr. W. H.* We need not go into this matter at any length; most scholars seem agreed on Henry Wriothesley, Earl of Southampton. (In a letter from Sir John Paston, written in 1471, I find Wriothesley written phonetically as Wrottsley, so that is doubtless the way it was pronounced—it is always so difficult to find out how the English do pronounce their proper names.) Granted that Shakespeare's young man was the Earl of Southampton, then he was doubly disguised first by being called "Mr." and secondly by having his initials reversed from H.W. to W.H.

Profane Love is represented by "the Dark Lady of the Sonnets." I have already quoted Shakespeare's uncomplimentary description of her. Again, the consensus concerning her identity is that she was Mary Fitton, one of Queen Elizabeth's maids of honor, who seems to have distributed her amatory favors with great liberality. I have a suspicion that the two existing portraits of Mary Fitton show her as a blonde, but my memory may be at fault. These would-be identifications of Mr. W.H. and the Dark Lady are really of no consequence except as a recreation. We shall never know who they were.

It is also taken for granted that Thomas Thorpe's 1609 edition of the sonnets was pirated and brought out without the collaboration or the knowledge of the author. This is probably true. Again, the order of the sonnets has been violently disputed. I feel almost dogmatically that the sonnets are correct as they stand; that, with a few possible exceptions, they follow each other in logical and effective sequence. The two sonnets at the end, adaptations from a Greek poet of the fifth century A.D., were written earlier than the others, but their place in the cycle is pleasantly appropriate: little conventional ornaments that they are, following the dark and disturbed moods that precede them, they stand as a commentary on the triviality of all things human, and bring down the curtain with a postlude of lighter music.

Selections from this sonnet sequence will be found in all anthologies of English poetry, so I shall limit my quotation. In any case, each sonnet is a stanza in what amounts to a long poem of great majesty and power. It is, of course, true that some of the stanzas fell below excellence. A masterwork of such length without a flaw would be almost a monstrosity, and eloquence maintained at too high a pitch would strain the attention.

The first seventeen sonnets are a plea to the young man to get married and have offspring, so that "you should live twice, in it and in my rhyme," and "You had a father: let your son say so." These seventeen are followed immediately by the famous "Shall I compare thee to a summer's day?" which I have already quoted. There follows a day-to-day account of Shakespeare's love and the moods of love, triumphant or downcast, now passionate, now recalling Platonic idealism:

> So then I am not lame, poor, or despis'd,
> Whilst that this shadow doth such substance give
> That I in thy abundance am suffic'd
> And by a part of all thy glory live.

In Sonnets XLI and XLII the Dark Lady makes her appearance. Shakespeare has already had an affair with her; now she is beginning to seduce his friend. Shortly thereafter Shakespeare goes on his travels, and, on his return, there is an outburst of happiness and radiance, broken in LXVI by a sudden weariness of life. He then begins to see his friend in relation to the world; he gives him advice:

> So thou be good, slander doth but approve
> Thy worth the greater, being woo'd of time;
> For canker vice the sweetest buds doth love,
> And thou present'st a pure unstainèd prime.
> Thou hast pass'd by the ambush of young days,
> Either not assail'd or victor. . . .

And Shakespeare is beginning to feel old; in four sonnets he thinks about impending death, and how his passing will affect his friend. The climax of this group is the well-known sonnet beginning

> That time of year thou mayst in me behold
> When yellow leaves, or none, or few, do hang
> Upon those boughs which shake against the cold,
> Bare ruin'd choirs, where late the sweet birds sang. . . .

Shortly after this a rival poet appears on the scene and through nine sonnets (LXXIX–LXXXVII) Shakespeare is consumed with jealousy and self-doubt. The rival poet is most often supposed to have been George Chapman, whose translation of Homer Keats so admired in later days, but again, we do not and cannot know who he was. It is enough to say that he troubled the situation sufficiently to make Shakespeare think that all was over between him and his young friend:

> Farewell! thou art too dear for my possessing,
> And like enough thou know'st thy estimate:

> The charter of thy worth gives thee releasing;
> My bonds in thee are all determinate.

The general mood of the sonnets becomes somewhat darker, more philosophical, and there are some wonderful observations on the relationship between human beings, as in Sonnet XCIV, beginning "They that have power to hurt and will do none." Then there are travels and absence again, and some self-examination,

> Alas! 'tis true I have gone here and there,
> And made myself a motley to the view,

leading up to the magnificent poem, Sonnet CXVI:

> Let me not to the marriage of true minds
> Admit impediments. Love is not love
> Which alters when it alteration finds,
> Or bends with the remover to remove:
> O, no! It is an ever-fixèd mark,
> That looks on tempests and is never shaken;
> It is the star to every wandering bark,
> Whose worth's unknown, although his height be taken.
> Love's not Time's fool, though rosy lips and cheeks
> Within his bending sickle's compass come;
> Love alters not with his brief hours and weeks,
> But bears it out even to the edge of doom.
>   If this be error and upon me proved,
>   I never writ, nor no man ever loved.

Number CXXVI is not a sonnet at all, but six couplets bringing to a conclusion the series to the friend. It is as though Shakespeare were extending the device that he frequently used in his plays of terminating a dramatic scene with couplets. The poem is a desperate warning that, although Nature may seem to defy Time in order to preserve the young man's beauty, yet, in the end, she must surrender him to Time. The last line, "And her quietus is to render (surrender) thee," has the sad finality of an epitaph to youth. Immediately following is an uncomplimentary sonnet to the Lady, and, two sonnets later, the anguished

> The expense of spirit in a waste of shame
> Is lust in action . . .

Shakespeare, as well as his young friend, is now caught in the toils of the Dark Lady. Sonnet CXXX is the scathing description of the lady that I quoted earlier.

The climax of the drama is in Sonnet CXLIV:

> Two loves I have of comfort and despair,
> Which like two spirits do suggest me still:
> The better angel is a man right fair,
> The worser spirit a woman colour'd ill.
> To win me soon to hell, my female evil
> Tempteth my better angel from my side,
> And would corrupt my saint to be a devil,
> Wooing his purity with her foul pride.
> And whether that my angel be turn'd fiend
> Suspect I may, but not directly tell;
> But being both from me, both to each friend,
> I guess one angel in another's hell:
>   Yet this shall I ne'er know, but live in doubt,
>   Till my bad angel fire my good one out.

Two sonnets later, there is the wonderful penitential poem, beginning "Poor soul, the centre of my sinful earth," with the triumphant conclusion:

> So shalt thou feed on Death, that feeds on men,
> And Death once dead, there's no more dying then.

Through six sonnets more, he feverishly pursues the Dark Lady, and then, with the two inconsequential little ornaments concerning Dian, Cupid, and "the little Love-god lying once asleep," the curtain falls. We have been in the presence of one of the great masterpieces of poetry, from which so often selections have been drawn, and which, alas, is commonly known only in selections.

John Donne, in other forms so free, has given us twenty-six strictly wrought and beautiful Petrarchan-Shakespearean sonnets. These are the *Holy Sonnets,* seven of them, arranged in a corona series, on the life of Christ, and a second group of *Holy Sonnets,* nineteen of them, on the hopes and fears of a personal religious experience. They all combine with the Petrarchan octave the Shakespearean terminal couplet. It is a temptation to choose one that is not so generally known, but the tenth is so triumphant that I shall succumb to it like others who have quoted from the sequence:

> Death be not proud, though some have callèd thee
> Mighty and dreadful, for thou art not so,
> For those who thou think'st thou dost overthrow,
> Die not, poor death, nor yet canst thou kill me.
> From rest and sleep, which but thy pictures be,
> Much pleasure, then from thee much more must flow,
> And soonest our best men with thee do go,
> Rest of their bones, and soul's delivery.
> Thou art slave to Fate, Chance, kings, and desperate men,
> And dost with poison, war, and sickness dwell,
> And poppy or charms can make us sleep as well,
> And better than thy stroke; why swell'st thou then?
> One short sleep past, we wake eternally,
> And death shall be no more; death, thou shalt die.

Wordsworth said that in Milton's hands the sonnet became a trumpet, thinking, perhaps of his terminal lines, to which the other thirteen are a prelude. Keeping the Petrarchan rhyme-scheme, Milton nevertheless overthrew the whole thought-form of the sonnet, not even pausing, as a rule, between the octave and sestet. Paragraphing was the hallmark of Milton's verse; the four-stress couplets of *L'Allegro* and *Il Penseroso* are written in paragraphs that pay small heed to the individual line; the great paragraph-structures of his blank verse are spoken of as "organ music" (to which I am tempted to reply that an organ has bellows, but a human being only lungs), and so with the sonnet. Milton's sonnets, indeed, can scarcely be spoken of as sonnets at all. Nevertheless, some are familiar poems, the most famous, I suppose, being the one on his blindness:

> When I consider how my light is spent;
> Ere half my days, in this dark world and wide,
> And that one Talent which is death to hide,
> Lodg'd with me useless, though my Soul more bent
> To serve therewith my Maker, and present
> My true account, lest he returning chide,
> Doth God exact day-labour, light denied,

I fondly ask; But patience to prevent
That murmur, soon replies, God doth not need
Either man's work or his own gifts, who best
Bear his mild yoke, they serve him best, his State
Is Kingly. Thousands at his bidding speed
And post o'er Land and Ocean without rest:
They also serve who only stand and wait.

The complex syntax flows over all the milestones of the sonnet form like a freshet, pausing only at the penultimate line to set off the climax of the last.

After Milton, the sonnet was almost abandoned for a century and a half, while Pope's heroic couplet swept everything before it, its reign broken only by the blank verse of Cowper, Young, and Thomson, the odes and elegiac stanzas of Thomas Gray, and, toward the end of the eighteenth century, the lyrics of William Blake. The heroic couplet did not die from within; at the end of its career it was still employed with sweetness and strength in Oliver Goldsmith's *The Deserted Village* and with almost modern realism by George Crabbe in *The Village*. But the publication in 1765 of Bishop Thomas Percy's *Reliques of Ancient English Poetry,* a miscellany of old ballads and Elizabethan lyrics, opened whole vistas of pre-Augustan work that fired the imagination of the early Romantic poets along with the Nature worship of Rousseau and the political upheaval of the French Revolution. In the midst of the ferment that boiled up dreams of a golden age and the brotherhood of man, there was also present a strong antiquarian spirit that looked back to the Gothic age and the age of Elizabeth for inspiration. Old forms and lyric measures were revived. In Coleridge's *Rime of the Ancient Mariner* and, later, John Keats's *La Belle Dame sans Merci,* the folk ballad reappeared in more sophisticated guise; the Spenserian stanza was revived by Byron, Shelley, and Keats, and the sonnet came back with Wordsworth and has been with us ever since.

Although Wordsworth wrote a long sequence of one hundred and thirty sonnets, divided into three parts, *Ecclesiastical Sonnets,* on the history of the Church of England, his most familiar works in the form are separate pieces much influenced by Milton. His two best-known sonnets, *Upon Westminster Bridge* and "The world is too much with us, late and soon," hold to the strict Petrarchan rhyme-scheme; his more usual practice is to change the rhyme sound in the two interior lines of the second quatrain, thus:

> It is a beauteous evening, calm and free,
> The holy time is quiet as a Nun
> Breathless with adoration; the broad sun
> Is sinking down in its tranquillity;
> The gentleness of heaven broods o'er the Sea:
> Listen! the mighty Being is awake,
> And doth with his eternal motion make
> A sound like thunder—everlastingly.
> Dear Child! dear Girl! that walkest with me here,
> If thou appear untouched by solemn thought,
> Thy nature is not therefore less divine:
> Thou liest in Abraham's bosom all the year;
> And worshipp'st at the temple's inner shrine,
> God being with thee when we know it not.

In the literature of the sonnet, none stands higher than Keats at his best. He used both rhyme-schemes. I have already quoted his Petrarchan sonnet *On First Looking into Chapman's Homer;* here is one of his Shakespearean sonnets:

> When I have fears that I may cease to be
> Before my pen has glean'd my teeming brain,
> Before high-pilèd books, in charact'ry
> Hold like rich garners the full-ripen'd grain;
> When I behold upon the night's starr'd face
> Huge cloudy symbols of a high romance,
> And feel that I may never live to trace
> Their shadows, with the magic hand of chance;
> And when I feel, fair creature of an hour!
> That I may never look upon thee more,
> Never have relish in the faery power
> Of unreflecting love;—then on the shore
>   Of the wide world I stand alone, and think,
>   Till Love and Fame to nothingness do sink.

The sonnet flourished during the mid-nineteenth century, not only in such single masterpieces as Matthew Arnold's on Shakespeare, Andrew Lang's on the *Odyssey,* and George Meredith's *Lucifer in*

Starlight, but also in two major sequences, Elizabeth Barrett Browning's love poems to her husband, Robert Browning, in strict Petrarchan form, and Dante Gabriel Rossetti's *The House of Life,* again strictly Petrarchan, which celebrated his love for Elizabeth Eleanor Siddal, who had been his model and whom he finally married.

Elizabeth Siddal was beautiful, but a simple, middle-class girl who was somewhat bewildered by the procession of painters and poets, feverishly arguing matters of art, who haunted Rossetti's house. She even tried to paint and write verse herself, so as not to be left out of things. But her case was hopeless. She was dying of tuberculosis and torn by jealousy of Rossetti's other loves. At the age of twenty-nine she committed suicide by taking an overdose of opium. Rossetti, in penitence and grief, was moved to bury the single manuscript of his sonnets, *The House of Life,* with her. He placed it between her hair and her cheek, and it remained with her in the grave for seven years. At the end of that period Rossetti was persuaded by friends to have Elizabeth disinterred and the manuscript recovered. When it was published, one sonnet in the series, *Nuptial Sleep,* was considered inordinately shocking and became the focus of a controversy that grew more and more embittered and darkened the last years of the poet's life. The main attack, *The Fleshly School of Poets,* was an article by a minor poet called Robert Buchanan, in which Rossetti and his circle, including Swinburne, were violently abused. Swinburne was delighted with the smoke of battle and published his *Under the Microscope* in reply, but the article had a deadening effect on Rossetti, already clouded with constant use of the drug chloral, and he became suspicious of everybody and of everything published, even Lewis Carroll's *Hunting of the Snark,* which he thought was written to make fun of him. Meanwhile Browning swung his big guns into action with a poem called *House* in which he dismissed with scorn the notion that sonnet sequences are personal records, apparently forgetting his own wife's *Sonnets from the Portuguese,* a title that misled no one. *House* is written in Browning's best rumbling-bumbling style; it takes as symbol a house from which one wall has been sheered so that the public can stand and gape at the owner's most private arrangements and gossip about his personal life. Here are three stanzas:

> Shall I sonnet-sing you about myself?
> Do I live in a house you would like to see?

Is it scant of gear, has it store of pelf?
    "Unlock my heart with a sonnet-key?" ...

"For a ticket, apply to the Publisher."
    No: thanking the public I must decline.
A peep through my window, if folk prefer;
    But, please you, no foot over threshold of mine. ...

"Hoity-toity! a street to explore,
    Your house the exception! *With this same key
Shakespeare unlocked his heart,* once more!"
    Did Shakespeare? If so, the less Shakespeare he!

We should not leave the subject of Rossetti's *The House of Life* without quoting his sonnet about the sonnet:

A sonnet is a moment's monument—
Memorial from the Soul's eternity
To one dead deathless hour. Look that it be,
Whether for lustral rite or dire portent,
Of its own arduous fullness reverent:
Carve it in ivory or in ebony,
As Day or Night may rule; and let Time see
Its flowering crest impearled and orient.

A sonnet is a coin; its face reveals
The Soul,—its converse, to what Power 'tis due:—
Whether for tribute to the august appeals
Of Life, or dower in Love's high retinue,
It serve; or, 'mid the dark wharf's cavernous breath,
In Charon's palm it pay the toll to Death.

At the end of the nineteenth century, there are two major sequences, Robert Bridges' *Growth of Love* and George Santayana's two unentitled series, all of them Petrarchan. Bridges' sequence, though eloquent and dignified, is not among his best works; Santayana's, on the other hand, is one of the great sequences of the language.

Santayana's consists of fifty sonnets divided into two series, the first of twenty and the second of thirty poems. They are Italian in form and Continental in feeling, though here and there we find an Elizabethan sestet. They invariably rise to a climax of sound and sense in the last line. An occasional echo from Dante of "love that moveth the celestial spheres," or from Petrarch, "Wherefore I walk already proud in hope," establishes loyalty to the long continuity of the tradition. The Platonic conception of beauty and love that is the major theme of most great sequences here gains extra conviction and vitality from the fact that the poet was also a philosopher whose experiences, thoughts, and feelings were illuminated, and to an extent shaped, by Plato. Also there stands in the background the Roman Catholic Church, whose faith Santayana had long since repudiated, but which he always looked back to as the source of his emotional imagery.

Although these poems are a celebration of love and the beloved, actually only sixteen out of the fifty are personal love poems. Yet love is over the whole sequence like light; the landscape of the poet's mind is transfigured with radiance and warmth, making familiar thoughts shiningly unfamiliar and paving worn paths of logic with illogical gold. There is a sense of the miraculous over his lines, as though the poet had discovered new territories within himself. The love was never to be confessed to the beloved; in numbers XXXVI and XXXVII, which go together, he reads some of the sonnets aloud to her, and she remarks casually, "I like the verses; they are written well," while he thinks to himself, "And I go by you as a cloud might go." Even when they are dead, they must be "divided in the tomb," for he "would lie among the hills of Spain," and she, "among thy kindred in the northern main." These sonnets were published in 1894, when Santayana was thirty-one.

In the twentieth century the sonnet has, if anything, become even more popular with poets who employ rhyme and meter. John Masefield's sonnets are memorable. Edna St. Vincent Millay's rank with the best of her work, especially the little sequence of twenty to be found in her posthumous volume *Mine the Harvest*. In Madeline Mason's *At the Ninth Hour,* the poet experiments with a new rhyme-scheme for the octave, *abcabccb;* and brings two of the rhymes down into the sestet: *dbadda.* The poems are good, but I think that nothing is gained and a good deal lost by this arrangement. The Shakespearean and Petrarchan forms have become instinctive with poets and expected by readers, and the rearrangement of rhymes gives a labored effect.

Wildly experimental are the so-called "sonnets" of Merrill Moore, who is said to have written a hundred thousand of them. The rhymes are placed wherever convenient to the author at a given moment, and the poems may or may not be of fourteen lines. They are improvisations, sometimes brilliant, more often slap-dash. They do fulfill Rossetti's doctrine of a "moment's monument" for most of them were extemporized very quickly; sometimes, it is said, while Dr. Moore was waiting for the traffic lights to change.

Published in a separate volume, but not to be regarded as a sequence, are Edwin Arlington Robinson's sonnets, sometimes philosophical, sometimes descriptions of characters in the wry and observant style he made his own. They are among the best of Robinson's work.

Robert Frost uses the sonnet occasionally, the best one being *A Silken Tent,* Shakespearean in form:

> She is as in a field a silken tent
> At midday when a sunny summer breeze
> Has dried the dew and all its ropes relent
> So that in guys it gently sways at ease,
> And its supporting central cedar pole
> That is its pinnacle to heavenward
> And signifies the sureness of the soul,
> Seems to owe naught to any single cord
> But strictly held by none, is loosely bound
> By countless silken ties of love and thought
> To everything on earth the compass round
> And only by one's going slightly taut
> In the capriciousness of summer air
> Is of the slightest bondage made aware.

Conrad Aiken, in my opinion, has never written better than in his sonnet sequence, *And in the Human Heart.* There are forty-three sonnets in Shakespearean form, modern exemplars of the great Elizabethan tradition. I looked in vain for the praise that I expected for this book; the reviewers were almost solidly against it. It seemed to me a not unsuccessful attempt to bring back the vigor of the Elizabethan sonnet—the sonnets of Sidney come to mind—into a modern idiom. Of course, being modern, they lack the pastoral quality of the high Renaissance. Here is the final sonnet of the sequence:

> Whip up the horses of the Yes and No!
> Day ends, night hurries, we have worlds to see.

Our chariot to these winds of thought that blow
magniloquent meanings betwixt you and me.
If the void sunders downward, let us fall,
nethermost whistling Nothing there to find—
these but our nightmares, our own dragons, all,
who through the chaos but extend the mind.
Nor shall our daybreaks hammered be of gold—
of love our empire, who all things shall love.
Morning and evening are at hand, behold,
and to one measure, by our blessing, move.
All's here that is, or will be, or has been.
Rejoice, my love, our histories begin!

It is strange, and almost inappropriate, to find in this sonnet the influence of Emily Dickinson.

In this brief account of the sonnet, I have tried to make evident how a seemingly arbitrary and artificial form should develop through the centuries and through several languages to become a natural and almost instinctive part of the poet's equipment. Somehow this fourteen-line stanza, with its statement and variations, proved exactly right for the quick embodiment of an idea or an emotion. All sorts of experiments have been tried with it, but it always emerges again as one of the most efficient vehicles of expression. It can be made beautiful or harsh, adoring or satirical, whimsical or philosophical. It has evolved almost as a language might evolve, beginning in conscious efforts to produce an effect or meaning and developing into a recognized form of communication.

The Kinds of Poetry

The old classification of the kinds of poetry into *epic, dramatic,* and *lyric* has loosened and blurred through the centuries and is now by no means all-inclusive.

The *epic* is a long sustained poem in one form of verse (in the classics, dactylic hexameter; with us, blank verse) dealing with a series of heroic events, and centering around a hero or heroes. In the tradition of Homer and Virgil, there are certain conventions that denote the pure epic, such as the invocation to the Muse, the narrative opening in the middle of the story, the account of games of skill and of battles, and, rhetorically, the use of the epic simile. A good example of this last, among scores of others that we could quote from Milton, is a famous simile from *Paradise Lost.* It is also one of the shortest:

> His Legions, Angel Forms, who lay intrans't
> Thick as Autumnal Leaves that strow the Brooks
> In *Vallambrosa* ...

Paradise Lost is the only true epic in English if we are to demand the strict conventions of the form. But the Old English *Beowulf* is surely an epic, dealing, as it does, with the feats of a single hero, even though some of the classic conventions are not to be found.

The *mock epic,* or *mock-heroic* poem, employs the high rhetorical devices of the classic epic and applies them humorously to some trivial episode. It is a travesty of the form. The perfect example is Pope's incomparable *The Rape of the Lock.* Byron's *Don Juan,* though episodic and digressive, could be classified as a mock epic.

In general, the word *epic* is now used very loosely, to denote a long, ambitious work on a theme removed from realism or simple story. For example, Michael Drayton's voluminous *Polyolbion* (meaning "manifoldly blest" and with a pun between *Olbion* and *Albion*) is a celebration of every geographical feature of England, the brooks, rivers, hills, and so forth. It has sometimes been called a *topographical epic.* On the other hand, we should not think of calling Masefield's long narrative poems, or E. A. Robinson's, epics, because their themes and treatment are too close to real life and lack the heightened, or heroic, quality that we look for in the epic. Tennyson's *Idylls of the King* might be called an Arthurian epic, except for the very curious title "Idylls," which denotes a series of episodes rather than a grand, heroic unity. Browning's *The Ring and the Book,* analytical and realistic, is not an epic except in its proportions. We might call Robert Bridges' *The Testament of Beauty* a *philosophical epic,* because of the exaltation of the theme and the epic length, but again, we are dealing with the looser connotations of the word. Is Dante's *Divine Comedy* a theological epic? Wordsworth's *Prelude* an autobiographical epic? Answer yea or nay; you cannot go wrong, for your answer depends on whether you are using the word in its strict or its modified sense.

Dramatic poetry, for the purposes of this book, is simply the form of verse in which poetic drama is cast. Elizabethan drama is in blank verse, though exceptions to this generalization may be found in the rhymed passages of Shakespeare's *Comedy of Errors* and other early plays and the rhymed couplets that he often used to close a scene in his later plays. Blank verse continues as the medium for drama in the Romantic period and in the dramas of Tennyson, Browning, and Robert Bridges and, as I have previously noted, the masques of Robert Frost. It is a standard form for plays, and may well be in use again. Clemence Dane's *Will Shakespeare,* a distinguished work of some thirty years ago, is in blank verse, as is Christopher Fry's *The Lady's Not for Burning*. T. S. Eliot's *Murder in the Cathedral,* departing from the traditional form, is in a variety of experimental units, loosely metrical.

When older critics, such as Dryden, spoke of dramatic poetry, they were not thinking so much of the form of verse as of the general structure, such as the three unities of time, place, and action, but these subjects, matters of debate from Greek times to the end of our eighteenth century, need not concern us here.

Lyric poetry, the most widely inclusive of all, originally referred, as its name implies, to a song-poem to be sung to the accompaniment of a lyre. The pure lyric is still a poem of musical intention that could appropriately be set to music. There is scarcely a poet in the annals, ancient or modern, who has not written pure lyrics. They are usually in three- or four-stress verse and divided into stanzas. Many recent poets are almost wholly lyrical, as, for example, James Stephens and A. E. Housman. In the pure lyric of Elizabethan times the art reaches a perfection by which all subsequent lyrics may be measured.

Besides the song, lyric poetry includes the *ode* (see page 77), the *sonnet* (see page 88), the *elegy,* and the *pastoral*. The pastoral is sometimes known by other names, the *idyl,* the *eclogue,* and the *bucolic*.

The *pastoral* originated in the *Idyls* of Theocritus, a Sicilian Greek who lived in the first half of the third century B.C. Associated with him are two lesser pastoral poets, Bion and Moschus. Their idyls are shepherd songs, usually in dialogues, on rustic subjects, love, and the seasons, set in a landscape where trees and flowering meadows hear the voice of Pan and are familiar to the nymphs and muses. The original pastorals are much less artificial than they may seem to a modern ear, for the actual shepherd songs of modern Greece are not far from Theocritan idyls—or were so at the beginning of this century. Their beauty has inspired all poets since, even those who have but read them in translation.

After the three Greek pastoral writers, the great master of the theme was Virgil (70–19 B.C.). His *Eclogues* abound in the celebration of country joys, with some reference to his own farm. The Fourth Eclogue, a mysterious prophecy of a glorious child who should bring peace to the world, was taken, in the early centuries of the Church, as a foreshadowing of the coming of Christ, and added much in mediaeval times to Virgil's reputation as a magus, or wizard.

In the Renaissance, the pastoral became popular with Italian, French, and English poets. The Elizabethan lyric was chiefly pastoral in tone.

Today the pastoral tradition as a song among shepherds and shepherdesses has been dropped, and since Dr. Johnson's time any country poetry has been designated as pastoral.

The *pastoral elegy* is one shepherd's lament for the death of another, and has its origin in Moschus' lament for the death of Bion. Many splendid poems in English follow the conventions of the pastoral elegy. They include Edmund Spenser's *Daphnaida,* Milton's *Lycidas,* Matthew Arnold's *Thyrsis,* and Shelley's *Adonais.*

The *elegy,* apart from the pastoral elegy, is a poem dealing with the death of an individual or with death in general, and, in its adjectival form, *elegiac,* may refer to any poem of somber exaltation or regret. Thomas Gray's *Elegy Written in a Country Churchyard* is the most famous elegiac poem in the language. Tennyson's *In Memoriam,* written after the death of his friend Arthur Hallam, is a major work not only of elegiac but also of philosophical import. Matthew Arnold's *Memorial Verses* on the death of Wordsworth (1850) is yet another fine elegy.

The lyric includes, besides all these classifications, the so-called French forms, *ballade, rondeau, villanelle,* etc.

The *incantation* is the oldest poetry of all, and has its origins in the first rhythmic shouts of battle and the abracadabra of magic spells. Today it refers to a kind of poetry in which the sounds and images predominate, suggesting moods or emotions that are never stated.

The *satire,* employing irony, sarcasm, exaggeration, and pointed wit, ridicules and denounces human vices or personal enemies. Satire usually takes the heroic couplet as its form. Dryden's *MacFlecknoe,*

Pope's *Dunciad,* and Byron's *English Bards and Scotch Reviewers* are among the best known satires in our poetry. *Light satire* is gentle ridicule without condemnation, such as is found in Chaucer's description of the characters in his Prologue to *The Canterbury Tales.*

In the *dramatic monologue,* which Browning invented, the plot and characterization are narrated and described from the point of view of a single participant in the action.

The varieties of poetry are so many that some poems do not fall into any established category but invite an individual definition.

PART **III** *A Brief Survey of the*
Background of Poetry in English

In his irregular ode, *Alexander's Feast,* Dryden represents Alexander the Great as swayed by one emotion after another
according to the various moods induced by the music of his bard,
Timotheus. The history of poetry begins with the bards, who took an
active and inspiriting part in great battles and events at court. Taillefer, William the Conqueror's minstrel, who is pictured in the Bayeux
tapestry, won permission to strike the first blow at the battle of Hastings. He led the Norman army, singing of the great deeds of
Charlemagne and Roland until he perished in the melée. Edward
Gibbon, in *The Decline and Fall of the Roman Empire,* has this to
say about the wild, Germanic tribes of about 300 A.D., some of whom
were to become the ancestors of the modern English: "The immortality so vainly promised by the priests was in some degree conferred by the bards. That singular order of men has most deservedly
attracted the attention of all who have attempted to investigate the
antiquities of the Celts, the Scandinavians, and the Germans. Their
genius and character, as well as the reverence paid to that important
office, have been sufficiently illustrated. But we can not so easily express, or even conceive, the enthusiasm of arms and glory which they
kindled in the breast of their audience. Among a polished people, a
taste for poetry is rather an amusement of the fancy than a passion
of the soul. And yet, when in calm retirement we peruse the combats
described by Homer and Tasso, we are insensibly seduced by the
fiction, and feel a momentary glow of martial ardour.... It was in
the hour of battle, or in the feast of victory, that the bards celebrated

the glory of heroes of ancient days, the ancestors of those warlike chieftains who listened with transport to the artless but animated strains."

We can easily discern the bardic quality in three Old English works, the long, heroic narrative of *Beowulf*, *The Battle of Maldon*, and *The Battle of Brunanburgh*. But these are polished works of an advancing civilization rather than improvisations as an immediate incitement to feats of arms; they are more reminiscent, and we may imagine them sung in the halls of earls as a diversion rather than as an accompaniment of the tumult of war.

The bardic spirit prevailed well into mediaeval times in Wales, where, as G. M. Trevelyan notes, it was difficult "to keep down the spirit of the Welsh, perpetually incited by bards recounting the glories of the House of Llewellyn." When Edward I conquered Wales at the end of the thirteenth century and overthrew Llewellyn, Prince of Wales, the people demanded that he give them a new Prince who could not speak one word of English. Whereupon Edward produced his infant son, afterwards Edward II, who could not speak a word of any language, and proclaimed him Prince of Wales, as the heirs to the English throne have been known ever since. Such is one story of this rather shadowy conquest. Another is to the effect that one of Edward's first acts was to call for a massacre of all the Welsh bards. Although J. R. Green dismisses this as a mere fable (as historians are apt to dismiss the more picturesque embellishments of their subject), it was accepted as truth for centuries, and inspired Thomas Gray's magnificent Pindaric ode, *The Bard*. In this work, in the form of a prophecy by the last of the Welsh bards, Gray traces an outline of English history up through the time of the Tudors, who were, like King Arthur, Welsh, and the poem ends with a note of triumph celebrating Elizabeth the Great.

Up to the time of the present dynasty, which came to the throne in 1714, English poetry was influenced not only by history but by many of the English monarchs personally. Geoffrey Chaucer was on familiar terms with kings, and served three of them, first as ambassador and then in public office, Edward III, Richard II, and, for the last year of his life, Henry IV, to whom he addressed this petition:

The Complaint of Chaucer to His Purse

To yow, my purse, and to noon other wight
Complayne I, for ye be my lady dere!

I am so sory, now that ye been lyght,
For certes, but ye make me hevy chere,
Me were as leef be layd upon my bere;
For which unto your mercy thus I crye:
Beth hevy ageyn, or elles mot I dye!

Now voucheth sauf this day, or yt be nyght,
That I of yow the blisful soun may here,
Or see your colour lyk the sonne bryght,
That of yelownesse hadde never pere.
Ye be my lyf, ye be myn hertes stere,
Quene of comfort and of good companye:
Beth hevy ageyn, or elles mot I dye.

Now purse, that ben to me my lyves lyght
And saveour, as doun in this world here,
Out of this toun helpe me thurgh your myght,
Sin that ye wole nat ben my tresorere;
For I am shave as nye as any frere.
But yet I pray unto your curtesye:
Beth hevy ageyn, or elles mot I dye.

LENVOY DE CHAUCER

O conquerour of Brutes Albyon,
Which that by lyne and free eleccioun
Been verray kyng, this song to yow I sende;
And ye, that mowen alle oure harmes amende,
Have mynde upon my supplicacioun!

Chaucer knew the world of his own time from every angle, as is
well reflected in the *Canterbury Tales*. He traveled in France and
Italy on royal errands, and though there is no evidence that he knew
Petrarch and Boccaccio in Italy, there is none to the contrary. It is
certain that he moved in French literary circles, and the French poet
Eustache Deschamps commemorated their friendship in a charming
Balade à Geffroy Chaucier in which he compared him to Socrates,
Seneca, and Ovid, and complimented him on his translation of the
Roman de la Rose. And all this while the Hundred Years' War was
in full swing!

Chaucer established our versification and helped establish the
English language, through the wide influence of his London dialect and his enrichments from the French. Of the many forms that

he perfected, the four-stress couplet, the five-stress couplet, and the rime royal were his favorites. He burlesqued the ballad in his *Tale of Sir Thopas* and laid the foundation for the Spenserian stanza in the *Monk's Tale*.

His influence is strong on our poets still, underlying but widespread, and, in the works of the present poet laureate, obvious and direct. He had imitators and disciples in his own day both in England and Scotland, and Spenser so loved his "well of English undefiled" and was so deeply under his enchantment that Ben Jonson was led to complain of Spenser's "Chaucerisms." Through Spenser, Chaucer was an influence on the young John Keats, and through Keats on scores of the poets of the nineteenth century. Matthew Arnold says, "of Chaucer's divine liquidness of diction, his divine fluidity of movement, it is difficult to speak temperately."

Arnold says also: "His language is a cause of difficulty for us ... it is a difficulty to be unhesitantly accepted and overcome." For the interested reader, I can give a few simple (though far from complete) rules that will enable him with a little practice to approximate the sounds of Chaucer's poetry. The three long vowels *a, e,* and *i* should be pronounced in the Continental manner: that is, long *a* is *ah;* long *e* is the modern long *a,* as in *ate;* long *i* is the modern long *e* as in *seen.* Chaucer's double-*o* should be pronounced like our long *o* as in *rose.* The terminal short *e* of a word should be lightly pronounced except when the following word begins with a vowel, and then it should not be sounded. In words ending in *ight,* such as *light* or *night,* the *ight* should be pronounced approximately like *isht.* In a word like *knight* or *know,* the *k* should be pronounced as well as the *n.* If you make these sounds your own and perhaps pursue the subject a little further, you may come to suspect, as I do, that Middle English was a much more beautiful and expressive language than ours.

No one would dispute Dryden's praise of Chaucer as the Father of English poetry. He was not only an inspired poet, he was widely read as well. Latin, Italian, and French were almost as familiar to him as English. The stories he told were not his own; nearly all of them have recognizable sources: his genius lay in giving them new life by his understanding of character, unsurpassed descriptions, and the ability to identify himself with every mood from the most delicate melancholy of Troilus's love for Criseyde to the gap-toothed laughter of the five-times-married Wife of Bath. Nothing, no smallest detail, eluded his eye, and his ear recorded with joyous accuracy the differing cadences of the human voice and the birdsong of springtime England. There is no poet, moreover, whose own personality is more clearly felt in his writings; his living presence is in every tale.

Even within the same form, he was able to fit the cadences to the material with a skill that defies analysis. The mirthful gusto of the Wife of Bath is inherent in every syllable of this passage:

> But, Lord Crist! whan that it remembreth me
> Upon my yowthe, and on my jolitee,
> It tikleth me aboute myn hertes roote.
> Unto this day it doth my herte boote
> That I have had my world as in my tyme.
> But age, allas! that al wole envenyme,
> Hath me beraft my beautee and my pith.
> Lat go, farewell! the devel go therwith!
> The flour is goon, ther is namoore to telle;
> The bren, as I best kan, now moste I selle;
> But yet to be right myrie wol I fonde.
> Now wol I tellen of my fourthe housbonde.

Compare with this passage those frightening, dark lines in *The Pardoner's Tale* when the three blaspheming rioters suddenly meet the old man on the blasted heath. One of them, not realizing that he represents Death, mocks him and asks why he lives so long at such a great age. He answers:

> ... For I ne kan nat finde
> A man, though that I walked into Inde,
> Neither in citee ne in no village
> That wolde chaunge his youthe for myn age;
> And therefore mote I han myn age stille,
> As longe tyme as it is Goddes wille.
> Ne Deeth, allas! ne wol nat han my lyf.
> Thus walke I, lyk a resteleer kaityf,
> And on the ground, which is my modres gate,
> I knokke with my staf, bothe erly and late,
> And seye, "Leeve mooder, leet me in!" ...

Troilus and Criseyde, Chaucer's second masterpiece, is not nearly so well known as *The Canterbury Tales,* but it deserves to be. It is more than a story; it is the embodiment of youth's romance and, tragedy, seven-line stanzas in rime royal unfolding musically in accord with the narrative moods. The following stanzas are part of Criseyde's plaint of love, when she is "among the Grekis stronge":

> Ful rewfully she loked upon Troie,
> Biheld the toures heigh and ek the halles:
> "Allas!" quod she, "the plesance and the joie,
> The which that now al torned into galle is,
> Had ich had ofte withinne the yonder walles!
> O Troilus, what dostow now?" she seyde.
> "Lord! wheyther thou yet thenke upon Criseyde?
>
> "Allas, I ne hadde trowed on youre loore.
> And went with yow, as ye me redde er this!
> Than hadde I now nat siked half so soore,
> Who myghte have seyd that I hadde don amys
> To stele awey with swich oon as he ys?
> But al to late comth the lectuarie,
> Whan men the cors unto the grave carie. . . ."

On the whole, I agree with Virginia Woolf, who says, "It is the peculiarity of Chaucer, however, that though we feel at once this quickening, this enchantment, we cannot prove it by quotation. . . . Chaucer is very equal, very even-paced, very unmetaphorical. If we take six or seven lines in the hope that the quality will be contained in them, it has escaped. . . . Chaucer, it seems, has some art by which the most ordinary words and the simplest feelings when laid side by side make each other shine; when separated they lose their lustre."

John Skelton, a merry poet-priest, was the brightest star between Chaucer and the great Elizabethans, and he, too, was closely connected with the royal court. In his youth he was the protégé of King Henry VII's mother and served as tutor to Prince Henry, subsequently King Henry VIII. His works are voluminous. The most characteristic are in a breathless, rough, two-stress verse, with many extra syllables and alliterations, giving somewhat the effect of Anglo-Saxon verse, in spite of the rhymes, that come thick and fast. Skelton called his verse "Skeltonical," and Skeltonic it is called to this day, and it has influenced the work of many modern poets, Edith Sitwell in particular. Skelton, Donne, and Browning are three classic examples of learned poets who deliberately strained English meter for striking effect. Skelton had this to say of his form:

> Though my rhyme be ragged,
> Tatter'd and jagged,
> Rudely rain-beaten,
> Rusty and moth-eaten;
> If ye take well therewith,
> It hath in it some pith.

Pith indeed! His satires against the greed and ignorance of the priesthood, and against Cardinal Wolsey in particular, were so bitter that the powerful churchman's wrath forced him to take sanctuary in Westminster Abbey for the closing years of his life. But Skelton could also sing beguilingly, as some of his lyrics to gentlewomen in his *Garland of Laurel* show:

To Mistress Isabel Pennell

> By Saint Mary, my lady,
> Your mammy and your daddy
> Brought forth a goodly baby!

> My maiden Isabel,
> Reflaring rosabel,
> The fragrant camomel,
> The ruddy rosary,
> The sovereign rosemary,
> The pretty strawberry;
> The columbine, the nept,
> The gillyflower well set,
> The proper violet;
> Ennewèd your colour
> Is like the daisy flower
> After the April shower;
> Star of the morrow gray,
> The blossom on the spray,
> The freshest flower of May;
> Maidenly demure,
> Of womanhood the lure;
> Wherefore I make you sure
> It were an heavenly health,
> It were an endless wealth,
> A life for God himself,

To hear this nightingale
Among the birdes smale
Warbling in the vale,
  Dug, dug,
  Jug, jug,
    Good year and good luck,
    With chuck, chuck, chuck, chuck.

Skelton's gusto was not often as innocently employed as here, and his bawdy passages and scenes of low life made him a figure of merriment in the popular imagination of the following century. But in his own time he was crowned as laureate by both Oxford and Cambridge, and since then he has been compared to Rabelais, Swift, and Hogarth. The great Erasmus called him *litterarum Anglicorum lumen et decus* —the light and glory of English letters—but Pope, two hundred years later, said that "Skelton's poems are all low and beastly; there is nothing in them worth reading." Between these two extreme opinions, Skelton's reputation rests as one of the most vigorous and fantastic in our poetry.

Sir Isaac Newton invented two words that have proved useful in physics, and we may employ them in the service of history as well. These are "centripetal"—proceeding toward a common center; and "centrifugal"—fleeing away from a common center. The Elizabethan Age was centripetal, and the poetry of the time, like other activities, was focused around that Queen who, in sacrificing her private motives, provided a period of tranquillity and prosperity, rich soil for the full bloom of the English Renaissance. She was learned, affable, and magnificent, and through the nearly forty-five years of her reign her ruling passion was the good of her people. To this "Most High, Mighty, and Magnificent Empress, Renowned for Piety, Virtue, and all Gracious Government," Spenser dedicated his *Faerie Queene,* in whose allegory she plays a central part. And of her Shakespeare wrote:

She shall be lov'd and fear'd; her own shall bless her;
Her foes shake like a field of beaten corn,
And hang their heads with sorrow; good grows with her.
In her days every man shall eat in safety
Under his own vine what he plants, and sing
The merry songs of peace to all his neighbours.

God shall be truly known; and those about her
From her shall read the perfect ways of honour,
And by those claim their greatness, not by blood.

During her lifetime the poets and musicians as well celebrated her
under a score of fanciful names, such as Gloriana, Oriana, Cynthia,
and Belphoebe, and after her death, composed memorial verses, of
which the two stanzas that follow are among the most touching.
(The Queen died on the eve of the Feast of the Virgin Mary, a fact
that was made much of.)

Sleep, dearest Queen; your virtue never sleepeth;
Rest in your bed of death; your honour waketh;
Slumber securely, for your glory keepeth
Continual guard, and living joy partaketh:
Dearest of dear, a rising doth remain,
For suns that sleeping set must rise again.

The blessed morn 'fore blessed Mary's day,
On Angel wings our Queen to Heaven flieth;
To sing a part of that celestial lay,
Which Alleluiah, Alleluiah crieth.
In Heaven's chorus so at once are seen
A Virgin Mother and a Maiden Queen.

It is astonishing how soon after the death of Queen Elizabeth, in
1603, the whole bright inspiration faded, and a centrifugal age set in.

Outside of the drama and the sonnet sequences, the Elizabethan
lyric was the distinctive accomplishment of the age. It was pure lyric
poetry; that is, poetry for singing, and no form of art before or since
has surpassed the perfection of its beauty. Coleridge has this to say
of it: "The imagery is almost general: sun, moon, flowers, breezes,
murmuring streams, warbling songsters.... The excellence at which
they aimed consisted in the excellent polish of the diction, combined
with perfect simplicity ... by the studied position of words and
phrases, so that not only each part should be melodious in itself, but
contribute to the harmony of the whole, each note referring and
conducting to the melody of all the foregoing and following words
of the same period or stanza: and lastly, with equal labour, the
greater because unbetrayed by the variation and various harmonies
of their metrical movement. [There are] countless modifications and

subtle balances of sound in the common metres of their country."

These lyrics are found in three places, in the Elizabethan drama, where they serve as musical adornments; in collections of poems, commonly called "Miscellanies"; and in song books. Musically, the lyrics were of two kinds, the *air,* written for a solo voice accompanied by an instrument, usually the lute; and the *madrigal,* a short composition for unaccompanied voices in four, five, or six parts, each being a melody complete in itself. All the poets of the time were at least amateur musicians; it was impossible to carry on any social life at all without being able to bear one's part in singing these elaborate part songs, as Thomas Morley, the composer, wrote in 1597: "Supper being ended, and Musick books (according to the customs) being brought to the table, the mistress of the house presented me with a part, earnestly requesting me to sing. But when, after many excuses, I protested unfeignedly that I could not, everybody began to wonder. Yea, some whispered to others, demaunding how I was brought up; so that, upon shame of my ignorance, I go now to seek out mine old friend, Master Gnorimus, to make myself his scholar." This is a charming example of Elizabethan advertising technique designed to impel the reader to study Morley's *Plaine and Easie Introduction to Practical Musicke.*

During a brief period of some twenty years, three hundred or more matchless lyrics were composed. The stanza forms are varied and ingenious; they echo courtly music and folk song; they show the effects of classical prosody as well as our old Anglo-Saxon versification; their themes range from the pastoral to satire, from carefree madrigals to slow-moving elegies; they transmute into purest English cadence, themes from Horace, Ovid, Virgil, Anacreon, the Greek Anthology, the French and Italian poets of the time, Arthurian myths, native ballads—and all new and spontaneous as the first notes of dawn.

Although these lyrics were ignored for two hundred years, they began to come back in the mid-eighteenth century, and by the time of William Blake, whose short poems they profoundly influenced, they flowed back into the main stream of our poetry, so that it may be said that few if any poets since the Romantic period have sat down to write without Elizabethan echoes in their ears.

The Elizabethan lyrics follow acknowledged conventions within the bounds of which the poets were able to express the subtlest nuances of emotion and humor, the music and meaning so delicately adjusted to each other that we simultaneously hear and feel. A large proportion of them are pastorals, the sources of which, as I have pointed out, go back to classic models.

I have chosen for illustration a few of these lyrics, each perfect in its way, that show the variety of music and mood. They should, of course, be read aloud, for they are addressed to the ear more than to the eye.

The first one is anonymous, though it may have been written by the composer, John Dowland, who set it to music. It belongs to the incantational kind of poetry: we cannot be sure whether the lady is, in fact, sleeping, or is dead, and our uncertainty, if anything, makes the poem even richer. In many of their poems, both sonnets and pure lyrics, the Elizabethans made much of the kinship between Death and Sleep:

> Weep you no more, sad fountains;
>   What need you flow so fast?
> Look how the snowy mountains
>   Heaven's sun doth gently waste!
>   But my Sun's heavenly eyes
>   View not your weeping,
>   That now lies sleeping,
>   Softly, now softly, lies
>   Sleeping.
>
> Sleep is a reconciling,
>   A rest that peace begets;
> Doth not the sun rise smiling
>   When fair at even he sets?
>   Rest you then, rest, sad eyes!
>   Melt not in weeping,
>   While she lies sleeping,
>   Softly, now softly, lies
>   Sleeping.

The rhythms of this poem are so subtle, the overtones so moving, that sometimes I think it is the most beautiful lyric ever written.

The following madrigal is one of the twenty-five written in honor of the Queen, under the fanciful name of Oriana, and composed by the best musicians of England at the invitation of one of the most accomplished of them, Thomas Morley. This was the one time in history when England led the world in music. The names of the poets who supplied the texts are not known; it may be that the composers themselves wrote them. All the poems have the same refrain: "Thus sang the shepherds and nymphs of Diana, long live fair Oriana." The collection was completed in 1601, but—sad coincidence —was not published until 1603, the year when both Queen Elizabeth and Thomas Morley died.

> Lightly she whipped o'er the dales,
> Making the woods proud with her presence;
>   Gently she trod the flowers;
> And as they gently kissed her tender feet
> The birds in their best language bade her welcome,
> Being proud that Oriana heard their song.
>   The clove-foot satyrs singing
>   Made music to the fauns a-dancing,
>   And both together with an emphasis
>   Sang Oriana's praises,
> Whilst the adjoining woods with melody
> Did entertain their sweet, sweet harmony.
> Then sang the shepherds and nymphs of Diana:
>   Long live fair Oriana.

Some of the Elizabethan madrigals had a satirical bite to them, as in the last line of this one, although the music to which it is set softens the effect by continuing in almost heartbreaking sadness:

> The silver swan, who living had no note,
> When death approached unlocked her silent throat;
> Leaning her breast against the reedy shore,
> Thus sung her first and last, and sung no more:
> Farewell, all joys; O death, come close my eyes;
> More geese than swans now live, more fools than wise.

The following madrigal, although it seems so light, has a grim undertone, and we are reminded how often in those days the "bells of death" rang out for victims of the plague, which swept London from time to time. It was one such visitation that moved Thomas

Nashe to write his beautiful *In Time of Pestilence,* that rose to a climax in the stanza

> Beauty is but a flower
> Which wrinkles will devour;
> Brightness falls from the air;
> Queens have died young and fair;
> Dust hath closed Helen's eye;
> I am sick, I must die—
>> Lord, have mercy on us!

The little hedonistic madrigal just touches on the subject in one line, as though glad to forget it:

> Hey nonny no!
> Men are fools that wish to die!
> Is't not fine to dance and sing
> When the bells of death do ring?
> Is't not fine to swim in wine,
> And turn upon the toe,
> And sing hey nonny no!
> When the winds blow and the seas flow?
> Hey nonny no!

"On a time the amorous Silvy," an anonymous poem, is one of the most beautiful of the pastorals. The slight change in the refrain at the end of the last stanza subtly conveys the feeling that now the world of love and fancy must be left behind and the world of everyday confronted:

> On a time the amorous Silvy
> Said to her shepherd, "Sweet, how do ye?
> Kiss me this once and then God be wi' ye,
>> My sweetest dear!
> Kiss me this once and then God be wi' ye,
> For now the morning draweth near."

> With that, her fairest bosom showing,
> Op'ning her lips, rich perfumes blowing,
> She said, "Now kiss me and be going,
>> My sweetest dear!

Kiss me this once and then be going,
For now the morning draweth near."

With that the shepherd waked from sleeping,
And spying where the day was peeping,
He said, "Now take my soul in keeping,
My sweetest dear!
Kiss me and take my soul in keeping,
Since I must go, now day is near."

The long pause after the word "go" and the finality of the words
"must" and "day" bring the idyl to an end with an almost stern
reality.

"Must" is also a key word in the dirge from Shakespeare's *Cymbeline*. That grim and imperative word, in a slight shift in the refrain
from an adjective to a verb, sums up the helplessness of man:

Fear no more the heat o' the sun,
Nor the furious winter's rages;
Thou thy worldly task hast done,
Home art gone and ta'en thy wages:
Golden lads and girls all must,
As chimney sweepers, come to dust.

Fear no more the frown o' the great,
Thou art past the tyrant's stroke;
Care no more to clothe and eat;
To thee the reed is as the oak:
The sceptre, learning, physic, must
All follow this, and come to dust.

Fear no more the lightning flash,
Nor the all-dreaded thunder-stone;
Fear not slander, censure rash;
Thou hast finish'd joy and moan:
All lovers young, all lovers must
Consign to thee, and come to dust.

No exorciser harm thee!
Nor no witchcraft charm thee!
Ghost unlaid forbear thee!
Nothing ill come near thee!

> Quiet consummation have,
> And renownèd be thy grave!

In line 5 of the third stanza, we have the opening phrase "All lovers young," and the expectation is for a matching adjective, such as "all lovers fair," instead of which we have the hammer-blow of the verb "must" again. It is a tremendous climax on one word. Note, too, how the form changes in the first four lines of the concluding strophe, with four staccato exclamations rhymed in three-stress couplets with feminine rhymes. It gives the effect of a magical incantation. Then in the last two lines the verse smooths out in a resumption of the four-stress line and brings the dirge to a quiet close.

The music of the Elizabethan lyrics is so persuasive that we may be caught unaware and pass by important meanings. This applies especially to the songs from Shakespeare's plays; for example, this one from *The Two Gentlemen of Verona:*

> Who is Silvia? What is she?
> > That all our swains commend her?
> Holy, fair, and wise is she;
> > The heaven such grace did lend her,
> That she might admirèd be.
>
> Is she kind as she is fair?
> > For beauty lives with kindness:
> Love doth to her eyes repair
> > To help him of his blindness;
> And, being help'd, inhabits there.
>
> Then to Silvia let us sing,
> > That Silvia is excelling;
> She excels each mortal thing
> > Upon the dull earth dwelling:
> To her let us garlands bring.

In *The Testament of Beauty,* Robert Bridges, speaking of perfect love, writes:

> > > of Sylvia 'tis enquired
> *why all the swains commend her,* and he replieth thereto
> *Holy, fair, and wise is she,* thus giving to Soul
> First place, thereafter to Body, and last of the trine
> Intelligence; and that is their right order in love.

Thus in three adjectives, carefully chosen and ordered, and without interrupting the casual flow of his song, Shakespeare embodied the whole philosophy of love.

The way the Elizabethans used classical models and built on them is excellently shown in a familiar poem by Ben Jonson, who, largely self-taught, was one of the best classicists of his time. The original poem by Agathias is in the Greek Anthology, and is thus translated by J. W. Mackail: "I am no wine-bibber; but if you will make me drunk, taste first and bring it to me, and I will take it. For if you should touch it with your lips, no longer is it easy to keep sober or to escape the sweet cup-bearer; for the cup carries me the kiss from you, and tells me of the favour that it had." Inspired by these lines, Ben Jonson went far beyond them:

> Drink to me only with thine eyes,
>   And I will pledge with mine;
> Or leave a kiss but in the cup
>   And I'll not look for wine.
> The thirst that from the soul doth rise
>   Doth ask a drink divine;
> But might I of Jove's nectar sup,
>   I would not change for thine. . . .

If we could follow, flash by flash, the thoughts that formed in Jonson's mind after the original hint from the Greek Anthology, we should be near to the mystery of poetic composition.

One of the reasons for the greatness of the Elizabethan poets is their many-sidedness. Caught up in the centripetal force of Elizabeth's reign, they were at home in their society and proud of their destinies as part of the new England that was taking form; they were not poets only, most of them were busy in the world of affairs: Shakespeare as actor, manager, as well as dramatist; Sir Walter Ralegh as courtier, explorer, and navigator; Sir Philip Sidney as courtier and soldier; Edmund Spenser as government agent in Ireland; Sir Edward Dyer as government agent on the Continent; Thomas Campion not only as poet but as one of the finest composers of music of his day. And whether or not they had attended one of the universities, they were all learned men and alert to apply their learning. One of the great paradoxes of literature is that men who led such strenuous lives should have had a touch so delicate.

The century succeeding the Elizabethan Age was indeed centrifugal and witnessed the execution of a king, the establishment of a Puritan dictatorship, misappropriately called the Commonwealth, the Restoration period, with its extravagant reaction against the virtues as well as the faults of Puritanism, the deposition of another king, and the enthronement of his daughter and son-in-law in a rather dull but peaceful reconciliation of contending forces. The violence of the century was the result of religious fanaticism, which has always been one of the most terrible agents of contention.

The poets of the century show no unity of purpose and little of idiom. The influence of John Donne and "metaphysical" symbolism are felt strongly in a number of poets, including such dissimilar writers as the Cavalier poets of Charles I's time, Sir John Suckling and Richard Lovelace, in whose work the music of the Elizabethans is supplanted by wit and epigram; the religious poets George Herbert and Richard Crashaw; the religious mystic Henry Vaughan; and the gentle Puritan, friend of the more fiery Milton, Andrew Marvell. Milton himself as a poet stands apart in isolated majesty, though as a man of action he was deeply involved in Cromwell's Commonwealth. Ben Jonson, who lived for thirty-seven years into the seventeenth century, had his own group of younger poets, "sealed in the tribe of Ben," into whom he instilled his own classical concepts of poetry amid a deal of vituperation against fellow poets and commendation of his own genius. When he was forty-six years old, he took a walking tour from London to Edinburgh, where he visited the Scotch poet William Drummond of Hawthornden, and gave vent to comments, when he was flown with wine, that Drummond set down as *Conversations*. Drummond himself seems not to have been free from malice when he wrote his general views of his distinguished guest: "He is a great lover and praiser of himself, a contemner and scorner of others, given rather to lose a friend than a jest, jealous of every word and thought of those about him (especially after drink, which is one of the elements in which he liveth) a dissembler of ill parts which reign in him, a bragger of some good that he wanteth, thinketh nothing well but what either he himself, or some of his friends and countrymen, hath said or done." In contrast to this biased opinion, we should quote one of the many tributes to Ben Jonson by the greatest of the "sons of Ben," Robert Herrick:

When I a verse shall make,
Know I have prayed thee,
For old religion's sake,
Saint Ben, to aid me.

Make the way smooth for me,
When I, thy Herrick,
Honouring thee, on my knee
Offer my lyric.

Candles I'll give to thee,
And a new altar;
And thou, Saint Ben, shalt be
Writ in my Psalter.

After its confusions, both political and poetic, the seventeenth century came to a distinguished close in the works of Dryden, who, because of his influence on Alexander Pope, set the tone for the more centripetal eighteenth century.

To emphasize the individualistic nature of the seventeenth century, we need only consider the poems of the three poet-priests, John Donne, Robert Herrick, and George Herbert. Except for the fact that they all took orders in the Anglican Church, they had almost nothing in common.

If we were to agree with Ben Jonson that Donne wrote all his best pieces before he was twenty-five, we should have only the love poems and should be forced to omit the Holy Sonnets, the Anniversaries, and other important works. What we do observe is that Donne wrote many of his most characteristic poems before 1598, and chronologically, therefore, is partly an Elizabethan. But he never was in accord with the Elizabethans; his satire on the court is extravagantly venomous, and his love poems are often mere mockeries of the conventions of the time and exercises in cynicism. When he fell in love with Anne Moore, whom he married, there is a change of tone. During his absence on the Continent he wrote some verses to his wife which for smoothness of music and delicacy of feeling are wholly Elizabethan:

Sweetest love, I do not go
For weariness of thee,
Nor in hope the world can show
A fitter love for me;

But since that I
Must die at last, 'tis best
To use myself in jest
    Thus by feign'd deaths to die....

Let not thy divining heart
    Forethink me any ill,
Destiny may take thy part,
    And may thy fears fulfill;
        But think that we
Are but turn'd aside to sleep;
They who one another keep
    Alive, ne'er parted be.

Even more beautiful and certainly more characteristic, is *The Ecstasy,*
which, in a flash, reveals the transfiguration of the lovers' bodies by
their souls, the immortal union in the triumph of love.

Donne was popular and influential in his own day and for two or
three decades after his death, then for two centuries he was almost
wholly neglected. Coleridge wrote of his poetry:

With Donne, whose muse on dromedary trots,
Wreathe iron pokers into true-love knots;
Rhyme's sturdy cripple, fancy's maze and clue,
With forge and fire-blast, meaning's press and screw.

In 1906 Arthur Symons wrote of him, "This morbid, nervous, hesi-
tating intellectually dispassionate creature is indeed an almost unknown person.... Donne is one of the worst and greatest poets in
English literature, a poet unlike any other. He has written some of
the most splendid single lines that were ever written, and hardly a
stanza without a flaw.... The subtlety of a great brain waits upon a
'naked thinking heart'; the result is a new kind of poetry, which
Donne invented for himself and in which he has had no successor."
This was written before the great Donne revival of the 1920s, for
which T. S. Eliot and his numerous school were responsible. The
complexities and angry frustrations of Donne's emotions appealed to
an age similarly confused, while the obscurities and elaborations of
his symbolism delighted a school of poet-critics whose main interest
lay in the analysis and interpretation (often the overinterpretation)
of a style that inspired yet further obscurities in their own.

The second of our poet-priests, Robert Herrick, was a belated

Elizabethan, although he was a boy of eight at the time of the Queen's death. His short religious poems, *Noble Numbers,* and his pagan pastorals and love poems, *Hesperides,* were published in the same volume in 1648, when he was fifty-seven and the vicar of Dean Prior in Devon. He was ejected from his living by the Puritans but returned to it after the Restoration, and died there at the age of eighty-three. At times he was in love with country life, the comforts of which he enumerates in *His Grange, or Private Wealth,* at others he was deeply bored and became homesick for London, although, as he acknowledged, he wrote better in Devon:

> More discontents I never had
>   Since I was born, than here;
> Where I have been and still am sad,
>   In this dull Devonshire.
>
> Yet justly, too, I must confess
>   I ne'er invented such
> Ennobled numbers for the press,
>   Than where I loath'd so much.

His *Farewell to Sack* (sherry wine) and *Welcome to Sack* are wonderful little mock-heroics. Except for his realistic details of country life, the flowers and rural festivals, Herrick's poems are wholly of an imaginary world where he had a succession of lovely, amorous mistresses, Julia, Sapho, Anthea, Electra, Myrha, Corinna, and Perilla, all of them summoned from the pages of classical literature and celebrated with the utmost grace and ardor. In his imaginary world, too, he made sacrifices to the gods and goddesses of antiquity and invoked their blessing on his friends and the seasonal joys of the English countryside. Combined with all this was a lack of taste almost innocent in its failure to select, and amid his most charming lyrics we find epigrams not even amusing in their flat indecency. We know very few of the details of Herrick's life at the rectory, other than that he had a faithful maidservant, Prudence Baldwin, whom he celebrates in his verses, and a pet pig whom he taught to drink beer from a tankard. But the character who comes to us from his work is of irresistible charm and lack of guile, of merriment and wistful sweetness. He tunes his lute to the old Elizabethan music, and the sound is as true and fresh as it ever was:

Fair daffodils, we weep to see
        You haste away so soon;
As yet the early-rising sun
        Has not attained his noon.
            Stay, stay,
        Until the hasting day
            Has run
        But to the even-song;
And having pray'd together, we
        Will go with you along.

We have short time to stay as you,
        We have as short a spring;
As quick a growth to meet decay
        As you, or anything.
            We die
        As your hours do, and dry
            Away,
        Like to the summer's rain;
Or as the pearls of morning's dew
        Ne'er to be found again.

The third of our poet-priests, George Herbert, has not unjustly
been called the one saint in English literature. Coming from a notable
and noble family he was ten at the time of the Queen's death and
grew up in an age when, the gates of high adventure being closed,
Englishmen were beginning to fall into introspection and melancholy. Herbert tells us how he was tempted by Beauty, Money, Glory,
and Wit and Conversation and how he let the Lord answer for him,
and put them all by. His restlessness was resolved by a serene love
for the Church of England, and he retired to the country and served
as a priest in love with the very stones of which his parish church
was built. His poems are suffused with symbols from the Bible and
the liturgy of the Anglican Church. There is an almost mediaeval
intensity in his use and elaboration of every reference, like the intricate designs with which the old monks illuminated their manuscripts. In a few pieces he even composed his stanzas so that they
would take the shape of his theme when printed, as in *Easter Wings,*
of which I quote the first two stanzas:

Lord, who createdst man in wealth and store
        Though foolishly he lost the same,
            Decaying more and more,
                Till he became
                    Most poor;

                    With thee
                O let me rise,
            As larks, harmoniously,
        And sing this day thy victories;
Then shall the fall further the flight in me.

When Herbert was forty, after consumption had long racked him,
he took his farewell—to borrow a phrase from Sir Thomas Browne
—in a colloquy with God. His poems, under the title of *The Temple*,
were published just after his death in 1633.

Henry Vaughan, the Welsh mystic and physician of a generation
later, was an acknowledged disciple "of that blessed man, Mr. George
Herbert, whose holy life and verse gained many pious converts, of
whom I am the least." Herbert was the unblemished genius in a
childlike soul; Vaughan, shut away in wild Wales, developed a
profounder, more conscious mysticism, which evoked in longing
retrospect the child's innocence that Herbert never lost. The emotion
is similar to the theme of Wordsworth's *Ode on the Intimations of
Immortality from Recollections of Early Childhood,* and is found
at its clearest in Vaughan's *The Retreat:*

            Happy those early days when I
            Shin'd in my Angel-infancy!
            Before I understood this place
            Appointed for my second race,
            Or taught my soul to fancy aught
            But a white celestial thought;
            When yet I had not walkt above
            A mile, or two, from my first Love,
            And looking back (at that short space)
            Could see a glimpse of His bright face;
            When on some gilded cloud or flow'r
            My gazing soul would dwell an hour,
            And in those weaker glories spy

Some shadows of eternity;
Before I taught my tongue to wound
My conscience with a sinful sound,
Or had the black art to dispense
A sev'ral sin to ev'ry sense;
But felt through all this fleshly dress
Bright shoots of everlastingness.
  O how I long to travel back
And tread again that ancient track!
That I might once more reach that plain
Where first I left my glorious train,
From whence th' enlightened spirit sees
That shady city of palm trees;
But ah! my soul with too much stay
Is drunk, and staggers in the way.
Some men a forward motion love,
But I by backward steps would move,
And when this dust falls to the urn,
In that state I came, return.

Two minor religious poets of the seventeenth century were discovered only recently: Thomas Traherne, some of whose yellowed manuscripts were discovered in a bookstall and others in the British Museum, and were published as *Poems of Felicity* in 1910; and Edward Taylor, whose poems were discovered in the Yale Library in 1937 by Thomas H. Johnson (later the editor and biographer of Emily Dickinson). Taylor was a Puritan minister in Western Massachusetts in the late seventeenth and early eighteenth centuries, but, under the influence of Herbert and Vaughan, he often wrote like a high-church Anglican. His contraband incense, altars, and candlelight would not have made him popular with his fellow Puritans, and his poems remained among the manuscripts of his grandson, Ezra Stiles, until their discovery two centuries later. Taylor was the first distinguished American poet; we were not to have another one for over a hundred years after his death.

A seventeenth-century poet who stood apart, as poet, from his professed Puritanism was Andrew Marvell. Marvell when he was studying at Cambridge was converted to Roman Catholicism by the Jesuits; he was then reconverted to the English church by his father, an Anglican priest, and finally joined the Puritans and became, for a while, secretary to John Milton. Two events in his life had a direct effect on his poetry: when he was thirty he was tutor to the daughter of the Lord General Fairfax of Appleton House, famous for its beautiful gardens; and two years later he was a tutor in the house of John Oxenbridge, who had made several trips to the Bermudas. Except for *To His Coy Mistress* and *The Definition of Love*, Marvell's best poems are concerned with gardens and include one on the *Bermudas*, whose luxuriant foliage twines into his other work as well. Marvell was the master of the four-stress couplet, in which these poems were written. When he indulged in the extravagances of metaphysical imagery, he did so with a humorous side-glance, as in his description of the homecoming of the salmon fishers:

> . . . like Antipodes in shoes,
> They shod their heads in their canoes.

Next to *To His Coy Mistress,* his poem *The Garden* is his best known:

> How vainly men themselves amaze
> To win the palm, the oak, or bays;
> And their uncessant labours see
> Crown'd from some single herb or tree,
> Whose short and narrow vergèd shade
> Does prudently their toils upbraid;
> While all the flow'rs and trees do close
> To weave the garlands of repose.
>
> Fair Quiet, have I found thee here,
> And Innocence thy sister dear!
> Mistaken long, I sought you then
> In busy companies of men.
> Your sacred plants, if here below,
> Only among the plants will grow.
> Society is all but rude,
> To this delicious solitude.
>
> No white nor red was ever seen
> So am'rous as this lovely green.
> Fond lovers, cruel as their flame,
> Cut in these trees their mistress' name.

Little, alas, they know, or heed,
How far these beauties hers exceed!
Fair trees! where s'e'er your barks I **wound**,
No name shall but your own be found.

When we have run our passions' heat,
Love hither makes his best retreat.
The gods, that mortal beauty chase,
Still in a tree did end their race.
Apollo hunted Daphne so,
Only that she might laurel grow.
And Pan did after Syrinx speed,
Not as a nymph, but for a reed.

What wondrous life in this I lead!
Ripe apples drop about my head;
The luscious clusters of the vine
Upon my mouth do crush their wine;
The nectarine, and curious peach,
Into my hands themselves do reach;
Stumbling on melons, as I pass,
Ensnar'd with flow'rs, I fall on grass.

Meanwhile the mind, from pleasure less
Withdraws into its happiness:
The mind, that Ocean where each kind
Does straight its own resemblance find;
Yet it creates, transcending these,
Far other worlds, and other seas;
Annihilating all that's made
To a green thought in a green shade.

Here at the fountain's sliding foot,
Or at some fruit-trees' mossy root,
Casting the body's vest aside,
My soul into the boughs does glide;
There like a bird it sits, and sings,
Then whets, and combs its silver wings;
And till prepar'd for longer flight,
Waves in its plumes the various light.

Such was that happy Garden-state,
While man there walk'd without a mate;
After a place so pure and sweet,
What other help could yet be meet!
But 'twas beyond a mortal's share
To wander solitary there;
Two paradises 'twere in one
To live in Paradise alone.

How well the skilful gard'ner drew
Of flow'rs and herbs this dial new,
Where, from above, the milder sun
Does through a fragrant zodiac run;
And, as it works, th' industrious bee
Computes its time as well as we.
How could such sweet and wholesome hours
Be reckon'd but with herbs and flow'rs!

The poet who dominates the seventeenth century is John Milton.
I have already spoken of the special qualities of his prosody, a subject
considered so important that Robert Bridges has devoted a book
to it. The majority of critics speak of Shakespeare and Milton in the
same breath, but I cannot agree with them, being, as I have already
said, a heretic on the subject. "Milton was of the Devil's party without knowing it," said William Blake, and many others have recognized in Satan the epic hero of *Paradise Lost*. Hero or not, he is
the most interesting figure, but even so, he is merely a supernatural
being, and I confess to a preference for human ones. Milton's God is
more like King Charles I than a beneficent deity; perhaps Milton
had a feeling of guilt in regard to that unfortunate monarch, whose
death he rejoiced in with such bloodthirsty glee, and whom he sneered
at for having read Shakespeare and Sidney's *Arcadia*—"a vain ama-
torious poem." Although Milton spoke of *Paradise Lost* as "things
unattempted yet in prose or rhyme" the parallels between his poem
and the *Carmen Paschale* of Sedulius (1475) are deadly.

Milton's prosody silenced the Elizabethan music of blank verse.
Until Tennyson, he overshadowed the work of all who used the
form. Poor Keats, who had nothing but his own instinct to save him
from idolatry of Milton, was alternately praising him, which he
knew he was expected to do, or blaming him, which was his natural

impulse. "The Paradise lost," he wrote to his brother and sister-in-law, "though so fine in itself is a corruption of our Language.... A northern dialect accommodating itself to greek and latin inversions and intonations.... I have but lately stood on my guard against Milton. Life to him would be death to me." He gave up his poem *Hyperion* because he could not free himself sufficiently from Milton's influence.

Nor can I find much to enjoy in Milton's minor poems, especially the wooden couplets of *Il Penseroso* and *L'Allegro,* which have, in schoolrooms, extinguished in so many the possibility of an interest in poetry. We have but to compare these couplets with Andrew Marvell's to make my point clear.

I can only conclude by saying that I regard Milton as a dead whale stranded on the beach of poetry from which no critic has been strong enough or brave enough to tow him out to deep water.

The centripetal force in the eighteenth century was a devotion to convention, form, and decorum, as a reaction to the hurly-burly of the seventeenth. Alexander Pope sharpened the heroic couplet of Dryden and used it for various ends: for satire, as in *The Dunciad* and the *Epistle to Dr. Arbuthnot,* for his exquisite mock-heroic fantasy, *The Rape of the Lock,* for *An Essay on Criticism,* and for his philosophical poem, *An Essay on Man.* Pope's work is always interesting; it is the sort of writing in which you may start to look up a single line and find yourself reading on for pages. It is not a poetry of mood or diffuse meditation; all is clear-cut, conversational, and memorable.

Pope was not fortunate in his pastoral verse, and that is hardly to be wondered at, considering the rules he set down for it: "... we are not to describe our shepherds as shepherds of this day really are, but as they may be conceived then to have been, when the best of men followed the employment. To carry this resemblance yet further, it would not be amiss to give these shepherds some skill in astronomy, as far as it may be useful to that way of life.... We must therefore use some illusion to render a pastoral delightful; and this consists in exposing only the best side of a shepherd's life, and in concealing its miseries." We should add that he wrote this when he was very young.

The ability of the eighteenth century to conceal its miseries has made it seem, in retrospect, one of the most attractive of all civilizations. But disillusionment toward the end of the century affected the pastoral among many larger things. George Crabbe is a poet seldom read today, but he is much admired by Robert Frost and was the subject of a sonnet by Edwin Arlington Robinson, another of his admirers. Crabbe attacked the pastoral artificiality of the poetry of his day. He saw rural life as it was, in all the squalor and anguish imposed by a neglectful age. He objected specifically to the influence of Virgil, "the Mantuan," whose *Eclogues,* great as they are, had no slightest relation to English rural life about 1800. At the beginning of his best-known poem, *The Village,* Crabbe demands, in impeccable heroic couplets, a more realistic poetry:

> Fled are those times when in harmonious strains
> The rustic poet praised his native plains;
> No shepherds now, in smooth alternate verse,
> Their country's beauty or their nymphs rehearse;
> Yet still for these we frame the tender strain,
> Still in our lays fond Corydons complain,
> And shepherd boys their amorous pains reveal,
> The only pains, alas! they never feel....
> Must sleepy bards the Mantuan dream prolong,
> Mechanic echoes of the Mantuan song?
> From Truth and Nature shall we widely stray,
> Where Virgil, not where fancy, leads the way?

Dr. Johnson had already broadened the scope of the pastoral, when, in the pages of *The Rambler,* he defined it as "a poem in which any action or passion is represented by its effects upon country life." Granted this definition, the works of Robert Frost and A. E. Housman are pastoral, and, to a large extent, those of Hardy and Bridges.

Pastoral in atmosphere, though not in the classic convention of Theocritus or Virgil, is Thomas Gray's incomparable *Elegy Written in a Country Churchyard.* Gray was caught between two great ages. He was one of the most learned men of his time, and his education impelled him toward the Augustan school, especially Dryden ("Remember Dryden and be blind to all his faults," he wrote). But his natural tendencies included many that were subsequently identified with the Romantic movement: antiquarianism, for example, that sent him back to old Icelandic poetry in his two "Norse Odes" and provided the inspiration for his ode *The Bard*; and these works, in turn, had an effect on Macpherson of the Ossianic poems, which profoundly influenced the Romantic movement not only in England but on the Continent. A melancholy nostalgia for his own childhood, a mood frequent in Romantic poetry, resulted in his *Ode on a Distant Prospect of Eton College*. The *Elegy* is, of course, his masterpiece, and the secondary theme of that perfect work is a profound sentiment for the humble people of the world, the same that Wordsworth developed as one of the main concerns of his poetry.

Matthew Arnold, in a rather stupid essay, made much of a quotation from one of Gray's friends to the effect that Gray "never spoke out." What Arnold expected from this shy, melancholy, and reclusive poet is impossible to conjecture. The same limitations that made him unable to appreciate the glories of Chaucer and Pope led Arnold to criticize Gray adversely for the reticence that is an essential virtue of his poetry. Dr. Johnson, on the other hand, found Gray lacking in Augustan proprieties. Standing between classicism and romanticism, Gray is a giant who was a target for the slings and arrows from both sides. He wrote comparatively few poems, but he will live forever in his *Elegy*.

At about the same time as Crabbe, Robert Burns was introducing realism into his country lyrics and a good many of those qualities that we have come to term *romantic*. And with the publication of William Blake's first book in 1783, many romantic tendencies, glimpses of which had appeared in the work of Thomas Gray and William Collins, became predominant.

Blake was a visionary, a mystic, whose symbolism was as elaborate as his lyric melodies were simple and fresh. In his *Songs of Innocence and Experience* he contrasted two worlds, one spiritual and unsullied, the other darkened with all the passions of materialism, and wrote companion pieces to emphasize the change; for example, the lamb,

> Little Lamb, who made thee?
> Dost thou know who made thee? ...

and the tiger,

> Tiger! Tiger! burning bright
> In the forests of the night,
> What immortal hand or eye
> Could frame thy fearful symmetry?

As a mystic, Blake belonged to that small but ever-present group of poets who are homesick for Paradise itself. The essence of its philosophy is the passionate desire of the individual soul for reunion with God. The mystical longing is a cosmic homesickness. These poets cut across centuries and schools; they say the same thing in Pentecostal tongues. There are traces of mysticism in some of the classic poets; in the sixth book of the *Aeneid,* for example, or the *Prometheus Bound* of Aeschylus. The mystical poets, though few in number, are nearly all masters: in English, George Herbert and his disciple Henry Vaughan, Thomas Traherne, William Blake, Emily Dickinson, parts of Walt Whitman, Ralph Waldo Emerson, and the Irish poets James Stephens and AE (George Edward Russell). I would not include William Butler Yeats in this group, for, strongly influenced by Blake as he was, he was an occultist and spiritualist rather than a mystic, and the symbolism of his poetry, beautiful as it may be, is an ornament, not a conviction. Wordsworth, because of the great *Ode on Immortality* and passages in *The Prelude,* is more touched with mysticism than Coleridge, who, like Yeats, was more interested in the occult or supernatural than in true mysticism.

Most mystical poets are humorous and playful at times. Both Herbert and Vaughan indulged in fanciful conceits and devised shapes to their printed stanzas with an ingenuity that went far beyond the seriousness of a high religious aim. Blake's epigrams, many of them Rabelaisian, are uproariously funny. As for James Stephens, his Irish wit capers through some of his best inspirations, and in one of his poems God enters a pub and makes himself unmistakably manifest to a bibulous character named Thomas an Buile. Emily Dickinson's is a kind of family humor that draws God into the details of everyday life with unquestioning trust.

Orthodox Christian mystics regard the Fall of Man in the light of the story of the Garden of Eden, using that at least as a symbol; others, like Blake and the Wordsworth of the *Ode on Immortality* follow the Platonic idea of prenatal existence, the Fall of Man consisting in the descent of the soul into a material and materialistic universe. There is always the desire to return to the original innocence of the human spirit, in Vaughan's words,

> Before I taught my tongue to wound
> My conscience with a sinful sound,

> Or had the black art to dispense
> A sev'ral sin to ev'ry sense; ...

or in Blake's,

> Ah! Sun-flower! weary of time,
> Who countest the steps of the sun;
> Seeking after that sweet golden clime
> Where the traveller's journey is done. ...

And since mysticism is essentially an optimistic philosophy, the soul of man will eventually be redeemed from the material world after the period of darkness. To quote Blake again:

> And did those feet in ancient time
> Walk upon England's mountains green?
> And was the holy Lamb of God
> On England's pleasant pastures seen?
>
> And did the countenance divine
> Shine forth upon our clouded hills?
> And was Jerusalem builded here
> Among these dark Satanic Mills?
>
> Bring me my bow of burning gold!
> Bring me my arrows of desire!
> Bring me my spear! Oh clouds, unfold!
> Bring me my chariot of fire!
>
> I will not cease from mental fight,
> Nor shall my sword sleep in my hand,
> Till we have built Jerusalem
> In England's green and pleasant land.

This material life is a shadowy interlude between two glories. To quote an early Italian mystic whose name I have forgotten, "Let us never, when we go down into the darkness, deny that we have seen the light." Mysticism, being intensely personal, is akin to romanticism.

The Romantic Revolt at the end of the eighteenth century was, in general, the insistence on the personal man as opposed to the social man. The words "classicism" and "romanticism" are so loosely and widely used that it might be well to examine them for a moment, always remembering that although the great poets may be classified as predominantly classic or romantic, they all show traces of the opposite quality. The classicist says, "The proper study of mankind is Man"; the romanticist says, "The proper study of mankind is Me." *"Man* is the measure of all things," says the one; *"I* am the measure of all things," replies the other. The essential doctrine of romanticism is every man for himself, and when carried to extreme lengths (as with many of the poets of our own time) it may become self-absorption, self-pity, and lost in the obscurity of purely personal symbols, thus becoming incomprehensible to the common reader.

The Romantic Revolt had so many causes that it would be impossible to summarize them all. Two of them are obvious: the philosophic explosion in the writings of Jean-Jacques Rousseau, who so insisted on the "natural" man that Voltaire remarked that when reading him he felt as though he ought to be going on all fours; and the political explosion of the French Revolution, which blew everything, society, humanism, religion, sky-high, and after a period of chaos, resulted, as violent revolutions nearly always do, in a tyrannical dictatorship. These causes would account for the individualistic and revolutionary aspects of romanticism.

Of course romanticism is a wholly centrifugal force; the core of its philosophy is to send each man on his personal mission, irrespective of society in general. Hence, it is foolish to speak of a romantic school; there is no school, except, perhaps, at recess, with everybody doing what he wants. "Romantic movement" is better. To speak of Wordsworth and Coleridge or of Shelley and Keats as though the pairing of the names indicated a similarity in their poetry is erroneous; there is little similarity between any two romantic poets.

There are many other romantic qualities, such as a love of wild nature as opposed to the gardens and parks and pastoral landscapes of classicism; a vision of man in a state of nature with the accompanying illusion of the Noble Savage; a belief that the human race, if properly taught, could live without government in a state of cultural anarchy, or could, at any rate, with universal suffrage and democracy, shape a wise and noble and totally incorruptible state, as Whitman dreamed. To the classicist's ideal of a beneficent Aristocracy the romantic opposes the vision of the enlightened Common Man. The classicist is a realist and is concerned with the present. The romanticist lives in the future and the past. This interest in the past resulted in a pleasant antiquarianism, with the revival, in the eighteenth century, of an interest in the old ballads and the Arthurian masterpiece of Sir Thomas Malory. We have already noted the antiquarianism of Gray's *The Bard,* and we find the same delight in mediaevalism and magic in Horace Walpole's romantic novel *The Castle of Otranto,* the original ancestor of the so-called "Gothic" spirit of Coleridge, Sir Walter Scott, John Keats, Tennyson, Dante Gabriel Rossetti, William Morris, Edgar Allan Poe, and, indirectly, the modern mystery story.

The older generation of English romantic poets, Wordsworth and Coleridge, published their poems together as *Lyrical Ballads* in 1798, and after that went their separate ways. To the edition of 1800 Wordsworth contributed his famous Preface, including his belief that poetry is to be found in the humbler, everyday aspects of people and that it should employ a simple and familiar diction. Poetry is the result of "emotion recollected in tranquillity." Coleridge, in his *Biographia Literaria,* speaks of the opposing points of view (though both within the scope of romanticism) with which he and Wordsworth embarked on their venture: "...it was agreed that my endeavours should be directed to persons and characters supernatural, or at least romantic" [*The Ancient Mariner* and *Christabel*], "so as to transfer from our inward nature a human interest and a semblance of truth sufficient to procure for these shadows of imagination that willing suspension of disbelief for the moment, which constitutes poetic faith. Mr. Wordsworth, on the other hand, was to propose to himself as his object, to give the charm of novelty to things of everyday, and to excite a feeling analogous to the supernatural, by awakening the mind's attention to the lethargy of custom, and directing it to the loveliness and wonders of the world before us...."

Wordsworth's Nature was not the stormy heights and wild seas that were to inspire Byron; it was halfway between those and the pastoral countryside, the scenery of the Lake District, with bold hills and waterfalls and sunny meadows. Nor were his people noble savages; they were humble folk like the shepherd Michael, whose son Luke left his native fields and went up to the city where

> he gave himself
> To evil courses: ignominy and shame

Fell on him so that he was driven at last
To seek a hiding-place beyond the seas,

or like Lucy, who

> ... dwelt among the untrodden ways
> Beside the springs of Dove,
> A Maid whom there were none to praise
> And very few to love.

The only beauty Wordsworth ever saw in a city was expressed in his sonnet *Composed upon Westminster Bridge,* written at dawn before anyone else was awake! The theme of Man-and-Nature, reiterated through the sometimes prosy blank verse of *The Prelude,* was more effectively expressed in the *Lines Composed a Few Miles Above Tintern Abbey,* where we find the poet returning after a sojourn in lonely rooms amid the din of towns and cities

> To look on nature, not as in the hour
> Of thoughtless youth; but hearing oftentimes
> The still, sad music of humanity,
> Not harsh nor grating, though of ample power
> To chasten and subdue. And I have felt
> A presence that disturbs me with the joy
> Of elevated thoughts; a sense sublime
> Of something far more deeply interfused,
> Whose dwelling is the light of setting suns,
> And the round ocean and the living air,
> And the blue sky, and in the mind of man:
> A motion and a spirit, that impels
> All thinking things, all objects of all thought,
> And rolls through all things. ...

Wordsworth is a poet most people come to appreciate more as they grow older. His limitations are a lack of intensity and of humor, but there is an impressiveness about his deep moral conviction of the rightness of the relationship between man and Nature that accumulates into the effect that only great poetry can give. When Wordsworth died in 1850 at the age of eighty, Matthew Arnold, in his noble *Memorial Verses* said:

> . . . He found us when the age had bound
> Our souls in its benumbing round;
> He spoke, and loosed our heart in tears.
> He laid us as we lay at birth
> On the cool flowery lap of earth,
> Smiles broke from us and we had ease;
> The hills were round us, and the breeze
> Went o'er the sun-lit fields again;
> Our foreheads felt the wind and rain.
> Our youth returned, for there was shed
> On spirits that had long been dead,
> Spirits dried up and closely furl'd,
> The freshness of the early world.
>
> Ah! since dark days still bring to light
> Man's prudence and man's fiery might,
> Time may restore us in his course
> Goethe's sage mind and Byron's force;
> But where will Europe's latter hour
> Again find Wordsworth's healing power? . . .

Although Wordsworth lived to be eighty and Coleridge sixty-two, it may be said that as poets they died early. The second generation of romantic poets actually died young, Byron at thirty-six, Shelley at thirty, and Keats at twenty-five. A good deal of amusing but useless speculation has toyed with imaginary futures for them had they lived on, of which the best-known is Francis Thompson's essay on Shelley. It is possible that Keats would have continued and enriched his work if he had had good health and had lived on. But, in my opinion, Byron and Shelley said all that they had to say, and, in the last analysis, it is not much.

Pope wisely remarked "that true self-love and social are the same," thus expressing the classic point of view of the responsibility of the poet to his own kind. Neither Shelley nor Byron expanded his self-love much beyond his own preferences and idiosyncrasies. Shelley's revolutionary passion was like a great pressure of steam escaping through the whistle but turning no machinery. The beauty, the goodness, the truth, the Platonic idealism, that inspired Shelley remained just that, abstract words unapplied to specific human problems and leading nowhere except to chaos. Matthew Arnold's description of Shelley as "a beautiful and ineffectual angel" remains the last word on the subject. Byron's revolutionary ideas were hopelessly confused, and his death at Missolonghi while on his way to fight for the oppressed Greeks belongs to his biography only, wherein it is almost the sole redeeming feature. Byron was at once a revolutionary and a snob, a foe to monarchy and, for a while, an admirer of that vulgar and bloodthirsty wrecker, Napoleon. There was no consistency in him.

Byron's masterpiece is *Don Juan;* cynical and hateful in many ways though it is, it is witty and Rabelaisian and contains passages of high poetry. Outside of that we have a few lyrics, and such would seem to be the sum and substance of Byron's bequest to us. But if I were writing this a hundred and twenty-five years ago, I should have a great deal more to say on the subject, for Byron's kind of unfettered romanticism, personal and social, swept Europe, where it was held in check only by the wiser and nobler influence of Goethe. Indeed, the adjective "Byronic" is still with us.

Shelley had charity and personal charm, but the fact is, he never grew up. He was hysterical, nervous, and given to self-pity:

> Though thou art ever fair and kind,
>   The forests ever green,
> Less oft is peace in Shelley's mind
>   Than calm in water seen.

So he concludes his lines "To Jane." In Dr. Johnson's use of the word, this is *disgusting.* Shelley's self-revelation in *Alastor* is the most mawkish and embarrassing in literature until we come to T. S. Eliot's *Love Song of J. Alfred Prufrock.*

"Radiant" was one of Shelley's favorite words, and at its best his poetry has a kind of radiance. It is this almost disembodied aspect, this quality of Ariel, that struck the young Robert Browning with admiration and inspired his poem *Memorabilia,* which was suggested by overhearing someone in a bookshop remark that he used to know Shelley:

i

> Ah, did you once see Shelley plain,
>   And did he stop and speak to you
> And did you speak to him again?
>   How strange it seems and new!

ii

But you were living before that,
    And also you are living after;
And the memory I started at—
    My starting moves your laughter.

iii

I crossed a moor, with a name of its own
    And a certain use in the world no doubt,
Yet a hand's-breadth of it shines alone
    'Mid the blank miles round about.

iv

For there I picked up on the heather
    And there I put inside my breast
A moulted feather, an eagle-feather!
    Well, I forget the rest.

Shelley has left us a few lyrics, almost Elizabethan in their beauty and music, such as these lines *To* ——:

One word is too often profaned
    For me to profane it,
One feeling too falsely disdained
    For thee to disdain it;
One hope is too like despair
    For prudence to smother,
And pity from thee more dear
    Than that from another.

I can give not what men call love,
    But wilt thou accept not
The worship the heart lifts above
    And the Heavens reject not—
The desire of the moth for the star,
    Of the night for the morrow,
The devotion to something afar
    From the sphere of our sorrow?

He has also left us the noble pastoral elegy for John Keats, *Adonais,* the *Ode to the West Wind,* and a few other pieces that survive the romantic limitations of their day. His influence has been small—

on the youthful Browning, on Francis Thompson, and, conspicuously, on the late Elinor Wylie, who was so enamoured of his genius that she considered herself his reincarnation and wrote a prose fantasy about him.

If Elinor Wylie was in love with Shelley, the late Amy Lowell was in love with Keats, a much better choice, in my opinion. Of the second generation of romantic poets, Keats was the sturdiest and the most gifted. Shelley and Byron were both well born and well provided for; the confusions and disasters that caused them to indulge in self-pity were of their own making. Keats was not well born, his education was not distinguished, and he had little money. He nursed his younger brother Tom on his deathbed and contracted tuberculosis from him. He was doubtless thinking of Tom when he wrote, in the *Ode to a Nightingale,*

> Where youth grows pale, and spectre-thin, and dies.

The reviewers who attacked his work so atrociously were thinking less of the poems than of Keats's association with Leigh Hunt, then a focus of so much conservative detestation, but there was nothing they left unsaid. They made fun not only of his poetry but of his background, the fact that he had been an apothecary's apprentice, even of the sound of his name. Just after his death, it was the current opinion that these assaults had killed him; Shelley says so eloquently in *Adonais* and Byron flippantly in *Don Juan.* It is, of course, an overstatement, but recent writers have passed over too casually the deep and festering wound he must have received from such public pronouncements of contempt. That desperate epitaph he composed for himself, "Here lies one whose name was writ in water," was not the result of tuberculosis or his frustrated love for Fanny Brawn but of a final conviction that he had failed as poet.

Poetry and the quest of beauty were the most important things in his life. They inspired him but they did not distort him. He had a good sense of humor, and except in those last terrible letters to Fanny, which never should have been made public, he was not one to succumb to self-pity. He had a large circle of warmly devoted friends, who appreciated his genius. He was manly and, as long as he was at least fairly well, he enjoyed life. No one could have been farther from the wandering phantom that Shelley conceived of as poet in *Alastor*. The variety of his work is impressive, especially considering the short period in which it was written, and the poetry of the English language would show a great gap without it. His best poems are all masterpieces of their kind: half a dozen sonnets, four great odes, *On a Grecian Urn, On Melancholy, To a Nightingale, Bards of Passion and of Mirth;* the poem *To Autumn,* which might well be called an ode; the romantic ballad *La Belle Dame sans Merci,* and the wonderful Gothic narrative, *The Eve of St. Agnes.* The main influence on Keats was the Elizabethans, particularly Spenser; and Milton was a minor influence in his younger days as was Dryden on his supernatural narrative poem, *Lamia,* which we should probably include among his masterpieces. His influence, in turn, was strong on Tennyson and Rossetti and on Oscar Wilde and the aesthetic school at the end of the nineteenth century. Of all the romantic poets, Keats, Coleridge, and Wordsworth have best stood the test of time.

Poetic fame is like quotations on the stock market; a poet's value goes up and down not only in his own time but for centuries thereafter. For example, John Donne exercised a huge influence on the first half of the seventeenth century, but with the coming of Waller he sank into obscurity in which he remained throughout the eighteenth and nineteenth centuries, to be revived and even overpraised by T. S. Eliot and his school during the three decades from 1920 to 1950. Byron in his own day, in spite of the scandals attached to his way of living, or perhaps because of them, was immensely popular. Ernest Boyd notes that "His publisher declared that in ten years Byron's pen had brought in $375,000, and the sale of 14,000 copies of one of his books in a single day is recorded." Pope's stock remained high for over half a century after his death, sank to almost nothing in the late nineteenth and early twentieth centuries, and now is high again, partly owing to the enthusiasm of that indomitable dame, Edith Sitwell. Shelley and Keats were almost unknown by their contemporaries.

Two of the great Victorian poets, Robert Browning and Alfred, Lord Tennyson, commanded a huge public in their own day; people waited for the publication of their new volumes with all the eagerness of a line waiting to buy tickets for a popular play. Browning Societies sprang up in England and America to study the works of the master; some of them still survive, though they have widened their scope. The third great Victorian poet, Matthew Arnold, wrote nearly all his verse before he was thirty-five, and his prose criticism, by which he achieved his contemporary fame, overshadowed it until comparatively recent years.

Tennyson, popular as he was in his own time, became a symbol of Victorianism. Attacks on his work began comparatively early with George Meredith's private opinion and publicly in 1870 with passages in Swinburne's *Under the Microscope.* These adverse comments during his lifetime did not have much effect on the reading public, but the first quarter of this present century found him the object of neglect and contempt. A large body of sentimental and dainty writing gave ammunition to the enemies of his work, but could not long obscure the fact that he was also the author of great poetry and a prophet of almost uncanny inspiration. The great elegy for his friend, Arthur Hallam, which he called *In Memoriam,* abounds in splendid passages, and, nine years before the publication of Darwin's *Origin of Species,* anticipates the theory of evolution and deals with it in the light of Christian faith. *The Palace of Art* is an allegory designed to refute Goethe's principle of "art for art's sake"; it is a self-argument, a conflict between Wisdom and Beauty, wherein the poet contends against his own aestheticism. The poem may also be interpreted more deeply as a conflict between different aspects of the human soul. In any case, it remains acutely applicable in our own day as a refutation of the aestheticism of the school of Pound and Eliot. *Locksley Hall,* freed of its irrelevant love story, is not only a wonderful poem but is lighted by flashes of prophecy, the more astounding because they were written back in 1842:

For I dipped into the future, far as human eye could see,
Saw the Vision of the world, and all the wonder that would be,

Saw the heavens fill with commerce, argosies of magic sails,
Pilots of the purple twilight, dropping down with costly bales;

Heard the heavens fill with shouting, and there rain'd a ghastly dew
From the nations' airy navies grappling in the central blue;

Far along the world-wide whisper of the south-wind rushing warm,
With the standards of the peoples plunging thro' the thunder-storm;

Till the war-drum throbb'd no longer, and the battle-flags were furl'd
In the Parliament of man, the Federation of the world.

There the common sense of most shall hold a fretful realm in awe,
And the kindly earth shall slumber, lapt in universal law.

We have seen the first part of this prophecy come true; let us
hope for the fulfillment of the second.

The long octameter couplets of this poem are representative of
Tennyson's experimental range; there was almost no form that he
left untried, and the new combinations of rhyme and rhythm in
his various stanza forms are innumerable. He was a superb
technician, patient and restrained; he had the "law of pure and
flawless workmanship" that Matthew Arnold described as the
artistic quality in poetry. His blank verse, as in his Arthurian poems
and many shorter pieces, such as *Tithonus* (from which Aldous
Huxley took the title for his novel, *After Many a Summer Dies
the Swan*), is more varied and melodious than any since Elizabethan
days and quite free from the heavy grandeur of the Miltonic
paragraph. Some of his early work, incantational and mysterious,
was admired by Poe, and even Whitman spoke of "Tennyson,
the boss of us all." No one lyric can represent his numerous
varieties of song-poem: I have chosen one from *The Princess*
because it is in blank verse and yet eminently singable:

> Now sleeps the crimson petal, now the white;
> Nor waves the cypress in the palace walk;
> Nor winks the gold fin in the porphyry font.
> The firefly wakens; waken thou with me.
>
> Now droops the milk-white peacock like a ghost,
> And like a ghost she glimmers on to me.
>
> Now lies the Earth all Danaë to the stars,
> And all thy heart lies open unto me.
>
> Now slides the silent meteor on, and leaves
> A shining furrow, as thy thoughts in me.
>
> Now folds the lily all her sweetness up,
> And slips into the bosom of the lake.
> So fold thyself, my dearest, thou, and slip
> Into my bosom and be lost in me.

Thomas Carlyle remarked that "Alfred was always carrying a bit of chaos around with him and turning it into cosmos." That was the method of his life and his work, a shaping strength that transformed sorrow into faith and confusion into the forms of beauty and hope. Tennyson's eventual optimism was not easily acquired. We think of him as Lord Tennyson, Poet Laureate, the intimate of all the great men of his day, beloved in England by everybody, from Queen Victoria to the old servant Susan Epton. We forget the unhappy childhood and the poverty that blighted him until he was in his mid-thirties. His character was complex and had its darker, almost self-defeating side, that left its traces in the self-questioning of many of his poems. In *The Two Voices,* one is that of suicidal despair. The emergence of the great artist brought solace to the man, and from his private triumph evolved the successful poet.

In leaving him, however, I should like to quote a children's poem of his that seems sheer magic and is almost unknown:

> Minnie and Winnie
> Slept in a shell.
> Sleep, little ladies!
> And they slept well.
>
> Pink was the shell within,
> Silver without;
> Sounds of the great sea
> Wander'd about.
>
> Sleep, little ladies!
> Wake not soon!
> Echo on echo
> Dies to the moon.
>
> Two bright stars
> Peep'd into the shell.
> "What are they dreaming of?
> Who can tell?"
>
> Started a green linnet
> Out of the croft;
> Wake, little ladies!
> The sun is aloft!

I would trade the *Idylls of the King* for that!

Like Tennyson, Browning was a master technician, but not all his experiments are concealed in the general effect of the poem; they often obtrude and we are aware of the bold metrical devices and the clever rhyming (when the poems are rhymed). Tennyson was the spokesman for the hopes and fears of the whole English-speaking world; Browning addressed a less numerous group drawn together by the feeling that they were an elite company who shared the secret of a cloudy but profound genius. He was interested in the out-of-the-ordinary, the eccentric, twisted, or ecstatic forms of human nature, and the Italian Renaissance, with its procession of remarkable and violent personages, provided the subject matter for the largest part of his compositions, among which the dramatic monologue was a new contribution to narrative and the analysis of character. Chaucer presented his people to us in the full sunlight of his present day; Browning shone his sun backward through time to reveal his extraordinary individuals, gesticulating and plotting, who were roused from their sleep in the pages of history. This is not romantic antiquarianism such as is expressed in Keats's "And they are gone: aye, ages long ago"; it is the transportation of the reader into the past where these Renaissance princes, philosophers, murderers, artists, and ecclesiastics are put through their paces before his eyes. Browning's early piece, *Sordello,* dealing with the tangled politics of mediaeval Italy, became a byword for obscurity. "It was a fine poem before he wrote it," said James Russell Lowell. Browning's subsequent works were less obscure, but still maintained a wide margin of interpretation to perplex the wits of those who like to solve puzzles and argue over their solutions. He delighted in the complexities of human character, and, becoming more and more interested in the workings of the criminal mind, in 1868 produced his—to me interminable—masterpiece, *The Ring and the Book,* in which the murder of a young wife by her husband is analyzed in twelve dramatic monologues, giving the different points of view of various people and the partisans of Rome, and finally of the Pope, who pronounces judgment. To me this is an eye-wearying bore, but there are those who still love it and may be called the true Browningites.

Browning was an optimist, but he acknowledged that life has more pain than pleasure:

I must say—or choke in silence—howsoever came my fate,
Sorrow did and joy did nowise—life well-weighed—predominate.

But we must match with that the self-description from the Epilogue
to *Asolando:*

> One who never turned his back but marched breast forward,
>   Never doubted clouds would break,
> Never dreamed, though right were worsted, wrong would triumph,
> Held we fall to rise, are baffled to fight better,
>   Sleep to wake.

To Browning, Evil was a proving ground for the Good.

Browning's romance with the poetess Elizabeth Barrett is familiar to the present generation through the popular play, *The Barretts of Wimpole Street.* It seems to have been one of those marriages made in Heaven, and Browning never recovered from his wife's death. However, the record of at least one family quarrel is preserved in his *Sludge, The Medium.* Mrs. Browning became deeply interested in a trance-medium named Daniel Dunglas Home, who practiced levitation, and on one occasion was seen to float out one window into another seventy feet above the ground. Browning became so jealous of his wife's interest in this medium that he devoted a dramatic monologue to the subject, ridiculing Home, under the name of Sludge, as a common cheat.

There were other evidences of Browning's temper. When, six years after Edward FitzGerald's death, his letters were published, the editors carelessly let slip through a foolish remark, intended for one person only, about Mrs. Browning's death. Browning attacked the dead translator of Omar Khayyam in a poem that howled with rage and sputtered with bad taste. The episode hastened his own death.

Browning's attack on Rossetti's sonnet sequence, in *House,* was wholly unprovoked and came at a time when his fellow poet was already on the verge of despair. Once Browning went to astonishing lengths to prove a point. In the usual controversary, which goes back to the days of Aristophanes, concerning the relative merits of Aeschylus and Euripides—as though to admire one, one must hate the other—Browning took the part of Euripides, and, to put Aeschylus in an unfavorable light, translated his *Agamemmon* in the most horribly discordant verse he could command.

There are few traces of Browning's direct influence in our century except in the works of E. A. Robinson, whose *Ben Jonson Entertains a Man from Stratford* is a dramatic monologue in the best Browning manner.

Of the three great Victorian poets, Arnold stands somewhat in the background, although his *Dover Beach* has become almost proverbial and his *Sohrab and Rustum* until recently was taught in the schools, though doubtless it would be thought too difficult for modern children. Arnold's chief inspiration was the Greeks, and among the Greeks, Sophocles, "who saw life steadily and saw it whole." He was well aware of the dangers to the future involved in the inventive and materialistic age in which he lived—nearly all the great Victorian writers issued their warnings concerning that —but went further and found human life itself inevitably tragic. His Scholar-Gipsy retreated from an insupportable epoch to the fringes of a world of phantoms, and his Empedocles went further and plunged to oblivion in the crater of Etna. His attitude toward "romantic" nature is inconsistent; *In Harmony with Nature* derides the notion that nature and man can ever be fast friends; elsewhere, as in *Quiet Work,* his philosophy of nature is almost Wordsworthian. Just once, in *The Forsaken Merman,* Arnold let himself go in the realm of pure fantasy, and the result is delightful. He recorded the chartless bewilderment of the culture of his time in *The Strayed Reveller.*

In this world of doubt and futility, Arnold recommends the same self-reliance that Emerson preached (he and Emerson were friends, and he wrote a sympathetic if somewhat condescending essay on Emerson) and a Stoic courage in the face of a hostile universe. His was the first of the doubting voices that through Hardy and many of the writers of our own day were to rise to a chorus of pessimism.

In both England and America the nineteenth century showed a preoccupation with moral values and a faith in material prosperity; a secondary rallying point in England was pride in the British Empire, and in America, after the Civil War, a commitment to Utopian vistas of democracy, the main theme of Whitman's work, although by the time he was recognized in a disillusioned age, he was valued for other qualities and credited with revolutionary trends that he never intended. His social philosophy of the love of comrades is merely a more intimate version of Tennyson's Federation of the

World, but the unconventionality of Whitman's diction and versification gave his message an all-embracing quality that the more restrained utterance of Tennyson sacrificed in favor of dignity.

In an atmosphere of optimism and dainty limitations, Henry Wadsworth Longfellow was the most popular of American poets not only in his own country but in England as well, where he stood third after Tennyson and Browning. Possibly he was more popular than Browning. Because of much sorry sentimentalism, the whole of Longfellow's work has in our own day been relegated to the scrap heap, where some of it, undoubtedly, does not belong. There is a small volume of excellent poetry to be winnowed from Longfellow's work, and Howard Nemerov has just this year (1960) edited such a selection with a sensitive and appreciative Introduction. (The Laurel Poetry Series, 35¢.) Robert Frost is an admirer of Longfellow's, and there are probably many others. Longfellow's aims were the same as Chaucer's: to provide a new nation with stories from foreign lands, to utilize native material, and to enrich versification. In the variety of his meters he included an English version of the hexameter for his *Courtship of Miles Standish* and his *Evangeline;* for *Hiawatha* he used the meter of the Finnish *Kalevala*. Longfellow, like Chaucer before him, was widely read in many languages and a well-traveled man. But alas! Longfellow was no Chaucer, nor would the age in which he lived have permitted him to get into print if he had been. The Wife of Bath would have been considered an offense to American womanhood, and the hairy wart on the Miller's nose a breach of good taste, not to mention more substantial improprieties. Longfellow expressed his admiration of Chaucer in a good sonnet, that concludes:

> He is the poet of the dawn, who wrote
> The Canterbury Tales, and his old age
> Made beautiful with song; and as I read
> I hear the crowing cock, I hear the note
> Of lark and linnet, and from every page
> Rise odours of plough'd field or flowery mead.

Of the four other notable American poets of the nineteenth century, Emerson, Poe, Emily Dickinson, and Walt Whitman, the last three predominantly belong to the twentieth. Emerson's poetry is on the whole rather wooden and not passionately inspired. We

remember him chiefly for his *Give All to Love,* with the memorable
ending:

> When half-gods go
> The gods arrive,

for his *Concord Hymn,* and his stanzas on Brahma. This last,
though one of Emerson's most inspired, is a paraphrase from the
Upanishads of the Hindus. The first stanza, from the *Katha
Upanishad,* is especially close. Here is R. E. Hume's translation from
the original:

> If the slayer think to slay,
> If the slain think himself slain,
> Both these understand not.
> This one slays not, nor is slain.

Emerson's poem begins:

> If the red slayer think he slays,
> Or if the slain think he is slain,
> They know not well the subtle ways
> I keep, and pass, and turn again.

The history of Edgar Allen Poe's poetry is one of the strangest
in literature. He was on only a few occasions a good poet; the best
of his work is probably these stanzas *To Helen:*

> Helen, thy beauty is to me
> Like those Nicëan barks of yore
> That gently, o'er a perfumed sea,
> The weary way-worn wanderer bore
> To his own native shore.
>
> On desperate seas long wont to roam,
> Thy hyacinth hair, thy classic face,
> Thy Naiad airs have brought me home
> To the glory that was Greece,
> And the grandeur that was Rome.
>
> Lo, in yon brilliant window-niche
> How statue-like I see thee stand,
> The agate lamp within thy hand,

Ah! Psyche, from the regions which
Are Holy Land!

This poem, like *Kubla Khan,* is a triumph of artifice, as a glance at the alliterations in line 4 and the arranged vowel sounds in the last two stanzas clearly shows. Poe was seldom so fortunate, and a contrivance like *The Bells* justifies Emerson's epithet for him, "the jingle-man." Furthermore, Poe looked upon the human race as corrupt and diseased, the victims of materialism. The French poet, Charles Baudelaire, found in Poe a congenial master, and his translations of the American poet had a lasting effect, which boomeranged back into American literature. Poe, translated into French, had a predominant influence on the French symbolists at the end of the nineteenth and beginning of the twentieth century; the French symbolists, especially Jules Laforgue, had a predominant influence on the young Ezra Pound and T. S. Eliot, and we may say that, in the powerful twentieth-century school of Pound and Eliot, Poe worked his revenge on his own country, that during his lifetime had left him in squalor and neglect.

Emily Dickinson, too, is chiefly important to the twentieth century, although her poems, published after her death, went through several editions in the 1890s. By 1920 she had been completely forgotten, at least by the general public interested in poetry. A collection of her poems called *The Single Hound* was given to me by a friend at Harvard in 1916 when I was a junior, and I was so enamored of it that I took it with me to France in World War I. As the years passed, I became more and more distressed that nobody seemed to have heard of her, and in 1922 I published an essay on her in *The Freeman,* beginning, "It is doubtful that Emily Dickinson will ever be famous." My most ambitious intention was to attract a few more sympathetic readers to her work. *The Freeman* was read by most people interested in literature, and the essay had a larger effect than I should have imagined possible. Many, including Thomas H. Johnson, her editor and biographer, have acknowledged the essay as the source of their interest in the poet. It came out just at the right moment, when her mystical quality and symbolic method were compared with William Blake's work, which at that time was at the height of an almost frantic revival, and her sharp images and suggestive diction accorded with the contemporary search for fresh means of expression. But though she was swept into popularity at the right psychological moment, she is not the toy of literary fashion, and has taken her place, with the modified enthusiasm demanded by critical reservations, among the great poets. Her influence, both direct and indirect, on the twentieth century has been considerable. It is chiefly manifested in the secondary meanings, both literal and metaphorical, that are combined in a single word or a single word in relation to the context. Examine, for example, the use of the word "cantons" in the following quatrain:

> My figures fail to tell me
> How far the Village lies—
> Whose peasants are the Angels—
> Whose Cantons dot the skies....

"When I state myself . . . it does not mean me, but a supposed person," she wrote. This evidence should be taken into account in reading her love-poems, which, perfervid and sentimental, are unfortunate, yet have occasioned volumes of foolish and sometimes offensive speculation concerning the identity of her "lover."

Her true genius is as the poet of revelation, lighting the New England landscape with a flash, momentary and yet eternal, so searching that every leaf, every grassblade, comes to view. Death is a low-lying cloud that chills her as she walks through it, to emerge in sunlight on the other side where "from those solemn abbeys such resurrection pours."

In her gradual retirement from human society she made an exception in the case of children, with whom she conspired against the adult world. She kept her lanes of communication open with scores of letters to chosen friends. These are almost as important as her poems, which she called her "letter to the world." She stands above all other American poets of her century: her jewel-like phrasing is inimitable, her perception of Nature is all-inclusive, and no poet has more convincingly revealed the eternal significance of transient things.

The first edition of Walt Whitman's *Leaves of Grass* came out in 1855, and he went on revising it and adding to it through several later editions. "I greet you at the beginning of a great career," wrote Emerson, and then recoiled to find that his compliment was emblazoned on the cover of the second edition of 1856. There was no trick to which Whitman did not descend to establish himself as a poet-prophet, writing anonymous eulogies of his work, and of himself as "the most masculine of beings," in the newspapers; and planting in provincial papers an account of one of his public appearances that had, in fact, been a catastrophe: "His gestures were few but significant...all the directors and officers of the Institute crowded around him & heartily thanked him." Esther Shephard in her deadly but incontrovertible book, *Walt Whitman's Pose,* follows him through the series of frauds and falsehoods with which he sought to transform himself into a gigantic prophet of male convictions, and a being to whom all nature was atune. I myself possess a memento of these astonishing tactics, the so-called "Butterfly Edition" of 1865, on the title page of which is a picture of a butterfly on Walt's outstretched finger. A friend, seeing the original photograph, asked Whitman how it happened that a butterfly was in a photographer's studio. "O I've always had the knack of attracting birds and butterflies and other wild critters. They know that I like 'em and won't hurt 'em, and so they come," answered Walt. In 1935 Miss Shephard located the butterfly, a pasteboard affair with a wire loop to attach it to the finger. I find more pathos than turpitude in all this.

Whitman was, in fact, playing a child's game all his life. He created an imaginary and ideal figure of himself and from that altitude he wrote his poems. Whatever grandeur and lyric sweetness they possess, as they do in many isolated passages, are the result of this self-transfiguration. At least during his periods of composition, he must have persuaded himself that he was the high personage he dreamed of and tried to foist on the public.

His philosophy was somewhat vague, influenced by transcendentalism and readings in Vedic literature, and though it would reward no one in search of logical thought, it gave to his landscapes and his emotional passages a mysterious power like a wind blowing through them from outer space. I have spoken of isolated passages, and it is true that Whitman is a poet best served by selections in an anthology. His elegy on Lincoln, *When Lilacs Last in the Dooryard Bloom'd,* and *Out of the Cradle Endlessly Rocking*—these long poems are sustained in beauty almost throughout. But his best work is mostly found in fragments or such short poems as *The Last Invocation*:

At the last, tenderly,
From the walls of the powerful fortress'd house,
From the clasp of the knitted locks, from the keep of the well-closed
    doors,
Let me be wafted.

Let me glide noiselessly forth;
With the key of softness unlock the locks—with a whisper,
Set ope the doors O soul.

Tenderly—be not impatient,
(Strong is your hold O mortal flesh,
Strong is your hold O love.)

The paradox concerning Whitman's work is that the common people, whom it was supposed to inspire, are indifferent to it. His devotees are to be found only among the sophisticated.

Another nineteenth-century poet, the English Jesuit, Gerard Manley Hopkins, influences a good many of the poets of our own time, and not always with happy effect. Hopkins is one of those eloquent eccentrics whose mannerisms usually find acceptance in their extreme form among their followers. At his extreme, he is hysterical and unintelligible, or, as in *The Golden Echo,* wherein, like the early fathers of the church, he advocates virginity as the best state for all beautiful girls, he frolics so amid puns and double meanings that his preachment becomes as distasteful as it is, in fact, unwholesome.

Hopkins's poems were not given to the public until 1918, when they were published by his friend and editor, Robert Bridges. His elaborate theory and practice of prosody cannot be examined in detail in a short account of him, and it is best to rely largely on what he himself had to say. In the first place, "take breath and read it with the ears, as I always wish to be read, and my verse becomes all right." *The Windhover,* "the best thing I ever wrote," is in "falling paeonic rhythm, sprung and outriding." "Falling rhythm" is, as I noted earlier in this book, the first paeon. "Sprung rhythm" is simply an extension of the old Anglo-Saxon principle of syllabic freedom; it is measured "by feet of from one to four syllables, regularly, and for particular effects any number of weak or slack syllables may be used.... In Sprung Rhythm...the feet are assumed to be equally long or strong and their seeming inequality is made up by pause or stressing." To the careful reader of this book, none of these principles will seem novel; Hopkins's idiosyncrasy lies in the sometimes excessive license with which he applied them. Hopkins himself never fully explained what he meant by "outriding"; he started an explanation but left it too unfinished to be more than a playground for speculation. Since Hopkins himself considered *The Windhover* his best work, I shall quote it here, though there are many other poems simpler and clearer:

To Christ Our Lord

I caught this morning morning's minion, king-
  dom of daylight's dauphin, dapple-dawn-drawn Falcon, in his riding
  Of the rolling level underneath him steady air, and striding
High there, how he rung upon the rein of a wimpling wing
In his ecstasy! then off, off forth on swing,
  As a skate's heel sweeps smooth on a bow-bend: the hurl and gliding
  Rebuffed the big wind. My heart in hiding
Stirred for a bird,—the achieve of, the mastery of the thing!

Brute beauty and valour and act, oh, air, pride, plume, here
  Buckle! AND the fire that breaks from thee then, a billion
Times told lovelier, more dangerous, O my chevalier!

  No wonder of it: shéer plód makes plough down sillion
Shine, and blue-bleak embers, ah my dear,
  Fall, gall themselves, and gash gold-vermilion.

A glance at the rhyme-scheme will show that this is Hopkins's version of a sonnet. In reading it, it is necessary to avoid the modern mispronouncing of the word "falcon"; it should be pronounced "fawcon" without the "l" sound, as in "walk" and "talk." The word "sillion" is not in any English dictionary; it is doubtless the French *sillon,* meaning a furrow. Read aloud several times, the poem will yield its music, rich and intricate, but, for more than a short passage, overburdened with assonances, internal rhymes, alliterations, and an effect of too much contrivance. As to the series of pictures and metaphors by which the poet transforms the windhover (a small falcon) into a symbol of Christ, I must leave that to the ingenuity of the reader. There are passages where I should not be a dependable guide. One poet like Hopkins is an interesting addition to the phenomena of literature; a general trend under his influence would be a literary decadence. It is natural that in an age like ours, some are attracted by the unusual, the obscure, and the distorted, and find in Hopkins's tortured syllables a congenial poetry; but for my part, when I read his more extreme pieces, I am haunted by old Richard Stanyhurst of four centuries ago.

In looking back over the centuries of the past, we are struck by the continuity of our poetry; how each poet, finding influences and sources to his liking, absorbs them and gives them new life in an expression wholly his own and, to some degree, colored by the age he lives in. Thus, taking a few names at random, we catch a glimpse of the French and Italian elements in Chaucer, the Elizabethan freshness in the lyrics of Blake, combined with the symbolism of so many mystics before him; the simple cadences of the hymn book in Emily Dickinson's work, with the shadow of George Herbert and Sir Thomas Browne over her mysterious phrasing. Every true poet is rooted in the past, selecting what nurture is best suited to his own growth, but retaining his identity, modified by the climate of his age. In his poetry he gives the best of himself and his experience of life as he has known it in his time.

PART IV *Poetry in the Twentieth Century*

Poetry in the first sixty years of the twentieth century is a segment of literary history so near to us that only the first two or three decades are sufficiently eroded by time for us to distinguish between the rock formations and the landslides. The closer we approach the present, the more confused becomes the picture, and there is the danger of subsiding into mere lists of names and evaluations more appropriate to a book review than a considered judgment set against the whole sweep of the poetic tradition. Having been a lively observer of much that has taken place during the past half century, and having early established definite criteria, I have found that my own reactions to these fifty years of poetical activity include admiration, amusement, and some disgust, all of which will be reflected in the account that follows.

At the beginning of the century, England and Ireland were poetically awake and vigorous. America was sunk in lethargy. Hence, the stir of revolt and experiment took place among Americans. There was no reason for it in England or Ireland, and it had almost no effect among British writers, although its course happened to be directed from England by the expatriate partners T. S. Eliot and Ezra Pound.

We shall deal first with the English and Irish poets.

Thomas Hardy's *Poems Past and Present* appeared in 1902 and his long epic drama, *The Dynasts,* in 1904. In considering his poetry, we must speak of pessimism of two kinds: *local,* in which the human race is excoriated, as in *Gulliver's Travels,* and *cosmic,* in which the whole scheme of the universe is shown to be adverse to man, who is scarcely more than a tragic accident or a plaything of malevolent gods. Swift was a priest of the Church of England and therefore could have no quarrel with the order of the universe but only with the perniciousness of mankind; he was bound by his professed religion to be a teleologist; that is, to believe that life has a definite purpose under a beneficent deity. He was limited to local pessimism. Matthew Arnold first introduced cosmic pessimism into English poetry, a philosophy lightened only by the love between individuals ("Ah, love, let us be true to one another") and the dignity of a Stoic acceptance of fate. Arnold's thought was shaped by Greek literature, Sophocles in particular, which exhibited a logical train of events, cause and effect, initiated by man's pride and concluded by his destruction. In Hardy's poetry, however, and most of his novels, the cast of thought was different.

The Greek Fates moved according to plan. The Fate of the Anglo-Saxons, Wyrd, was not logical but struck suddenly and causelessly as in a bolt of lightning or the foundering of a ship. Hardy, whose fate was a modern Wyrd, attempted to meet the charge that he was a pessimist by pointing out that his Deity was merely senseless, not malevolent. God, the sense-sealed, purposeless Creator, "went on working...in his unweeting way," unaware of the existence of man and grinding on like a machine through eternity. The ruthless Fates of the Greeks seem to me a less repellent conception.

Hardy is an extraordinary metrist. He is seldom purely lyric; he roughened much of his verse deliberately. The range of his forms is enormous, from the simple ballad stanza of *The Subalterns,* which deals with the universal slavery to fate, to the intricate paeons of *In the Servants' Quarters,* on St. Peter's denial of Christ, which is so difficult that some practice is required for reading it aloud. He was one of the boldest of experimenters, but always within the bounds of meter and rhyme. Often, in a kind of mysterious onomatopoeia, the taunting syllables echo the theme of his fatalism.

One small rift in his pessimism is in an exquisite little lyric called *The Darkling Thrush.* On a bleak winter day that seemed the symbol of the "Century's corpse," suddenly "a voice burst forth...of joy illimited." It was the ecstatic song of "an aged thrush, frail, gaunt, and small," and

> So little cause for carolings
> Of such ecstatic sound

Was written on terrestrial things
   Afar or nigh around,
That I could think there trembled through
   His happy good-night air
Some blessed hope, whereof he knew
   And I was unaware.

In the final Chorus of Hardy's *Dynasts,* there is yet another departure from his conception of the blind, sense-sealed Creator, and Hardy himself would probably have called it optimistic. The Chorus affirms that at some future date the senseless Creator may awake, and, observing the horrible universe that he has fashioned, make haste to wipe it out altogether. This is the philosophy of nihilism, the belief that being in iself is evil and that non-being is the cosmic salvation. It goes beyond the Hindu desire for the extinction of the individual in Nirvana, and celebrates the annihilation of everything.

Pity and terror, the two qualities that Aristotle deemed necessary for the purging of the soul, are plentiful in Hardy's poems, but there is something added, something that we do not often find in his novels: a mockery of human aspirations that adds satire to tragedy, the local pessimism of his *Satires of Circumstance.*

With A. E. Housman we are again dealing with nihilistic convictions. His wonderful, singing lyrics, a combination of the simplest folk forms with the intensity of the classic epigram, so sweetly persuade us to the grave that we shed tears with the bystanders at our own dissolution. In Housman's poems there are no old people; everyone is lovely, young, and doomed. The entire substance of Housman's work can be found in a single poem by one greater than he, the *Ode on a Distant Prospect of Eton College* of Thomas Gray.

Gray always looked back on his boyhood years at Eton, in company with his friends Richard West and Horace Walpole, as the golden age of his life. In his stanzaic ode he describes in the first five strophes the joys of youth, the games, the spring weather, the easy, changing moods; and in the last five, the terrors that lie in wait for the boys as they grow up: Misfortune, Anger, Fear, Passion, unhappy Love, Ambition, and, finally, Death. Each of these personifications and several others are effectively sketched in with a phrase or an adjective. The poem ends:

To each his sufferings: all are men,
   Condemn'd alike to groan;
The tender for another's pain,
   The unfeeling for his own.
Yet, ah! why should they know their fate,
Since sorrow never comes too late,
   And happiness too swiftly flies?
Thought would destroy their paradise.
No more;—where ignorance is bliss,
   'Tis folly to be wise.

How close this is to Housman's

Think no more; 't is only thinking
Lays lads underground.

Housman's almost unremitting gloom would become laughable or sentimental were it not for his lyric power and his wit, which, breaking through openly in such a couplet as

And malt does more than Milton can
To justify God's ways to man,

is in the background of even his darkest stanzas, saving, with a single turn of phrase, something that otherwise might have been mawkish. Housman has another virtue that deserves mention; he is a good poet who is also popular, and the attraction of his verse has lured many a reader to explore beyond him into the wider reaches of poetry.

Robert Bridges, who became poet laureate in 1913, stands out in sunlit grandeur against the muse of midnight and of death. Well acquainted with human suffering and degradation in his early years as a doctor attached to St. Bartholomew's Hospital in London, he was in charge of the "out-patients" and treated about one hundred a day, from the slums of the city. He retired for reasons of health when he was thirty-eight and settled down in the country. There he devoted himself to poetry and a number of scholarly pursuits allied to it, especially the study of prosody, classic and English, wherein he had no superior in all the range of poetry in the English language. His volume of *Shorter Poems* is my constant companion, and no flurry of excitement or spate of worry is proof against a glance into its pages. With Bridges are the

> Days that the thought of grief refuse,
> Days that are one with human art,
> Worthy of the Virgilian muse,
> Fit for the gaiety of Mozart.

It should be noted that Bridges was skilled in music. On his eightieth birthday the English nation presented him with a splendid harpsichord.

Bridges' lyrics have to be read again and again until one has them almost by heart. They are beguilingly simple, so much so that one might easily read through them rather than into them. They present difficulties to the modern reader, in spite of their simplicity. Bridges has a Spenserian boldness in using archaisms (notably the pronouns *thou* and *thee* and the old form of the verb that goes with *thou*) and in many other ways defies the conventions of modern speech. His idiom is his own, but the mastering of it is a small task compared to the reward.

> O soul, be patient: thou shalt find
> A little matter mend all this;
> Some strain of music to thy mind,
> Some praise for skill not spent amiss.

The lyrics in the *Shorter Poems* are so diverse that the quotation of one would seem an injustice to the rest.

> Ah heavenly joy! But who hath ever heard,
> Who hath seen joy, or who shall ever find
> Joy's language? There is neither speech nor word;
> Nought but itself to teach it to mankind.

The best essay on these lyrics is by Charles Williams, in his *Poetry at Present,* published by Oxford in 1930. "Love, diligence, wit, justice, courage, temperance, reason," says Mr. Williams in part, "—these are the qualities Mr. Bridges praises and recommends to the young adventurer. They are, transmuted into poetry, the qualities of his verse; they are the analyzed elements of its beauty as it praises Beauty. They are the method of his experience, and the things his genius chooses to experience are selected by them. Besides great art, a few things are pre-eminent in his poetic knowledge—the English landscape, man in society, Hellenism, solitude, piety. These things, communicated by those virtuous Pleiades named above, cause a profound and still delight. But it is a delight which may require a certain similarity of temperament or a certain prolonged discipline before it can be accepted, especially by a reader used to more violent effects. Violence attends on the steps of a number of our poets...and even violence may have its work to do. But it is an uncertain slave, and one whom Mr. Bridges would never spend a farthing to buy or shelter."

Bridges had a long career as poet; his philosophical masterpiece, *The Testament of Beauty,* from which we can turn only to Lucretius's *De Rerum Natura* for comparison and contrast, was published when he was eighty-five. This difficult and beautiful work sold 40,000 copies in this country alone, but, as I have said before, our century is distinguished by an almost senile loss of memory, and already the poem seems to be forgotten. It is difficult as well as beautiful, and I shall be content if my readers will get the *Shorter Poems* and read and reread.

> I have lain in the sun,
> I have toil'd as I might,
> I have thought as I would,
> And now it is night.
>
> My bed full of sleep,
> My heart of content
> For friends that I met
> The way that I went....
>
> To dream as I may
> And awake when I will
> With the song of the birds
> And the sun on the hill.
>
> Or death—were it death—
> To what should I wake
> Who loved in my home
> All life for its sake?
>
> What good have I wrought?
> I laugh to have learned
> That joy cannot come
> Unless it be earned;

For a happier lot
Than God giveth me
It never hath been
Nor ever shall be.

It will be noted that there is just one adjective in the poem. Bridges is not an adjectival poet.

Besides such giants as Hardy and Bridges, the early part of the century in England still had echoes from the recently departed aesthetic school. In the mid-nineteenth century, Dante Gabriel Rossetti created a small world, the Pre-Raphaelite Brotherhood, in which only artists dwelt and where poetry and painting and sculpture were the only subjects worth considering. It had its ally in Algernon Charles Swinburne, who romanticized the prostitute, celebrated leprosy, and, in general, set a frantic paganism swirling through his elaborate meters in interminable poems that shocked the Victorians but from us can gain scarcely the tribute of a yawn.

The aesthetic school was influenced by Rossetti's preoccupation with art and Swinburne's delight in literary depravity. "Art for art's sake" was the motto of the aesthetes at the end of the century, and Oscar Wilde maintained that "the first duty in life is to be as artificial as possible." Though Wilde was the most conspicuous of the aesthetes, owing to the tragic scandal that put an end to him, there were better poets than he in the aesthetic group, such as Ernest Dowson, William Butler Yeats, and Lionel Johnson.

Except for Yeats's work—and the best of it came later—almost nothing remains from these poets. Perhaps Lionel Johnson's *By the Statue of King Charles at Charing Cross,* with its midnight evocation of the royal martyr, will survive:

> Sombre and rich, the skies,
> Great glooms, and starry plains;
> Gently the night wind sighs;
> Else a vast silence reigns.
>
> The splendid silence clings
> Around me: and around
> The saddest of all kings,
> Crown'd and again discrown'd.

Comely and calm, he rides
Hard by his own Whitehall:
Only the night wind glides:
No crowds, nor rebels, brawl.

Gone, too, his Court: and yet,
The stars his courtiers are:
Stars in their stations set;
And every wandering star....

Yeats was nearly forty when he outgrew (or nearly outgrew) aestheticism and became the central figure of the Irish Renaissance. By the time of his death in 1939 many critics called him the greatest lyric poet of his period. Perhaps he was; certainly such poems as *The Rose of the World, Sailing to Byzantium, The Wild Swans at Coole,* part of *Meditations in Time of Civil War, Among School Children* and a score of others are of lasting beauty. But much of his work is marred by an occult symbolism that needs interpretation yet defeats it by the highly personal character of his revelations. He took his symbols from dreams, from spiritualism, and from the home-made occultism of his prose apocalypse, *A Vision.* This is an age of interpretative criticism, and a poet is often praised according to the amount of obscurity he provides for analysis. When reading, for example, *The Golden Nightingale,* the late Donald A. Stauffer's book on Yeats, we are led to wonder if poems that need such pages and pages of analysis (much of it questionable) can stand, as works of art, without them. I shall conclude, however, with a note of personal gratitude: it was Yeats who presented me with my first copy of the *Shorter Poems* of Robert Bridges.

I prefer, on the whole, the lyrics of James Stephens to those of Yeats. They recall the music of the Elizabethans and seem to have been composed in another world, where magical incantation is the common speech; and there are bursts of laughter, partly from fairyland and partly from the pub. Stephens is a true mystic, not an occultist, and the very simplicity of his revelations affirms their authenticity. I have always liked the mixture of laughter and vision in *What Thomas an Buile Said in a Pub:*

I saw God. Do you doubt it?
Do you dare to doubt it?

I saw the Almighty Man. His hand
Was resting on a mountain, and
He looked upon the World and all about it:
I saw him plainer than you see me now,
 You mustn't doubt it.

He was not satisfied;
 His look was all dissatisfied.
His beard swung on a wind far out of sight
Behind the world's curve, and there was light
Most fearful from His forehead, and He sighed,
"That star went always wrong, and from the start
 I was dissatisfied."

He lifted up His hand—
 I say He heaved a dreadful hand
Over the spinning Earth. Then I said, "Stay,
You must not strike it, God; I'm in the way;
And I will never move from where I stand."
He said, "Dear child, I feared that you were dead,"
 And stayed His hand.

There is not much to be said of "AE" (George William Russell),
important though he was in the Irish Renaissance, both poetically
and politically. (It should be remembered that he and Yeats and
Gogarty were all active in the Irish government before the advent
of De Valera.) AE's bushy red beard and shock of red hair belied
a nature essentially gentle and dreamy. Like James Stephens, he
was a true mystic, so much so that his poems have little to communicate; they are wrapped in a pale vapor of abstractions from
which only occasionally does a real object mistily come to view.
Hence, his poems are uninteresting and make small bid for any
audience.

 Yeats, Stephens, and AE were all devotees of the English mystic,
William Blake; in fact, Yeats's edition of that poet started the
Blake hurricane that blew for some twenty years, until, in the
1920s, the wind shifted to another quarter, and Donne came blasting
out of the horizon for another thirty years. All such convulsions
of taste end in tedium, and about 1920 an English poet complained
that with Shakespeare and other great poets at their elbow, he

had no patience with the fools who sat up all night to mutter about Blake. In the poem I quoted from Stephens, it will be noted how closely the description of God, with his beard swinging on a wind far out of sight, resembles Blake's drawing of the Ancient of Days.

One Irish poet who had scarcely a touch of mysticism was Oliver St. John Gogarty. As with most poets, there is mystery in his work, a sense of the eternal radiance shining through the ephemeral, but he is satisfied with the earth and her seasons.

> I thank the gods who gave to me
> The yearly privilege to see,
> Under the orchard's galaxy,
> April reveal her new-drenched skin;
> And for the timeless touch within
> Whereby I recognize my kin.

The Plum Tree by the House, one of his best, is too long to quote, but we cannot forget the climax:

> Branches that Chinese draughtsmen drew,
> Which none may find an equal to,
> Unless he enter there
> Where none may live—and more's the pity!—
> The Perfect, The Forbidden City,
> That's built—Ah, God knows where!

Gogarty was full of exuberance as well as classical and Elizabethan lore (he was one of the most learned poets I have ever known), and I shall depend on my readers to look up his wonderful paean beginning

> O Boys, the times I've seen!
> The things I've done and known!
> If you knew where I have been
> Or half the joys I've had,
> You never would leave me alone....

Yeats said of Gogarty, "His poetry fits the incident, a gay, stoical—no, I will not withhold the word—heroic song.... I think him one of the great lyric poets of our age." His *Collected Poems* came out in 1954 and seems to have suffered, like so many less important books, from the blank indifference to poetry of the modern public. To my wife and me it is a personal grief that this so recently dead poet should be so soon forgotten, for he was our especial friend, witty and well loved.

Returning to England in the early years of the century, we cannot pass over—as the anthologists do—John Masefield. He won his fame—I am afraid much of it was notoriety—with his long narrative poem, *The Everlasting Mercy*. The first parts of this poem, dealing with the redemption of what we should today call a juvenile delinquent, sink into non-poetry by a brave but undiscriminating attempt to mirror reality, sordid reality, in somewhat its own terms. My "somewhat" indicates that the poet went far but not far enough to realize a convincing narrative. Even so, the poem was found shocking. The last part, with its ecstatic revelation, is watered-down Blake.

Bit by bit Chaucer's influence permeated Masefield—one might almost say *redeemed* Masefield—but, as his narratives became better and better, his public became less and less. *Dauber* is a good, if not a great, poem, and *King Cole,* in spite of its unabashed sentimentality, has some fine passages. His best poems are about ships; I should choose "The Wanderer" as his likeliest passport to immortality.

> And as we watched, there came a rush of feet
> Charging the fo'c's'le till the hatchway shook.
> Men all about us thrust their way, or beat,
> Crying, "The *Wanderer!* Down the river! Look!"
>
> I looked with them towards the dimness; there
> Gleamed like a spirit striding out of night,
> A full-rigged ship unutterably fair,
> Her masts like trees in winter, frosty-bright.
>
> Foam trembled at her bows like wisps of wool;
> She trembled as she towed. I had not dreamed
> That work of man could be so beautiful,
> In its own presence and in what it seemed.

I, who have seen the frigate *Constellation* under full sail, may be prejudiced by my love of the subject toward his ship-poems, but even in his prose, ships inspire his most beautiful writing, as well they may, and he knows them from truck to keel.

Masefield succeeded Robert Bridges as poet laureate, and among innumerable differences between the two, Masefield's readiness to turn out verses in celebration of royal or ceremonious occasions contrasts with Bridges' firm refusal to write one line on such subjects.

Meanwhile, new and gifted poets were beginning their careers at the time King George V came to the throne (1910) and they became known as Georgians for a while. The war beginning in 1914 involved most of them and killed off many of them, and the group was, for a while, known as the War Poets. Among those who died were Rupert Brooke, Wilfred Owen, Isaac Rosenberg, Edward Thomas (Robert Frost's great friend), and Charles Hamilton Sorley (who was only twenty but of ripening promise)— that was a massacre of poets if there ever was one.

Rupert Brooke was the last poet to write about the heroism and nobility of war. I suppose he will remain in that position for the rest of history. He had the old vision of personal courage, the release in war from the shabbiness and pettiness of civilian routine, and the glory of death for one's country. Brooke died of a fever on one of the Greek islands on his way to active service; he never saw what a modern war was like, so he died illusioned. His work was ridiculously overpraised during the war and for some years after; then it sank into oblivion. He deserves a better fate than that. Some of the charm and beauty of his own personality can be found in his Georgian lyrics, and his war sonnets, granting their inadvertent falsity, are deeply moving. But with so many greater poets than he being lost by the neglect of the reading public, we cannot pause with too many tears over the grave of Rupert Brooke. He was, on the whole, a fortunate poet to die with his visions unshattered.

Not so young Sorley, killed in action, who wrote, "There is no such thing as a just war. What we are doing is casting out Satan by Satan." This was also the point of view of Robert Graves and Siegfried Sassoon, who survived the war and wrote about it realistically—Sassoon with a magnificent and effective bitterness that caused an uproar, Graves with a more detached and almost whimsical touch. One of the most fantastic of Graves's war poems is an account of the hallucinations of a soldier in the trenches, with the refrain, "It's a queer time."

Both Graves and Sassoon, in the natural course, outgrew their wartime selves, and are still with us, Graves the myth-maker, with his brilliant re-creations of the past, as well as occasional poems; Sassoon in his beautifully written biographical volumes and his poetry, which is better than ever, but, again, is almost lost to public notice. His *Collected Poems* appeared in 1949, Graves's in 1947, and they are both still active as poets.

The lyrics of a major poet are usually fragmentary expressions of the central philosophy of his major work. Thus, Hardy's lyrics, in general, conform to the pessimism of his novels and of *The Dynasts,* and the lyrics of Bridges are bathed in the same light that gathers full force in *The Testament of Beauty*. This is not to say that the lyrics of major poets lack variety; on the contrary, they may be as various as the facets of the minds that produced them. Then there are the poems that do not play true to form: one may find a few carefree songs in Hardy, and, in Bridges, several poems of deep melancholy. But, on the whole, there is a prevailing tone in such poets that unifies their work and makes it possible to discuss it from one point of view.

Poets who have devoted themselves wholly to short poems elude the commentator unless he is to turn his volume into a series of inadequate references or quote more extensively than would be possible except in an anthology. Both Graves and Sassoon, for example, have changed and evolved during the years and written scores of poems in many moods and on many subjects. We note the jaunty pleasure with which Graves passes through life, often using Skeltonic and folk measures to sharpen his quick, light thrusts at his material. In Sassoon we observe the return to country serenity of a spirit once racked with indignation, his lightly satirical view of people and events, his occasional ecstasy, as in that poem of transfiguring delight concerning the Armistice, "Everyone suddenly burst out singing":

Everyone suddenly burst out singing;
And I was filled with such delight
As prisoned birds must find in freedom,
Winging wildly across the white
Orchards and dark-green fields; on—on—and out of sight.

Everyone's voice was suddenly lifted,
And beauty came like the setting sun.
My heart was shaken with tears, and horror
Drifted away.... Oh, but everyone
Was a bird, and the song was wordless—the singing will never be done.

In view of this, and of the many excellent poems of his later
years, it is a pity that the interest focused on Sassoon when he was
a poet of protest during and after the First World War has turned
away from him in his richer period of creation. Well, as Robert Frost
said to me one day about good work that is neglected: "The books
are there. Someone some time will take them down from the
shelf."

Ralph Hodgson and Walter de la Mare have not been so lost
to view as Sassoon. These are both pure lyric poets, among the
best that the century can show, and very different from each other,
sharing in common only the fortunate fact that they were too old
to be drawn into the war in which so many other poets were killed
or, spiritually as well as physically, wounded.

Ralph Hodgson, at this writing, is eighty-eight and living with
his American wife in a remote and ancient farmhouse near Minerva,
Ohio. He calls it Owlacres, and there, in these later years, he has
written, and had privately printed, a series of broadsides called
Flying Scrolls, in which the imaginative beauty of his earlier work
flies off into fantasy borne on quick couplets to the margin of
surrealism. In his earlier work, his *Song of Honour,* together with
his numerous poems on the sufferings of the small creatures of the
world and his kinship with them, places him among the poets of
mysticism, with an especial affinity with James Stephens.

> 'Twould ring the bells of Heaven
> The wildest peal for years,
> If Parson lost his senses
> And people came to theirs,
> And he and they together
> Knelt down with angry prayers
> For tamed and shabby tigers
> And dancing dogs and bears,
> And wretched, blind pit ponies,
> And little hunted hares.

The Song of Honour is an account of the translation of the human soul beyond death to the heart of Being, of "Beauty in her naked blaze."

In 1960, *The Skylark,* Hodgson's first book in forty-three years, appeared, and is already beginning to attract the attention that his work deserves. The lyric voice is as clear as ever in the shorter poems. A long poem, *The Muse and the Mastiff,* is an extraordinary fantasy of an old dog dreaming of a bear. The poem expresses the bear's point of view as he wanders, watching with increasing hostility the other wild creatures of the nightmare forest. It is an elaborate and whimsical allegory of a world grown old, a world which, in any case, is only an illusion soon to be dispelled. *The Weaving of the Wing,* one of the most beautiful of Hodgson's lyrics, ends thus:

> Ay, this I surely know:
> An aeon and a day
> From this, the crown of spring,
> As down the wild I go
> I'll tap that knotted spray
> And start a yellow wing!
>
> 'The work is done,' I'll hear
> And let my lips rejoice,
> 'Is done' I'll echo there
> The Universal Voice.

What this poet said of De la Mare—"He was rather like a cup under a sparkling fountain"—may also be applied to Hodgson himself.

Walter de la Mare's many lyrics have a unity that would seem to indicate the existence of some long major work behind them, but there is none, unless it be written in invisible ink on some wizard's parchment. All his work comes from ghost-land or fairy-land. There is always a deliberate incompleteness in his poems; it is as though he took us to a certain place of mystery and there left us to go forward by the light of our own imaginations. The results are, in every sense, enchanting. *The Listeners* is known to everybody, and, in general, de la Mare may be said to be another of those rare specimens, a fine lyric poet who is also popular.

Only Housman outranks him in that respect among modern English poets.

Such were the poets who were writing in England and Ireland at the beginning of the century, though the majority of them came to their full blooming later. They all took delight in experimenting within traditional forms; they were all virtuosi in rhyme and meter, and they all showed that the old forms are never really old but capable of infinite rejuvenation by poets who work in them with the steady rapture of artists who are also craftsmen. With such excitement and stirring in English poetry, who would wish to rise up in revolt against the ancient measures? Who would find any inclination—not to speak of necessity—to relapse into formless measures, into free verse? Not one poet. The eccentricity and confusion of twentieth-century poetry are, originally, the product of America.

The reason for this is quite clear. During the first decade of the century in America, E. A. Robinson was writing and had published two volumes, but, with the honorable exception of the Theodore Roosevelt family, he had almost no readers or outspoken admirers. Robert Frost was writing but was as yet unpublished. Emily Dickinson had already been forgotten. Outwardly, there were no American poets at all, merely a few genteel versifiers who, reducing the great traditions to weak conventions, made them highly vulnerable.

Until the publication of Frost's first book, *North of Boston,* in 1914 and the first book of Robinson's to bring him fame, *The Man Against the Sky* in 1916, there was a complete lack of contemporary American poetry in the great tradition. Into this vacuum rushed two powerful personages, Ezra Pound of Idaho and Amy Lowell of Boston.

Pound had been an expatriate since 1908 and he revisited his native land only once before his indictment for treason after the Second World War. Amy Lowell was Boston to the core. Previous to their meeting in London, Pound had published several volumes of verse that seemed little more than echoes of the lyrics of the aesthetic period, and a volume called *Ripostes,* the first indulgence in that polyglot style that would have us believe that the author was at ease in the classic languages, Provençal, French, Italian, Anglo-Saxon, and—though this came later—Chinese; Amy Lowell was the author of a single volume in the genteel convention, *A Dome of Many-coloured Glass*. Pound and Amy Lowell struck sparks like flint and steel and set the Imagist bonfire ablaze.

In 1914, the two collaborated in the editing of *Des Imagistes*, which included work by Pound, Lowell, H.D. (Hilda Doolittle), John Gould Fletcher, Richard Aldington (an Englishman), and others. A dinner of the group in July, to celebrate the anthology, was the last occasion at which most of them met in amity. The involved and numerous quarrels among the original Imagists provide fascinating gossip; the interested reader will find them recounted in Fletcher's autobiography *Life Is My Song* and hear echoes of them in almost any work reminiscent of the period.

The split between Amy Lowell and Pound was furious and almost immediate. The result was that Amy Lowell, back in Boston, got out the second anthology, *Some Imagist Poets*, alone. This book was much like the other, except for the omission of Pound and the addition of, strangely enough, D. H. Lawrence. As an introduction, there was a somewhat pompous little manifesto, standard poetical principles except for the defense of free verse and the insistence that poetry must always create pictorial images. "To the Imagists," wrote Robert Graves and Laura Riding in their *Survey of Modernist Poetry*, "style meant the 'use of language of common speech,' but in a careful way, as in a paint-box." Elsewhere they note that "Imagism is one of the earliest and the most typical of these twentieth-century dead movements. It had the look of a movement of pure experimentalism and reformation in poetry. But the issuing of a public manifesto of Imagism, its massed organization as a literary party with a defined political programme, the war it carried on with reviewers, the annual appearance of an Imagist anthology—all this revealed it as a stunt of commercial advertisers of poetry to whom poetic results meant a popular demand for their work...."

There is no reason to condemn further a group of poets most of whom are forgotten and all tiresome to read. I suppose that Amy Lowell's dramatic monologue, *Patterns,* is still popular, but most of her work is merely a shattered dome of many-colored glass, overgrown with weeds and largely neglected. It was with some surprise that I received last year a copy of a book called *A Shard of Silence*—selections from Amy Lowell's work—edited by an enthusiast, G. R. Ruihley. Although he had chosen the best of her pieces his title impressed me as being the last word on the subject.

The only contribution of the Imagists to poetry was indirect: they aroused so much public interest in the subject that the work of the two great poets, Frost and Robinson, probably benefited from the general excitement.

Nor was the excitement confined to the eastern poets. *Poetry, a Magazine of Verse,* was founded by Harriet Monroe of Chicago in 1912. With Ezra Pound as her European editor, Miss Monroe's magazine soon acquired an international and experimental savor which, in general, it has preserved down to the present day. Carl Sandburg's *Chicago Poems,* Edgar Lee Masters' *Spoon River Anthology,* and Vachel Lindsay's *The Congo* gave substance to the claims that Harriet Monroe was making for the Midwest.

In spite of the high respect in which I hold Carl Sandburg, and the deserved affection he has won from his fellow countrymen, his volumes of free verse are too far from my conception of what poetry should be to deal with here. But I can recommend *The People, Yes* as a rich collection of American folk epigram, humorous and shrewd.

The Spoon River Anthology was a sensational success in its day, but these character sketches in broken prose, supposed epitaphs of a Midwestern village, now call for an epitaph of their own.

A slight flurry of interest in Vachel Lindsay has been aroused by two recent biographies, the tragic narratives of a life smashed by a dominant mother. These may send us in curiosity back to *The Congo* or *The Chinese Nightingale,* but we return disappointed by their prolixity. Their rhythms are interesting, and in *The Chinese Nightingale* especially there are passages of promised beauty that are never quite fulfilled. It is not likely that we shall turn back to them again; perhaps they needed Lindsay's own spirited performance of them to keep them alive.

Some of the shorter pieces might be retrieved. There linger in my mind, for example, the two charming lines that end his poem about the moon:

> O traveler, abiding not
> Where he pretends to be.

Unfortunately, the rest of the poem is childish and banal. The Midwestern School, that Harriet Monroe viewed with such pride and whose works she so often published in *Poetry,* was an isolated phenomenon. It had no roots and it has produced no followers.

The two expatriates, Ezra Pound, the peripatetic Bohemian, and T. S. Eliot, the staid British bank clerk, met in London and, different externally though they were, became devoted partners in their theory of style, in their random excursions into the literature of other times and other nations, and the acceptance of the tenets of the French Symbolists, especially and quite obviously of Jules Laforgue. This symbolism that Pound and Eliot adopted, which had a crippling effect on American poetry for a period of about thirty years, consists of a series of unrelated and jarring references. "Eliot pasted fragments of the Elizabethan ornate," says Robert Graves, "against the modern nasty . . . and in his notes asked the reader to find, despite the continual change of subject and meter, a connecting thread of sense" from the various quotations woven into the text without quotation-marks and set in glaring incongruity to the context.

Five years after the publication of *The Waste Land,* Eliot declared himself a royalist, an Anglo-Catholic, and a classicist. Royalism is politically reasonable; it is obvious that the European nations that have kept their kings and queens are better off than those that have lost them. One can have no quarrel with Anglo-Catholicism—or, as it is in America, High Church Episcopalianism. But Eliot's "classicism" is something else again. His espousal of the eccentricities of the metaphysical school, the lack of clarity and proportion in his work, and the highly personal—almost confessional—quality of his poetry, stamp him as a belated, though chilly, romantic.

The Waste Land will always remain Eliot's typical masterwork, even though after its publication he so radically changed his point of view. Pound had so much to do with the editing and revising of this poem that it might almost be said to be the result of their collaboration. I well remember the stir it caused when it first appeared in *The Dial.* It was published without notes, and enthusiasts were often embarrassed to find that their quotations from it belonged to some other poet who had been incorporated without acknowledgment. A large proportion of such borrowings gives us, at least, the pleasures of recognition, and makes us feel a little superior to the unknowing.

Much of the effect of Eliot's poetry in general has been an appeal to the innate snobbishness of man. This desire to be a member of the elite was organized in the "new" criticism. When *The Waste Land* was republished, Eliot added fifty-one notes that accounted for his borrowings. Sometimes a quotation is twisted: thus in the line of Webster's "But keep the wolf far thence, that's foe to men," the "wolf" is changed to "Dog" and "foe" to "friend," not only perverting Webster's effect, but ironically implying that the dog is either a false friend or a very stupid one. (T. S. Eliot is devoted to cats, about whom he has written amusingly.)

Here is Webster's wonderful dirge from *The White Devil:*

> Call for the robin-redbreast and the wren,
> Since o'er shady groves they hover,
> And with leaves and flowers do cover
> The friendless bodies of unburied men.
> Call unto his funeral dole
> The ant, the field-mouse, and the mole,
> To rear him hillocks that shall keep him warm,
> And (when gay tombs are robb'd) sustain no harm;
> But keep the wolf far thence, that's foe to men,
> For with his nails he'll dig them up again.

And here is the echo in *The Waste Land:*

> That corpse you planted last year in your garden,
> Has it begun to sprout? will it bloom this year?
> Or has the sudden frost disturbed its bed?
> Oh keep the Dog far hence, that's friend to men,
> Or with his nails he'll dig it up again!
> "You! hypocrite lecteur!—mon semblable,—mon frère!"

The last line of all being an echo from Baudelaire, the poet may well say, at the end of *The Waste Land,* "These fragments I have shored against my ruins."

The only reason for explaining this mosaic style is that so many young Americans adopted it. They also adopted the general theme of *The Waste Land,* a romantic nostalgia for the past combined with a fastidious scorn for the present. The weary frustration of Pound and Eliot during the first war would indicate that they had been among its victims, yet it in no wise touched them. "But why," asks Robert Graves, "is he [Eliot] complaining? Who forced him, during the Battle of the Somme, to attend London tea-parties presided over by boring hostesses?"

In Eliot's later poems, such as *Ash-Wednesday* and the *Four Quartets,* the symbolism becomes less literary and more personal. The result is that interpretation becomes even more difficult. *The Waste Land* has certainly produced a more voluminous body of criticism than any other modern poem, but the later works run a close second. In fact, the entire school of so-called (I believe by John Crowe Ransom) "New Criticism" came into being not only under Eliot's influence but as an instrument for the analysis of his work.

Though Eliot dominated American criticism and poetry from 1922 until about 1950, he was not unchallenged. In 1933 Llewellyn Powys tried to analyze the reasons for his wide popularity. "We may well enquire," he says, "how it has come about that this poet with the predilections of London society, has enjoyed so universal a recognition.... His popularity may be accounted for in two ways. First from his disposition to champion orthodoxy.... Secondly, because of the dramatic interest of his personal predicament.... Mr. Eliot is a poet who, partly through accident, has allowed himself to become entrammeled by convention and society, and the reading world has been as intent to watch his spiritual struggles as it would be intent to watch an animal in a lethal chamber."

It is true that the public has followed his "personal predicament" with widespread curiosity. His royalism, Anglicanism, and classicism in 1927 were headline news. His conversion to the works of John Milton some years later had less conspicuous but more far-reaching effects. Quite suddenly, like St. Paul, he turned completely around, and what he had once reviled he came to love. The effect of this conversion was to bring Original Sin into fashion again, and the works of many of our younger poets are strewn with phrases of penitence to be recited outside the barred doors of Eden. Considering that *The Waste Land* is still the most influential of Eliot's poems, the combination of Original Sin, a distaste for the present, and elaborate personal symbolism has made much that passes for poetry these days incomprehensible. Nor must we omit mention of *self-pity,* a dreadful element in any art, which, implicit in Eliot's work, is almost openly expressed in much that we read.

"There is the overwhelming possibility—which I consider a probability—that our descendants will not like this generation's most characteristic poetry at all," wrote Ben Ray Redman in 1949. "They may well think that we have set too high a value on verbal mysteries, prosodic eccentricities, ambiguities, and ambivalent symbolism.... His [Eliot's] most serious and mature poems may, indeed, largely disintegrate into quotations."

Though the symbolism of T. S. Eliot's poetry and the incoherence of Ezra Pound's *Cantos* have served as damaging models for younger men, the more nearly complete sterilization and confusion of recent American poetry were accomplished by the New Criticism (most of whose adherents now deprecate the term). Vanderbilt University, in Nashville, Tennessee, was the focus of a group of poets who first called themselves The Fugitives, and then, under the leadership of John Crowe Ransom, turned from poetry to criticism.

The best commentary on the New Criticism is by St. Paul:

For if the trumpet give an uncertain sound, who shall prepare himself to the battle?

So likewise ye, except ye utter by the tongue words easy to be understood, how shall it be known what is spoken? for ye shall speak into the air....

"Brethren, be not children in understanding: howbeit in malice ye are children, but in understanding be men."

Next to St. Paul's, the best comment is by Professor Douglas Bush of Harvard: "The new criticism ... may be said to have reacted against historical, impressionistic, and moralistic approaches to poetry and to have concentrated upon direct and precise analysis of form and texture.... For a select though large number of literary students the new criticism has been an advanced course in remedial reading.... And one cannot miss the tone of conscious intellectual superiority, a superiority which arouses envious despair in the less highly endowed...."

The analysis applied to each phrase of a poem is always elaborate, frequently goes beyond the intentions or even the knowledge of the author, and is sometimes questionable if not inaccurate. Ludicrous mistakes in interpretation often occur when the New critic (who ideally would have to know *everything* that symbolism can refer to) slips beyond his depth. For example, Skelton and some of the

Elizabethan poets used the syllables "jug jug jug" to indicate the first part of the song of the nightingale. The phrase appears in *The Waste Land* with the same connotation. But a commentator in *The Saturday Review,* apparently ignorant of Tudor poetry, applauded the poet's skill in changing his tone with "jug jug"—to indicate a chamber pot!

Basically, the school of Eliot and Pound with its attendant "new" criticism is the old aestheticism of Wilde and his associates—art for art's sake—but directed into erudite and intellectual areas. Although in general literature it has declined almost to the point where we may speak of it in the past tense, it is still powerful in the English departments of our colleges and even some of our preparatory schools. Many a student dazzles his family with words culled from aesthetic jargon, such as *oxymoron, pejorative,* and the favorite of all, *dichotomy,* and impresses them with the supreme importance of *irony* in great poetry. Yet, so closely have his studies been focused on texts without reference to their general place in literature or the historical background, that he would be unable to say what poet came when, or, for example, who ruled England in the time of Shakespeare. Analysis and interpretation carried to fantastic lengths are the entire program, thus leaving the poem in a vacuum and detached from the spirit of the age that shaped the author's mind and directed his sensibilities.

With so many critics eager to analyze, it is scarcely to be wondered at that many poets yielded to the temptation to make their works a rich field for such examination, an Easter-egg hunt for hidden references. Some of these referential poems will stand up even though the reader be ignorant of their outside associations, in the same way that Emerson's *Brahma* can please one who has no knowledge of the *Upanishads,* and Yeats's *Sailing to Byzantium* cast its spell over one who has no familiarity with Byzantine mosaics. Too often, however, the symbolism of much recent poetry has been esoteric, a kind of abracadabra addressed by the poet-wizard to the critic-warlocks, and to even the most sympathetic reader yielding little more than the pleasure of solving a crossword puzzle instead of emotion and thought.

Several experimental poets who grew up with the century, although independent of the Imagist group or the aestheticism of

Eliot and Pound, went off on explorations of their own. First published in the more advanced little magazines or the handsome *Dial*—which printed both traditional writers, such as George Santayana, and innovators—these poets became the center of cults and by the mid-century had gained a more general audience that either jeered at them, read them out of curiosity, or hotly defended them. Two of the most important of them are Wallace Stevens and the poet who characteristically writes his name in small letters, e. e. cummings. In discussing these poets, and some of the younger poets later on, I shall have to quote more extensively than has been my custom so far, for with the experimental poets, much is to be explained, and, with the younger poets, much introduced.

It is important to remember that Cummings is a painter as well as a poet. He grew up in as cultured and conventional a household as the early 1900s in America could show. His father was the noted Dr. Edward Cummings, pastor of the church in Boston that had been Edward Everett Hale's. The son's tribute to the father, "my father moved through dooms of love," an elegy in seventeen quatrains, shows that dominant spirit as the embodiment of tenderness, courage, truth, and love. The son's tricks with syntax are not absent here, but they are used for concentration, not whim, and the careful reader will not find much difficulty in discovering the portrait of a splendid man set against the background of a degenerate age and inevitable death:

> ... Scorning the pomp of must and shall
> my father moved through dooms of feel;
> his anger was as right as rain
> his pity was as green as grain. . . .
>
> My father moved through theys of we,
> singing each new leaf out of each tree
> (and every child was sure that spring
> danced when she heard my father sing) . . .
>
> though dull were all we taste as bright,
> bitter all utterly things sweet,
> maggoty minus and dumb death
> all we inherit, all bequeath

and nothing quite so least as truth
—i say though hate were why men breathe—
because my father lived his soul
love is the whole and more than all

This poet has developed so consistently from his earliest work that
he is able to include without incongruity in his *100 selected poems*
of 1959 a sonnet, "it may not always be so; and i say," that first
appeared in *The Harvard Monthly* and was reprinted in that oft-
sought but rarely-found volume, *Eight Harvard Poets,* published
in 1917. The elements in his work that have increased with the
passing years are wit, punning, and social criticism voiced in the
most uninhibited satire. His joyous attack on the Communists
goes deeper than it may seem to on first reading; it is a summary
of characters controlled by envy and hatred:

kumrads die because they're told)
kumrads die before they're old
(kumrads aren't afraid to die
kumrads don't
and kumrads won't
believe in life)and death knows whie

(all good kumrads you can tell
by their altruistic smell
moscow pipes good kumrads dance)
kumrads enjoy
s. freud knows whoy
the hope that you may mess your pance

every kumrad is a bit
of quite unmitigated hate
(traveling in a futile groove
god knows why)
and so do i
(because they are afraid to love

The fear of love is not in this poet. His love poems, both carnal
and elegiac, form a large part of his work. The central group of
these poems are highly "poetic" in the adjectival style of such
early influences as Swinburne and Francis Thompson; they are

decorated, somewhat crepuscular, and move one strangely and vaguely like the music of Debussy. Some of these poems sound like Emily Dickinson, a most surprising influence in Cummings's work. As we move away from the central group of the love poems, at one extreme we find a not unamusing obscenity, at the other, old-fashioned sentimentality.

There are, in general, three degrees of technical performance in Cummings's work: the first—except for the absence of capital letters and some oddities of punctuation—traditional and formal; the second, showing a good deal of typographical trickery, in which words are broken in places or several words run together, or as onomatopoeia to the ear, suggesting to the eye the theme of the poem by typographical arrangement; the third, in which both typography and syntax are so confused that I, for one, cannot follow him. In his *100 selected poems,* he has wisely chosen, for the most part, poems in the first or second degree. In this volume Cummings's sprightliness, tenderness, humor, and satire are at their best. Forewarned that he must not be put off by occasional jeering, bawdiness, and sentimentality, the reader will be rewarded with magical surprises like the unpredictable sparkles of fireflies in the summer night. Beneath the playful extension of language, the poet's thoughts and points of view, as well as his emotions, emerge clearly. Cummings has a love of love, of the earth at the spring, of individuals who play truant from conventional responsibility, and a detestation for the mechanical and advertising age, for fossilized societies such as Communism, and for hypocrisy. Much of what he has written is childish or self-exhibiting—the wry young man who refused to grow up—but at his best he is a poet who is greater than his experiments.

Though Wallace Stevens was fifteen years older than Cummings, his poems came over the horizon later and more slowly. *Harmonium,* his first book, appeared in 1923, and was so disregarded that copies of the first edition could still be picked up at a bargain price as late as 1928. It is unlikely that Stevens himself cared much about this lack of popularity. To a poet who had called his work "bric-a-brac" he responded with a copy of a new book, inscribed "More bric-a-brac." Besides, he led a double life; he was not only a poet but a highly successful lawyer and businessman who became president of one of the great Hartford insurance companies. The success of his public career gave confidence to his private muse; he was a poet who felt in no need of being subsidized by applause. Fastidious and detached, he has gained enthusiastic devotees who, perhaps, overrate him, and read between his cryptic lines—as he gave them every opportunity to do—more weighty meanings than a less sympathetic audience would take the trouble to extract.

Much of his poetry is in the method of Coleridge's *Kubla Khan*, highly colored visual images constantly shifting one into the other like the fragmentary designs in a kaleidoscope. To these he adds, like a commentator from the wings, ironic observations that bid us take nothing seriously. But he is serious; his mockery is directed at a world in which emotions and intelligence have gone stale. He would not deny the hope of creating a fresh world in the mind of the artist. For example, he says in *The Idea of a Colony:*

> Nota: his soil is man's intelligence.
> That's better. That's worth crossing seas to find.
> Crispin in one laconic phrase laid bare
> His cloudy drift and planned a colony.
> Exit the mental moonlight, exit lex,
> Rex and principium, exit the whole
> Shebang. Exeunt omnes. Here was prose
> More exquisite than any tumbling verse:
> A still new continent in which to dwell.
> What was the purpose of his pilgrimage,
> Whatever shape it took in Crispin's mind,
> If not, when all is said, to drive away
> The shadows of his fellows from the skies,
> And, from their stale intelligence released,
> To make a new intelligence prevail? ...

The reader may object that in this passage of calm blank verse, typical of Stevens's technique, there are none of those images I spoke of. But read on:

> ... The natives of the rain are rainy men.
> Although they paint effulgent, azure lakes,
> And April hillsides wooded white and pink,
> Their azure has a cloudy edge, their white
> And pink, the water bright that dogwood bears.

And in their music showering sounds intone.
On what strange froth does the gross Indian dote,
What Eden sapling gum, what honeyed gore,
What pulpy dram distilled of innocence,
That streaking gold should speak in him
Or bask within his images and words? ...

One suspects that Stevens himself is inhabiting this colony he speaks of. The dreamlike non-sequiturs that he presents to us are those fragments of the real world that he deemed worth taking with him, bathed in the light of the "still new continent." Or else he sends back fragments that he has rejected, scored with his satire. His whimsical titles, which sometimes seem to have no connection with the poems they are attached to, are another evidence of his disdain for the commonplace. You will find no cup of tea in *Tea at the Palaz of Hoon,* and *LeMonocle de Mon Oncle* looks out on a varied series of pictures, twelve strophes dealing symbolically with human experience and aspiration and snapping suddenly into unexpected and unforgettable epigrams like this one:

The honey of heaven may or may not come,
But that of earth both comes and goes at once.

To One of Fictive Music is a title that sends us back to the "defunctive music" of Shakespeare's *Phoenix and the Turtle,* and, incidentally, introduces one of Stevens's best poems, an invocation to

Sister and mother and diviner love,
And of the sisterhood of the living dead
Most near, most clear, and of the clearest bloom....

She is the eternal muse, lost in a shallow and deadened age, and the poem ends with a plea:

Unreal, give back to us what once you gave:
The imagination that we spurned and crave.

Stevens's obscurity and the extravagance of his humor are deliberate nose-thumbings of a poet who does not care whether he is read or not. When his personal idiom is extreme, only his enthusiasts will follow him, but the reader should not be too easily put off. Many passages are not obscure but merely difficult, and many more are as clear as illustrative images can make them. There is much beauty in this poetry both in these images and in the iambic measures wherein they have their being. Whether or not there is enough to ensure long life to Stevens's work is a question that must be left to the definitive critic, Time.

Two modern poets of British origin may be mentioned to balance the two Americans I have discussed: W. H. Auden and Dylan Thomas.

Auden was born an Englishman but left England for America when the second world war broke out, and became an American citizen. There is an almost ironical pattern in this: America gave T. S. Eliot to England; then, after Eliot's influence had passed its peak, England presented America with W. H. Auden. He is too conspicuous a poet to pass over, but I should willingly do so, for nearly everything he has written increases my reluctance to deal with him.

To describe the general tenor of his work, I have been looking in vain for an English word that has all the overtones of the French *ignoble*. A Frenchman accompanies the word with a gesture that implies something to be rejected, and that is approximately my feeling for Auden's poetry. The wit sparkles, the clever meters dash to fulfill their functions, but "all is not sweet, all is not sound." It is as though this poet, with his nervous variations on the theme of personal and social decay, were writing in and for a period more advanced in dissolution than our own. There is worry but no tragedy; jest but no comedy; there is tension without strength and restlessness without a goal. It may be true that persons disintegrate, that the monstrous State, made infallible by democracy, consumes their efforts and their economy, but we have not reached—we are still far from reaching—the moral collapse from the imagined rubble of which these poems issue.

"It is not the passion of a mind struggling with misfortune, or the hopelessness of its desires, but of a mind preying upon itself, and disgusted with, or indifferent to all other things. There is nothing less poetical than this sort of unaccommodating selfishness. There is nothing more repulsive than this sort of ideal absorption of all the interests of others, of the good and ills of life, in the ruling passion and moody abstraction of a single mind; as if it would make itself the center of the universe, and there was nothing worth cherishing but its intellectual diseases. It is like a cancer, eating into the heart of poetry. But still there is power; and power rivets attention...." Hazlitt's description of Byron's poetry applies so well to Auden's that I need hardly add to it.

The core of the matter is that this poetry is completely *heartless*. Nothing is to be cherished, nothing glorified, and pity speaks only through the lips of contempt. It would be difficult to find a more repulsive work than *Miss Gee. A Ballad,* from which I shall quote a few stanzas. It is an early poem, but the author thought well enough of it to include it in his *Selected Poems* of 1958.

> Let me tell you a little story
>   About Miss Edith Gee;
> She lived in Clevedon Terrace
>   At Number 83.
>
> She'd a slight squint in her left eye,
>   Her lips they were thin and small,
> She had narrow sloping shoulders
>   And she had no bust at all.
>
> She'd a velvet hat with trimmings,
>   And a dark grey serge costume;
> She lived in Clevedon Terrace
>   In a small bed-sitting room....
>
> Miss Gee looked up at the starlight
>   And said: "Does anyone care
> That I live in Clevedon Terrace
>   On one hundred pounds a year?"
>
> She dreamed a dream one evening
>   That she was Queen of France
> And the Vicar of Saint Aloysius
>   Asked Her Majesty to dance.
>
> But a storm blew down the palace,
>   She was biking through a field of corn,
> And a bull with the face of the Vicar
>   Was charging with lowered horn....

Summer made the trees a picture,
    Winter made them a wreck;
She bicycled to the evening service
    With her clothes buttoned up to her neck.

She passed by the loving couples,
    She turned her head away;
She passed by the loving couples
    And they didn't ask her to stay....

Miss Gee knelt down in the side-aisle,
    She knelt down on her knees:
"Lead me not into temptation
    But make me a good girl, please." ...

She bicycled down to the doctor,
    And rang the surgery bell:
"O, doctor, I've a pain inside me,
    And I don't feel very well." ...

Doctor Thomas sat over his dinner,
    Though his wife was waiting to ring;
Rolling his bread into pellets,
    Said, "Cancer's a funny thing."

His wife she rang for the servant,
    Said, "Don't be so morbid, dear."
He said: "I saw Miss Gee this evening
    And she's a goner, I fear."

They took Miss Gee to the hospital,
    She lay there a total wreck,
Lay in the ward for women
    With her bedclothes right up to her neck.

They laid her on the table,
    The students began to laugh;
And Mr Rose the surgeon
    He cut Miss Gee in half.

Mr Rose he turned to his students,
    Said, "Gentlemen, if you please,

We seldom see a sarcoma
    As far advanced as this."

They took her off the table,
    They wheeled away Miss Gee
Down to another department
    Where they study Anatomy.

They hung her from the ceiling,
    Yes, they hung up Miss Gee;
And a couple of Oxford Groupers
    Carefully dissected her knee.

Further than this one cannot go. I am aware that admirers of
Auden would defend the poem as a shock that produces pity, but
the defense is nullified by the Freudian mockery and the presence
of the Oxford Groupers. Pity is absent; the central figure is con-
demned beyond reprieve, and we see her typical spinsterhood and
subconscious desire for the Vicar—resulting in religiosity—as objects
of a prancing Freudian joke. But to the reader, it is the poet, and not
Miss Gee, who calls for contempt.

This general rejection of humanity, this stripping away of all
mystery and aspiration, is the result of a materialistic, mechanistic
point of view so closely allied to the self-destructive elements of
the age that the poet's continuous complaints about them become
a colloquy between the pot and the kettle. We are responsible only
to our physical anatomy—the mind, too, being a part of that:

> ... our own wronged flesh
> May work undisturbed, restoring
> The order we try to destroy, the rhythm
> We spoil out of spite: valves close
> And open exactly, glands secrete,
> Vessels contract and expand
> At the right moment, essential fluids
> Flow to renew exhausted cells....

To mention the human soul in the presence of such poetry would
be embarrassing.

Are there no exceptions to the general qualities I have found in
his work? Naturally there are.

There is a series of poems on the characters in Shakespeare's *Tempest* that are interesting and lively. A few—a very few—of his lyrics have the quality of tenderness, none more so than "Lullaby," which is pure romance and melody, as the first and last stanzas may illustrate:

> Lay your sleeping head, my love,
> Human on my faithless arm;
> Time and fevers burn away
> Individual beauty from
> Thoughtful children, and the grave
> Proves the child ephemeral;
> But in my arms till break of day
> Let the living creature lie,
> Mortal, guilty, but to me
> The entirely beautiful. . . .
>
> Beauty, midnight, vision dies:
> Let the winds of dawn that blow
> Softly round your dreaming head
> Such a day of sweetness show
> Eye and knocking heart may bless,
> Find the mortal world enough;
> Noons of dryness see you fed
> By the involuntary powers,
> Nights of insult let you pass
> Watched by every human love.

Against the prevailing intellectualism of Auden's poetry and that of his followers, Dylan Thomas's lyric romanticism blows from the opposite quarter, and it is a vigorous, gusty wind, his Welsh spirit singing in intricate though musical stanzas reminiscent of the Irish poets at the turn of the century (especially Stephens and Gogarty) and the Elizabethans.

Thomas read beautifully, and his public readings in America gained him a large audience more quickly than printed pages could have done. His presence on the platform was modest and a little shy, and I have heard him become so absorbed in the poems of Thomas Hardy, whom he seemed to admire above all other poets, that he had to be reminded to read some of his own. It is unfortunate that his personal tragedy, his fatal alcoholism, was exploited by irresponsible and often self-seeking people to the detriment of his reputation as poet, and gained him a wide notoriety among those who care nothing for poetry but only for morbid sensationalism.

Another difficulty in approaching Thomas—and this one is intrinsic in his work—is the wide margin of interpretation he left in many of his lyrics wherein the effects are so clear, yet so unrelated, that the result is surrealistic. For example, such lines as

> The planet-ducted pelican of circles
> Weans on an artery the gender's strip

only half-yield, even with their context around them, an intelligible meaning. He has been speaking of Capricorn and Cancer, so we may take the "planet-ducted" pelican as a symbol of the universe, our interpretation supported by the "circles" that imply orbits. We are also aware of the legendary pelican that nourishes its young with its own blood. But when I, at least, come to "gender's strip," I throw up my hands in surrender. I suppose that such passages must be left to flow over one rather than into one. Read aloud, as Thomas read them, their lack of clear significance is almost compensated for by their incantational power, but they do not recommend themselves as something to be cherished and learned by heart.

Luckily, his work is not wholly in this vein. In modified form, it results in beautiful surprises in diction, such as the "dark-vowelled birds" at the end of his poem on the October wind. And when it is subordinated to the general meaning of the poem, as in the line

> As I rode to sleep the owls were bearing the farm away,

we are captivated by metaphorical verbs that sting us with reminiscent sensation. *Fern Hill,* the poem in which the line occurs, seems to me his finest lyric, and I shall quote it in full:

> Now as I was young and easy under the apple boughs
> About the lilting house and happy as the grass was green,
> The night above the dingle starry,
>   Time let me hail and climb
> Golden in the heydays of his eyes,

And honored among wagons I was prince of the apple towns
And once below a time I lordly had the trees and leaves
     Trail with daisies and barley
     Down the rivers of the windfall night.

And I was happy and carefree, famous among the barns
About the happy yard and singing as the farm was home,
     In the sun that is young once only,
          Time let me play and be
     Golden in the mercy of his means,
And green and golden I was huntsman and herdsman, the calves
Sang to my horn, the foxes on the hills barked clear and cold,
     And the sabbath rang slowly
     In the pebbles of the holy streams.

All the sun long it was running, it was lovely, the hay-
Fields high as the house, the tunes from the chimneys, it was air
     And playing, lovely and watery
          And fire green as grass.
     And nightly under the simple stars
As I rode to sleep the owls were bearing the farm away,
All the moon long I heard, blessed among stables, the nightjars
     Flying with the ricks, and horses
          Flashing into the dark

And then to awake, and the farm, like a wanderer white
With the dew, come back, the cock on his shoulder: it was all
     Shining, it was Adam and maiden,
          The sky gathered again
     And the sun grew round that very day.
So it must have been after the birth of the simple light
In the first, spinning place, the spellbound horses walking warm
     Out of the whinnying green stable
          On to the fields of praise.

And honored among foxes and pheasants by the gay house
Under the new-made clouds and happy as the heart was long
     In the sun born over and over,
          I ran my heedless ways,
     My wishes raced through the house-high hay
And nothing I cared, at my sky-blue trades, that time allows

In all his tuneful turning so few and such morning songs
    Before the children green and golden
        Follow him out of grace.

Nothing I cared, in the lamb white days, that time would take me
Up to the swallow-thronged loft by the shadow of my hand
    In the moon that is always rising,
        Nor that riding to sleep
    I should hear him fly with the high fields
And awake to the farm forever fled from the childless land.
Oh as I was young and easy in the mercy of his means,
        Time held me green and dying
    Though I sang in my chains like the sea.

The poems of Vernon Watkins, another Welsh poet, who was
Thomas's friend and mentor, are not well known in America, but
I prefer them to Thomas's work. They are very different, of course;
Watkins's lyric quality is more concentrated, less free-wheeling,
than Thomas's, and he is eloquently at ease among traditional forms.
His phrasing has a certain magnificence unusual in contemporary
poetry, and his long discipline in rhyme and meter gives him the
assured music that we often look for elsewhere in vain. If the names
of great poets in lyric mood occur to us in reading him, it is not
from any derivative element in Watkins's work, but because of his
equal claim on our attention. Images that are fresh yet inevitable
embody large themes, philosophical or religious, which indicate a
contemplative mind and profound emotions. Any poem from his
latest book, *Cypress and Acacia* (1959) would support my view. It
is a temptation to quote the splendid *Ode at the Spring Equinox,*
which echoes the wild weather and windswept voices of the seasonal
apocalypse in six sixteen-line strophes, but it is somewhat long for
our pages. Instead, I shall quote *Poets, in Whom Truth Lives* which
has a perfection and tone that recall the poems of Robert Bridges:

        Poets, in whom truth lives
        Until you say you know,
        Gone are the birds; the leaves
        Drop, drift away, and snow
        Surrounds you where you sing,
        A silent ring.

Lives of the dead you share,
Earth-hid, in tender trust.
Passion builds the air;
The beautiful and just
Through your tongues' ecstasy
Can hear and see.

Christ, where the cold stream ran
Which now lies locked in doubt,
A proud cock-pheasant can
Stretching its plumage out
More praise you than the rest
With his gold crest.

So hear those shepherds come,
Drawn by a secret fire,
Though Vergil's voice is dumb
Proclaiming to the lyre,
Through time by Winter torn,
The boy, new-born.

The abounding river stops.
Time in a flash grows less
True than these glittering drops
Caught on a thread of glass
Two frosty branches bear
In trance-like air.

Stoop, for the hollow ground
Integrity yet keeps
True as a viol's sound
Though the musician sleeps.
Strong is your trust; then wait:
Your King comes late.

The scope and intention of this book do not include a careful consideration of the many gifted poets, men and women, of our time, and a mere list of names would signify nothing and would doubtless give offense to those I neglected to mention. Even the enumeration of tendencies would be confusing at a time when individualism is encouraged to the point where a single poet may well embody an entire tendency in himself. We cannot attribute the disparate qualities of American poets wholly to the centrifugal force of this century; the size of the country has had a great effect in cultivating the widely different phenomena of their isolation. We have no center like London or Paris in times past. Our poets work apart in widely scattered sections of the continent, and though their eventual fate may be dictated by reviewers in the periodicals of New York, the metropolis itself has no literary community proportionate to its size. Many colleges and universities over the country have their professor-poets, and many an otherwise undistinguished provincial town has its resident laureate. The situation is rich but overcrowded. Were I to yield to the temptation to discuss the score of poets who occur to me as I write, I should not be able to disentangle myself from the subject for a hundred pages or more.

I can best solve my problem by speaking of three of our younger poets—in their early forties—who seem to me representative of our hopes for the future.

The three whose work seems to me especially significant are Howard Nemerov, Howard Moss, and Richard Wilbur. Their art is both vigorous and sensitive, and they are all masters of the traditional forms within which they experiment boldly, as all our best poets have done. They are free from the influence of the neo-aesthetes and passing affectations of style. It is not too soon to say that they are established, for they all are, by a considerable body of work. I have taken great joy in their poetry, not only for its beauty, but also because it is what I have long hoped for, a return to clarity, balance, and affirmation.

Nemerov is a humanistic poet. Observation always accompanies inner experience and keeps him safe from the school of private emotion. He communicates, he shares, and by the play of an extraordinarily agile imagination combines reminiscences and scenery familiar to us all in unexpected juxtapositions and conclusions. We respond to his emotions, and that is the great test for any poetry.

The music of his verse is persuasive, well attuned to his originality. Many of his poems, though retaining their lyric quality, are of substantial length, such as *Moses* (a poem of the Exodus) and *To Lu Chi*. In these re-creations of past figures, as well as in the shorter poems, Nemerov's philosophy of life is clear. Unterrified by the radical changes of our time that have moved others, Eliot, Pound, and Auden in particular, to fastidious despair or unseemly panic, he regards them as the natural sequence of human history:

> I live in a great and terrifying time,
> As Descartes did. For both of us the dream
> Has turned like milk, and the straight, slender tree
> Twisted at root and branch hysterically.

Not only are all things moving together as on a great tide, the current here accelerated and here retarded yet always in motion, but every individual act, every aspect of nature or human experience, however small it may seem in itself, is eternal; just as a pebble cast in the water sends out a series of ripples in sequence never ended. It is this dramatic importance of all things felt and observed that gives such emphasis to his pictures, as in the two opening stanzas of *The Loon's Cry:*

> On a cold evening, summer almost gone,
> I walked alone down where the railroad bridge
> Divides the river from the estuary.
> There was a silence over both the waters,
> The river's concentrated reach, the wide
> Diffusion of the delta, marsh and sea,
> Which in the distance misted out of sight.
>
> As on the seaward side the sun went down,
> The river answered with the rising moon,
> Full moon, its craters, mountains, and still seas
> Shining like snow and shadows on the snow.
> The balanced silence centered where I stood,
> The fulcrum of two poised immensities,
> Which offered to be weighed at either hand....

Much of Nemerov's poetry shows metaphysical wit. In *The Dancer's Reply,* for example, he employs an unusual image for the concept of reincarnation. Here are three of the seven stanzas:

> ... For isn't it your shame,
> Old gentleman, to live in time
> Our terrible dream, and lose the beat of it?

But if you have such wit,
Then go, become a timeless thought,
But when our bodies and souls, on the last day,

Couple and dance away,
Your soul will be made to stay
And learn its dancing-lesson after school....

Nemerov's symbols are usually simple and direct, as in *The Gulls,* where the sea birds, over the bleak spaciousness of ocean, flying into the storm, "white wanderers" over the "wide rage of the waters," are blessed for their pride and courage,

Compassed in calm amid the cloud-white storm.

Sometimes he is more elaborate, though easily decipherable. In *I Only Am Escaped Alone to Tell Thee,* with its reference to the verse from the Bible that Melville used as his superscription to *Moby Dick,* the poet flashes his light on a nineteenth-century woman standing before a mirror, itself recalling the sea—

the long inaccurate glass
Whose pictures were as troubled water.

She is encased in whalebone corsets, "no rig for dallying"—and with the word *rig* again we return to the sea—

...maybe only marriage could
Derange that queenly scaffolding—
As when a great ship, coming home,
Coasts in the harbor, dropping sail
And loosing all the tackle that had laced
Her in the long lanes....

After the link with the whale-ship, the blended images expand more darkly into the vast reaches of ocean and to the death of the whale, the little female vanity set against the agonizing mystery that engulfs all:

I see her standing in the hall,
Where the mirror's lashed to blood and foam,
And the black flukes of agony
Beat at the air till the light goes out.

This poem is from the author's *The Salt Garden* (1955), and I cannot close his book without citing *The Pond*. This is a four-page requiem for a little boy who was drowned. We see the pond through the seasons, concluding with the junglelike luxuriance of summer. The end of this poem is so moving that two sections demand quotation:

> The long year has turned away, and the pond
> Is drying up, while its remaining life
> Grasps at its own throat; the proud lilies wilt,
> The milfoil withers, catkins crack and fall
> The dragonfly glitters over it all;
> All that your body and your given name
> Could do in accidental consecrations
> Against nature, returns to nature now,
> And so, Christopher, goodbye. . . .
> . . . in nature too there is a history. . . .
> And thinking so, I saw with a new eye
> How nothing given us to keep is lost
> Till we are lost, and immortality
> Is ours until we have no use for it
> And live anonymous in nature's name
> Though named in human memory and art. . . .
> And I made this song for a memorial
> Of yourself, boy, and the dragonfly together.

Howard Moss has some qualities in common with Nemerov, a skillful technique, clear communication, and an appreciation of the values of overtones. His humor is more direct, less ironic than Nemerov's, and—here they part company—Moss in many of his poems is the celebrant of love. This is not romantic love, which he deals with satirically, or the love that boasts it has "the only fingerprint that can be changed at will," but love as the gift, as in the last two stanzas of *The Falls of Love:*

> They rise up shining who have love to give;
> Who give love freely may all things receive.
> Though streams they cross can never be the same,
> They know the waters of the earth are one;
> They see the waking face inside the dream
> Who know the variations are the theme.

I know so many stories marred by love,
What faces tell its crooked narrative.
Only lovers rest in summer's grove;
A winter comes where love will never live.
A body without love is in its grave—
They rise up shining who have love to give.

Moss is a seasonal poet, as the title of his latest book, *A Winter Come, a Summer Gone* (1960), shows. We are usually conscious of the time of year, even when it is conveyed indirectly, and in changing weather "the wind weighs roses as it swings the snow." In the poem called *Rounds* the four parts follow the cycle, summer, autumn, winter, and back to spring:

Black and white go down,
Spring's petals spring,
One by one, to life;
Pink, or vermilion,
Upon the branch's sling
Is born and is brief.
A longing for the sun
Stretches along the limb
And hangs the shapely leaf....

Angels, earth has shown
Its heart to be too big;
Standing in spring we sniff
A newness all our own,
And though its whirligig
Can spin us through one life,
And only one, on loan,
We dance a joyous jig
On limbs soon stiff.

A Swimmer in the Air, the title poem of one of Moss's books, represents man, who has evolved from a sea creature and become "part man, dry fish, and wingless bird," living in a world he was not originally designed for and into which he can fit himself only by repeated struggle and achievement. Moss says in another poem, "the true world's in our dreams." The dreamlike quality is in nearly all this poetry, not misty as a dream remembered, but bright and sharp as during the course of the dream. So it is in *Cry from Montauk* where after a series of reminiscent details, pictures that come and go, we are left with the one reality:

> I hope, some summer night, someone,
> Turning his less than empty eyes
> To see the lavish emptiness,
> Remembers in this starlit grove
> Love is the only place we live.

However we may deprecate our explosive period, Moss and other poets of his generation seem braced for the recoil. They are often dark, but they are not, like many of their immediate predecessors, negative and confused. On the contrary, they sniff the winds and take in all the sights with unusual vigor, stimulated, it would seem, by the profusion of things to be observed. Their work has a variety that defeats the best intentions of one who would describe it.

Richard Wilbur has a delicate, confident touch. Clarity and precision, which suggest the French language, sharpen his statements. With complete suspension of disbelief, we accept his most extravagant conceptions. Take, for example, his *Lamarck Elaborated* "The environment creates the organ," from his latest book *Things of This World* (1956):

> The Greeks were wrong who said our eyes have rays;
> Not from these sockets or these sparkling poles
> Comes the illumination of our days.
> It was the sun that bored these two blue holes.
>
> It was the song of doves begot the ear
> And not the ear that first conceived of sound:
> That organ bloomed in vibrant atmosphere,
> As music conjured Ilium from the ground....

In the last line of the second stanza he has casually inserted another related example of cause-and-effect, that Ilium came into being at the summons of art. We may pause over this, but finally we have to admit its truth: of a hundred dead cities to which antiquity may accord romance, only Ilium actually exists, conjured up by the music of Homer, Virgil, and the scores of poets who have echoed them. It is still with us, living though doomed, the topless towers awaiting the destructive torch that beauty has kindled.

Thus Wilbur often uses examples from the past—"the thronged Atlantis of personal sleep"—but they are, literally, brought up to date. He is the poet of the immediate; he dwells less on reminiscence than any other poet I can think of. There is no nostalgia for the past. Just once does he recall his boyhood, and then in statements so cool that one might almost miss the pathos and the general truth: that illusion may release us for a moment from the facts that limit and frustrate us. The poem is called *Digging for China,* and I shall quote the first and last sections:

> "Far enough down is China," somebody said.
> "Dig deep enough and you might see the sky
> As clear as at the bottom of a well.
> Except it would be real—a different sky.
> Then you could burrow down until you came
> To China! Oh, it's nothing like New Jersey.
> There's people, trees, and houses, and all that,
> But much, much different. Nothing looks the same." ...

So the boy got his trowel and dug until he "sweated like a coolie," and

> Before the dream could weary of itself
> My eyes were tired of looking into darkness,
> My sunbaked head of hanging down a hole.
> I stood up in a place I had forgotten,
> Blinking and staggering while the earth went round
> And showed me silver barns, the fields dozing
> In palls of brightness, pattens growing and gone
> In the tides of leaves, and the whole sky china blue.
> Until I got my balance back again
> All that I saw was China, China, China.

Wilbur is not a visionary; he has not even a touch of mysticism. When we read his *Love Calls Us to the Things of this World* we may remember, inappropriately, young William Blake's dooryard tree full of bright angels, coming and going. In Wilbur's version, the half-awake man sees outside the open window that "the morning air is all awash with angels."

> ... Some are in bed-sheets, some are in blouses
> Some are in smocks; but truly there they are.

Now they are rising together in calm swells
Of halcyon feeling, filling whatever they wear
With the deep joy of their impersonal breathing;

Now they are flying in space, conveying
The terrible speed of their omnipresence, moving
And staying like white water; and now of a sudden
They swoon down into so rapt a quiet
That nobody seems to be there.

                       The soul shrinks
   From all that it is about to remember,
From the punctual rape of every blessed day,
And cries,

          "Oh, let there be nothing on earth but laundry,
Nothing but rosy hands in the rising steam
And clear dances done in the sight of heaven. . . .

Here again we have the interlude of bright illusion before the man, wide awake, must plunge into the world of facts. This is a kind of fantasy, a tantalizing and impermanent transformation of prosaic details. Wilbur is willing to pay his spiritual taxes to reality. His poetry is, on the whole, that of a happy man comfortably at ease in life, and if reality sometimes frustrates him, it is, nevertheless, the substance of his work.

Like Nemerov and Moss, Wilbur maintains the disinterestedness —the aloofness from fashion and public events—that Matthew Arnold deemed so important for the writer. Furthermore, the three poets are all equable and mature artists. They have no juvenilia, nor do any of their poems fall markedly below the standard of their best. Whether this is the result of sound self-criticism and a judicious use of the waste basket, or of inspiration trained to excellent achievement, we cannot tell. At any rate, they all seem to have sprung full-armed from the brow of Euterpe.

The pattern of such performance, undeviatingly pursuing its highest aim, was set by our living classic, Robert Frost, from the first poem he ever published to the present. He is still with us, having gone his own way unruffled while so many vogues sprang up around him and vanished. Sturdy, wise, and active, he remains unconfused in times when personal confusion is almost a fad, unafraid in what lesser folk have called an age of anxiety. The effect of his influence is incalculable. Recording people and nature acutely and often humorously, he reawakens and sustains our faith in human destiny and, in particular, the importance of man as a responsible individual. He is the bearer of good tidings, knowing that

> The bearer of evil tidings,
> When he was half-way there,
> Remembered that evil tidings
> Were a dangerous thing to bear.

Sorrow is in his poetry as well as joy, love most of all, and a light, satirical scorn for what is too unworthy to be dwelt upon. His most playful sentence may suddenly be discovered to be one of his most serious. When we are with him, at his slightest remark we turn, and find ourselves as in a mountain meadow with all the expanse of the world spread out below us.

We chose our destiny before we were born, he says, and it is our lifework to make the most of it, rebounding from failure to try something else:

> There is our wildest mount, a headless horse.
> And though it runs unbridled off its course,
> And all our blandishments would seem defied,
> We have ideas yet that we haven't tried.

He bids us take a chance on life:

> Have I not walked without an upward look
> Of caution under stars that very well
> Might not have missed me when they shot and fell?
> It was a risk I had to take—and took.

"For me," he says, "the initial delight is in the surprise of remembering something I didn't know I knew." And a poem "begins in delight and ends in wisdom." This is the true quality of his work, and since, as I have remarked, much of his poetry is a dialogue between Frost and his reader, nothing remains unshared or unexplored between the two.

I have already defined the great poet as the one who gives us the best of himself and his experience of life as he has known it in his time. This is an accurate description of Frost. Were I writing music instead of prose, this paragraph would be a tremendous chorale, a sounding finale, in his honor. As it is, I can only say that Frost towers over every other twentieth-century American poet, our undisputed master beyond time.

Thus I leave my reader in the best of company. We are still in pursuit of poetry, and in the pursuit—as with most things—lie all the joy and the excitement. But since to pursue blindly is to lose the path altogether, we need some experience, some knowledge, and, above all, practice.

> The lips at Hallelujah
> Long years of practice bore,

says Emily Dickinson. That is true for the poet—and for his reader.

Some Recommended Reading

Most of the poems cited in this book will be found either in *The Oxford Book of English Verse 1250–1918* edited by Sir Arthur Quiller-Couch and published in Oxford by The Clarendon Press (1939) or in the one-volume, combined edition of *Modern American Poetry* and *Modern British Poetry, Midcentury Edition,* edited by Louis Untermeyer and published by Harcourt, Brace, and Company (1950). It is recommended that the reader provide himself with both these books.

The standard edition of Chaucer is edited by F. N. Robinson and published by Houghton, Mifflin Company (1933).

Norman Ault's collection of *Elizabethan Lyrics* (Longmans, Green and Co., 1925) is excellent, as is E. H. Fellowe's edition of *English Madrigal Verse, 1588–1632* (Oxford at the Clarendon Press, 1920).

Hyder Edward Rollins's Variorum Edition of *Shakespeare The Poems* and *Shakespeare The Sonnets* (2 volumes), published by J. B. Lippincott Company in 1944, contains all that has been said by scholars, commentators, and editors about these works as well as a careful reprint of the works themselves, and is of absorbing interest to the reader who wishes to do a little research.

For the general reader, I heartily recommend Edward Hubler's one-volume edition of *Shakespeare's Songs and Poems,* published by McGraw-Hill Book Company in 1959. This is a beautiful volume, with a clear, carefully edited text, and the notes printed conveniently on the opposite page from the poems.

Samuel Daniel's *Poems and a Defense of Rhyme* are edited, with an excellent introduction, by Arthur Colby Sprague (Harvard University Press, 1930).

All the books I have spoken of so far are in print. Out of print, but occasionally to be found in secondhand bookshops, is Arthur Symons's *A Pageant of Elizabethan Poetry* (Blackie and Son, 1906). I would advise the fortunate reader who finds a copy to snap it up. Out of print also, but to be found in most big libraries, is Sir Sidney Lee's two-volume edition of *Elizabethan Sonnets,* wherein will be found the sonnet sequences of Spenser, Sidney, Drayton, Daniel, and many lesser writers (E. P. Dutton Company). I should warn the reader against Lee's introduction, however, which is a masterpiece of stupidity. As Arthur Symons says, "Lee's fixed idea is that poets are very prosaic people at heart and that the Elizabethan poets in particular were persons rather lacking in emotion and imagination, who translated and adapted the poems of French and Italian writers with great ability."

In print are the following:

The one-volume combined edition of the complete poems of John Donne and William Blake, together with selected prose of Donne, with an introduction by the present writer (Modern Library Giant edition: Random House, 1946).

Seventeenth Century Lyrics, edited by Norman Ault (Longmans, Green and Company, 1927).

Metaphysical Lyrics and Poems of the Seventeenth Century, Donne to Butler, edited, with an Essay, by Herbert J. C. Grierson (Oxford, at the Clarendon Press, 1921).

The works of the more notable poets mentioned in my text will easily be found in standard editions, often in paperbacks. For example, Howard Nemerov has selected from the works of Longfellow and contributed a discriminating introduction for a paperback edition published by Dell's Laurel Poetry Series in 1959. This is the volume I speak of as necessary for the rehabilitation of this neglected poet. Milton, Pope, Wordsworth, Keats, Tennyson, Browning—all poets of this stature can be found in paperbacks, well edited and annotated. There is, in fact, no longer any financial excuse for an ignorance of literature, except in the case of Emily Dickinson. Dr. Thomas H. Johnson's three-volume edition of her poems, published by the Belknap Press of the Harvard University Press (1955), costs twenty-five dollars, and is, furthermore, the only authoritative and corrected text.

Although in my text I give some sketchy rules for the reading of Chaucer's work, the general reader who wishes the poems in modern

English will find Theodore Morrison's *The Portable Chaucer* (The Viking Press, 1949) well-nigh perfect in its approximation of the poet's intention. Mr. Morrison has also contributed an interesting and informative introduction.

For the reader interested in the subject of poetical celebrations of Queen Elizabeth, Elkin Calhoun Wilson's *England's Eliza* (Harvard University Press, 1939) is a comprehensive and fascinating compendium.

William Gaunt's *The Preraphaelite Tragedy* and his *The Aesthetic Adventure* are as lively as fiction in recording the people and events of these movements in nineteenth-century England.

For editions of contemporary poets, the reader is advised to consult the list of acknowledgments, which will serve as a bibilography of the modern poets mentioned in the text.

Index

Accent, 32, 34, 42
Adonais, Shelley, 71, 117, 155–156
Adornments, 38–41
AE (George William Russell), 148, 180
Aeneid, Virgil, 2, 21, 24, 81
Aiken, Conrad, 113–114
Aim was Song, The, Frost, 59
Airs, 128
Alastor, Shelley, 154, 157
Aldington, Richard, 188
Alexander's Feast, Dryden, 79, 119
Alexandrine, 38, 49
Alexandrine couplet, 61, 86
Alliteration, 38–39
Amaranth, Robinson, 83
American poets, 141, 163–171
  twentieth century, 187–200, 209–218
Amoretti, Spenser, 97, 99
And in the Human Heart, Aiken, 113
Anglo-Saxon verse, 23, 27
Annus Mirabilis, Dryden, 17, 66
Antiquarianism, 151
Arnold, Matthew, 29, 79, 109, 117, 122, 147, 152–154, 158–159, 163, 173, 216
Assonance, 39–40
Astrophel and Stella, Sidney, 97, 100
At the Ninth Hour, Mason, 112
Auden, W. H., 40, 200–204
Autumnal, The, Donne, 61

Bait, The, Donne, 54–55
Balade a Geffroy Chaucier, Deschamps, 121
Ballad stanza, 52, 54, 58
Ballade, 83–86
Ballade of Broken Flutes, Robinson, 84
Ballads, 55–56, 58
Bard, The, Gray, 79, 120, 146
Bards, 119–120
Bards of Passion and of Mirth, Keats, 157
Barnes, Barnaby, 97
Barrett, Elizabeth (*see* Browning, Elizabeth Barrett)

Bates, Katherine Lee, 99
Battle of the Books, Swift, 7
Battle of Brunanburgh, The, 120
Battle of Maldon, The, 120
Baudelaire, Charles, 166
Bellay, Joachim du, 91
Bells, The, Poe, 166
Ben Jonson Entertains a Man from Stratford, Robinson, 163
Beowulf, 115
Bion, 116–117
Birches, Frost, 82
Blake, William, 4, 10, 108, 128, 144, 147–149, 166, 180, 215
Blank verse, 24, 45, 80–83, 144, 159
Border Ballads, 58
Boyd, Ernest, quoted, 157
Bridges, Robert, 8, 27, 29, 44, 50, 74–76, 84, 88, 111, 115, 133, 144, 175–177, 207
Brooke, Rupert, 183
Browning, Elizabeth Barrett, 110, 162
Browning, Robert, 12–13, 28, 80, 98, 110–111, 115, 118, 154–155, 157, 161–163
Browning Societies, 157
Brut d'Angleterre, Layamon, 22–23
Buchanan, Robert, 110
Burns, Robert, 71, 147
Bush, Douglas, quoted, 193
By the Statue of King Charles at Charing Cross, Johnson, 178
Byron, Lord, 71–74, 90–91, 108, 115, 118, 153–154, 201

Campion, Thomas, 24–25, 78
Canterbury Tales, Chaucer, 28, 52, 61, 68, 118, 121–123
Cantos, Pound, 28, 193
Carlyle, Thomas, quoted, 160
Carman Paschale, Sedulius, 144
Carpe diem, 4
Carroll, Lewis, 110
Chambered Nautilus, The, Holmes, 14
Chapman, George, 104

Chaucer, 28–29, 52, 61, 68, 70–71, 85,
    118, 120–124, 161, 164
Chevy Chase, 56
Chicago Poems, Sandburg, 189
Chinese Nightingale, The, Lindsay, 189
Chloris, Smith, 97
Christabel, Coleridge, 26
Classicism, 24, 149–150
Closed couplet, 61
Coleridge, Samuel Taylor, 5, 13, 26–27,
    56, 79, 108, 127, 137, 148, 151, 157
Collins, William, 78, 147
Comedy of Errors, The, Shakespeare, 81
Concord Hymn, Emerson, 165
Congo, The, Lindsay, 189
Conversational style, 17–18
Conversations, Drummond, 135
Copper Sun, Cullen, 69
Courtship of Miles Standish, The, Long-
    fellow, 164
Cowley, Abraham, 22, 79
Crabbe, George, 108, 146
Crane, Stephen, 28
Crashaw, Richard, 135
Critics, 21, 29, 193–194
Cry from Montauk, Moss, 214
Cullen, Countee, 69–70
Cummings, E. E., 195–196
Cymbeline, Shakespeare, 132
Cypress and Acacia, Watkins, 207

Daffodil Fields, The, Masefield, 68–69
Dancer's Reply, The, Nemerov, 210
Dane, Clemence, 116
Daniel, Samuel, 24, 68, 97–99
Dante, 74, 89–90, 111
d'Arezzo, Guittone, 89
"Dark Lady of the Sonnets," 103–106
Dauber, Masefield, 69, 182
Davies, Sir John, quoted, 66
Death of the Hired Man, Frost, 83
Defense of Rhyme, Daniel, 24
Dejection, Coleridge, 79
De la Mare, Walter, 37, 49, 185–187
Delia, Daniel, 97, 99
Des Imagistes, 188
Deschamps, Eustache, 121
Deserted Village, The, Goldsmith, 108
Desportes, Philippe, 91
Dickinson, Emily, 6, 58–59, 114, 141,
    148, 164, 166–167, 187, 218
Diction, 9

Digging for China, Wilbur, 215
Dithyrambic verse, 27–28
Divine Comedy, Dante, 74
Don Juan, Byron, 72–74, 115, 154, 156
Donne, John, 8, 11–12, 25–26, 28, 34,
    47, 54–55, 61, 99, 106–107, 135–
    137, 157
Dover Beach, Arnold, 79, 163
Dowland, John, 129
Dowson, Ernest, 85–86, 178
Dr. Faustus, Marlowe, 61
Dramatic monologue, 118
Dramatic poetry, 115–116
Drayton, Michael, 19, 68, 92–94, 98,
    101–102, 115
Drummond, William, 135
Dryden, John, 5, 17, 26, 61, 66, 79, 117,
    122, 145–146
Dunciad, Pope, 118, 145
Dyer, Sir Edward, 134
Dynasts, The, Hardy, 172, 174, 184

Earthly Paradise, Morris, 68
Easter Wings, Herbert, 139–140
Ecclesiastical Sonnets, Wordsworth, 108
Eclogues, Virgil, 91, 117
Ecstasy, The, Donne, 137
Elegy, 117, 168
Elegy for a Nature Poet, Nemerov, 67
Elegy Written in a Country Churchyard,
    Gray, 20, 66, 117, 146–147
Eliot, T. S., 26, 29, 39, 50, 116, 137,
    154, 157, 166, 172, 190–195, 200
Elite, literary, 21–22, 191
Elizabeth, Queen, 126–127, 129
Elizabethan drama, 80, 127–128
Elizabethan poets and poetry, 23–25, 27–
    28, 56, 72, 117, 126, 135–136, 144,
    194
Emerson, Ralph Waldo, 148, 163–166,
    168
Emotions, 12
Endymion, Keats, 26, 62
English Bards and Scotch Reviewers,
    Byron, 118
English poets, early, 120–126
    Elizabethan (*see* Elizabethan poets)
    modern, 27–29
    Restoration, 135–145
    twentieth century, 172–178, 182–187,
    200–218
    Victorian, 157–163

Enjambment, 45–47
Epic poetry, 114–115
Epigram, 5, 93, 148
Erasmus, 126
Essay on Criticism, An, Pope, 145
Essay on Man, An, Pope, 145
Euphuists, 7
Evangeline, Longfellow, 36, 164
Eve of St. Agnes, Keats, 71
Everlasting Mercy, The, Masefield, 182

Faerie Queen, The, Spenser, 71, 126
Falls of Love, The, Moss, 212
Fame, 157
Fern Hill, Thomas, 205
Fidessa, Griffin, 97
Fitton, Mary, 103
FitzGerald, Edward, 20, 50, 162
Five-stress couplet, 60–63
Fletcher, Giles, 25, 97
Fletcher, John Gould, 188
Flying Scrolls, Hodgson, 185
Folk ballad, 108
Forsaken Mermaid, The, Arnold, 163
Four-stress couplet, 52
Four-stress quatrain, 59
France, 91
Frederick II, King of Sicily, 89
Free verse, 7, 27
French forms, 23, 83–88
Frost, Robert, 4, 6–7, 17, 20, 25, 30, 59–
    60, 64–65, 82, 113, 145, 164, 185,
    187, 189, 216–218
Fry, Christopher, 116
Fugitives, The, 193

Garden, The, Marvell, 142
Garland of Laurel, Skelton, 125
George III, King, quoted, 80
Gibbon, Edward, quoted, 7–8, 119
Give All to Love, Emerson, 165
Go, lovely rose, Waller, 62
Gogarty, Oliver St. John, 181–182, 204
Golden Echo, The, Hopkins, 169
Goldsmith, Oliver, 108
Gorboduc, 81
Graves, Robert, 183–184, 188, 190–192
Gray, Thomas, 20, 66, 79, 108, 117, 120,
    146–147, 174–175
Greek Anthology, 51, 134
Green, J. R., 120
Griffin, Bartholomew, 97

Growth of Love, Bridges, 111
Guest, Edgar, 20

Hallam, Arthur, 60, 158
Hardy, Thomas, 172–174, 184, 204
Harvey, Gabriel, 24
Hazlitt, quoted, 200–201
H. D. (Hilda Doolittle), 188
Henry the Eighth, Shakespeare, 25
Heraclitus, quoted, 2
Herbert, George, 59, 135–136, 139–140,
    148
Heroic couplet, 26, 61–63, 108, 145
Heroic quatrain, 65–68
Herrick, Robert, 4, 21, 61, 135–139
Hesperides, Herrick, 138
Hexameters, classic, 24
Hiawatha, Longfellow, 164
Hodgson, Ralph, 185–186
Holmes, Oliver Wendell, 14–16
Holy Sonnets, Donne, 99, 106, 136
Home, Daniel Dunglas, 162
Homer, 95
Homesickness, 3–5
Hopkins, Gerard Manley, 27, 37, 169–
    171
Horace, 4, 77–78, 84–85
*Horatian Ode upon Cromwell's Return
    from Ireland,* Marvell, 77
Hotson, Leslie, 102
House, Browning, 110, 162
House of Fame, Chaucer, 52
House on the Hill, The, Robinson, 86
House of Life, The, Rossetti, 111
Housman, A. E., 29–30, 44, 59, 174–175,
    187
Howard, Henry, Earl of Surrey, 81, 96–
    97
Humanism, 209–210
Hunt, Leigh, 156
Hunting of the Snark, Carroll, 110
Huxley, Aldous, 159
Hymn to God my God, in my Sickness,
    Donne, 11
Hyperion, Keats, 145

Iambic feet, 32–34, 38
Iambic pentameter, 34, 43, 76
Idea, Drayton, 92–93, 97, 101–102
Idea of a Colony, The, Stevens, 198
Idyls, Theocritus, 116
Idylls of the King, Tennyson, 115

Il Penseroso, Milton, 52, 107, 145
Imagism, 22
Imagists, 188–189
In Bohemia, Bates, 99
In Flanders Fields, McCrae, 87
In Harmony with Nature, Arnold, 163
In Memoriam, Tennyson, 60, 158
In Time of Pestilence, Nashe, 131
Incantation, 117
Irish poets, 29, 148, 178–182, 204
Irish Renaissance, 179

James I of Scotland, King, 68
Jensen, Johannes V., 3
Johnson, Dr. Samuel, 11–12, 20, 146–147
Johnson, Lionel, 178–179
Johnson, Thomas H., 141, 166
Jonson, Ben, 26, 31–32, 73–74, 79, 122, 134–135

Keats, John, 3, 13–16, 26, 43, 56, 62–63, 71, 78, 80, 95, 108–109, 122, 144–145, 153, 155–156, 161
King Cole, Masefield, 63, 182
Kubla Khan, Coleridge, 5, 13

La Belle Dame sans Merci, Keats, 56, 108, 157
Lady's Not for Burning, The, Fry, 116
L'Allegro, Milton, 52, 107, 145
Lamb, Charles, quoted, 101
Lamia, Keats, 157
Landor, Walter Savage, 1
Lang, Andrew, 109
Last Invocation, The, Whitman, 169
Laura, Tofte, 97
Lawrence, D. H., 188
Layamon, 21, 23
Leaves of Grass, Whitman, 167
Lee, Sir Sidney, 98
Lentino, Giacomo da, 89
Licia, Fletcher, 97
Lindsay, Vachel, 189
Line length, 9, 38, 55
Listeners, The, De la Mare, 37, 49, 186
Locksley Hall, Tennyson, 158
Lodge, Thomas, 97
London Snow, Bridges, 74–75, 84
Long meter, 59
Longfellow, Henry Wadsworth, 36, 164
Loon's Cry, The, Nemerov, 210
Lotos Eaters, Tennyson, 39

Love Calls Us to the Things of this World, Wilbur, 215
Love Song of J. Alfred Prufrock, Eliot, 154
Lovelace, Richard, 135
Lowell, Amy, 22, 156, 187–188
Lowell, James Russell, 161
Lucifer in Starlight, Meredith, 109–110
Lycidas, Milton, 79, 117
Lyric poetry, 108, 116–118, 127–134, 159, 186, 204, 207, 209
Lyrical Ballads, 151

McCrae, John, 87–88
MacFlecknoe, Dryden, 117
Macleish, Archibald, 40
Madrigals, 128–133
Man Against the Sky, Robinson, 79, 187
Marlowe, Christopher, 45–46, 52–53, 61, 81
Marot, Clément, 91
Marvell, Andrew, 17–18, 47–48, 77–78, 135, 141–144
Masefield, John, 9–10, 52, 63, 66–69, 112, 182–183
Mason, Madeline, 112
Masters, Edgar Lee, 189
Memorial Verses, Arnold, 117
Meredith, George, 49, 158
Meres, Francis, quoted, 93
Metaphysical writing, 11–12, 54, 135, 210
Meter, 23, 25–26, 52
    irregularities in, 34–37
    rhythm and, 31–33
Metrical foot, 9, 33
Millay, Edna St. Vincent, 20–21, 112
Milton, John, 33, 40–41, 44–47, 52, 79–80, 107–108, 115, 117, 135, 142, 144–145, 157, 192
Mine the Harvest, Millay, 21, 112
"Miscellanies," 128
Miss Gee: A Ballad, Auden, 201
Mock epic, 115
Modulated verse, 79
Monk's Tale, Chaucer, 70, 85, 122
Monroe, Harriet, 189
Moods, 12–13
Moore, Merrill, 112–113
Morality, 14–16, 163
Morley, Thomas, 128, 130
Morris, William, 68

226

Moschus, 116–117
Moss, Howard, 209, 212–214
Murder in the Cathedral, Eliot, 39, 50, 116
Mystics, 147–149, 166, 180–181, 185–186

Nashe, Thomas, 130–131
Nature, poetry and, 29–30, 108, 146, 151–153, 163, 167
Nemerov, Howard, 67–68, 164, 209–212
"New criticism," school of, 192–193
New Yorker, The, 67, 69
Newton, Sir Isaac, 126
Nicolson, Harold, quoted, 2
North of Boston, Frost, 187
Nosce Teipsum (Know thyself) Davies, 66
Nuptial Sleep, Rossetti, 110
Nymph's Reply to the Shepherd, The, Ralegh, 53–54

Obscurantists, 7–8
Observations in the Art of English Poesie, Campion, 24
Ode, the, 77–79, 108
Ode on a Distant Prospect of Eton College, Gray, 147, 174
Ode to Evening, Collins, 78
Ode on a Grecian Urn, Keats, 14–15, 78, 157
Ode to the Immortal Memory . . . , Jonson, 79
Ode on the Intimations of Immortality . . . , Wordsworth, 79, 148
Ode to a Nightingale, Keats, 3, 78, 156
Ode to the West Wind, Shelley, 74, 78, 83, 155
On First Looking into Chapman's Homer, Keats, 43, 94–95, 109
On a Girdle, Waller, 62
On Melancholy, Keats, 157
On the Virgin Mary, Herrick, 61
Othello, Shakespeare, 81
Ottava rima, 68, 72–74
Overtones, 9–11

Paeons, 33, 37
Palace of Art, The, Tennyson, 158
Parlement of Foules, The, Chaucer, 68
Pastoral, 91, 116–117, 145–147
Pastoral elegy, 117, 155

Paradise Lost, Milton, 115, 144
Parthenophil and Parthenophe, Barnes, 97
Passionate Shepherd to His Love, The, Marlowe, 52–53
Pater, Walter, quoted, 4
Patterns, Lowell, 188
Pentameters, 27
Percy, Thomas, 56, 108
Pessimism, 172–174
Petrarch, 89–90, 97, 111
Phillis, Lodge, 97
Phoenix and the Turtle, Shakespeare, 60
Pindar, 78–79
Pindaric ode, 77–79
Pitch, 45
Plaine and Easie Introduction to Practical Musicke, Morley, 128
Platitudes, 6
Plato, 112
Pléiade, the, 91
Plum Tree by the House, The, Gogarty, 181
Poe, Edgar Allan, 12, 159, 164–166
Poems, intention of, 13–16, 18–22
  rereading of, 2
  revision of, 12–13
  style of, 16–17
  timelessness of, 2–3, 29
Poems of Felicity, Traherne, 141
Poetic diction, 11, 18
Poetic style, conversational, 17
  development of, 22–51
  rhetorical, 16–17
Poetry, appreciation of, 21
  civilization and, 1–2
  classic, 28, 30
  and the commonplace, 6
  English, background of, 119–171
  great, 29
  kinds of, 114–118
  moods in, 3–5
  prose and, 8–9
  root of, 30
  rules of, 19
Poetry, a Magazine of Verse, 189
Poets, and diction, 9
  experimental, 194–200
  good, 8
  judging of, 21
  modern, 27–29
  popularity of, 20–21

Poets, and diction, religious, 136–141
   task of, 6–7
Polyolbion, Drayton, 115
Pond, The, Nemerov, 212
Pope, Alexander, 5, 19, 26, 28, 62–63,
   95, 108, 115, 118, 126, 145–146
Pound, Ezra, 28, 166, 172, 187–190,
   193–195
Powys, Llewellyn, 192
Prelude, The, Wordsworth, 6
Pre-Raphaelite Brotherhood, 178
Princess, The, Tennyson, 78, 159
Prodigal Son, The, Robinson, 63
Progress of Poesy, Gray, 79

Quarles, Francis, 61
Quatorzains, 74
Quiet Work, Arnold, 163

Ralegh, Sir Walter, 53–54, 135
Ransom, John Crowe, 193
Rape of the Lock, The, Pope, 115, 145
Reading aloud, 41–52
Realism, 30
Redman, Ben Ray, 192–193
Refrains, 9, 56
Religious poets, 136–141
Reliques of Ancient English Poetry,
   Percy, 56, 108
Renaissance, the, 90, 94, 102, 117, 161
Restoration, the, 135
Reynard the Fox, Masefield, 52
Rhetorical style, 16–18
Rhyme, 24, 40–41
Rhyme-schemes, 55, 60
Rhymesters, 20
Rhythm, meter and, 31–33
   time, 42
Right Royal, Masefield, 52
Rime of the Ancient Mariner, Coleridge,
   56, 108
Rime royal, 68–70
Ring and the Book, The, Browning, 115,
   161
Robinson, E. A., 25, 63–64, 79–80, 82–
   87, 113, 146, 163, 187, 189
Rollins, Hyder, Edward, 102
Romantic poets, 17, 56, 71–72, 108, 147–
   149, 157
Romantic Revolt, 149–150
Romanticism, 149–153
Rondeau, 87–88

Rondel, 88
Ronsard, Pierre de, 91
Rose-cheeked Laura, Campion, 24, 78
Rossetti, Dante Gabriel, 10–11, 84, 90,
   110–111, 157, 162, 178
Rousseau, Jean-Jacques, 150
Rubaiyat, FitzGerald, 20

St. Paul, quoted, 193
Salt Garden, The, Nemerov, 212
Sandburg, Carl, 28, 189
Sandys, George, 60
Santayana, George, 95–96, 111–112, 195
Sassoon, Siegfried, 183–185
Satire, 117–118, 145, 174
Scansion, 33
Scotland, ballads of, 55
Scott, Sir Walter, 56
Sedulius, 144
Sestina, 88
Shakespeare, William, 4, 13, 21, 25, 42,
   44, 46, 61, 68, 73, 76, 80–82, 92–94,
   97–98, 102, 104–106, 116, 126–127,
   132–134
Shelley, Percy Bysshe, 12, 50, 71–75, 77–
   78, 80, 83, 117, 153–154, 156–157
Shephard, Esther, 168
Shorter Poems, Bridges, 175–177
Siddal, Elizabeth, 110
Sidney, Sir Philip, 56, 90, 97–98, 100–
   101, 135
Single Hound, The, Dickinson, 166
Sitwell, Edith, 157
Skelton, John, 68, 124–126, 193
Skylark, The, Hodgson, 186
Sleep and Poetry, Keats, 62
Sludge, the Medium, Browning, 162
Smith, William, 97
Sofonisba, Trissino, 81
Sohrab and Rustum, Arnold, 163
Song of Honour, The, Hodgson, 185–186
Song for St. Cecelia's Day, Dryden, 79
Songs of Innocence and Experience,
   Blake, 147
Sonnet sequences, 97–100, 110–111, 113
Sonnets, 88–114, 170
Sonnets, Shakespeare, 97
Sonnets from the Portuguese, Browning,
   110
Sorley, Charles Hamilton, 183
Spenser, Edmund, 68, 71, 90, 97–100,
   117, 122, 126, 134, 157

Spenserian stanza, 68–72, 108, 122
Sphinx, The, Wilde, 60
Spondee, 32–34, 43
Spoon River Anthology, Masters, 189
Stanyhurst, Richard, 24, 171
Stanza, 9, 52
Stanza forms, 52–77
Stauffer, Donald A., 179
Stephens, James, 116, 148, 179–180, 199, 204
Stevens, Wallace, 194, 197–200
Strayed Reveller, The, Arnold, 163
Suckling, Sir John, 135
Sunflower, Blake, 10
Sweet, George Elliott, 102
Swinburne, Charles Algernon, 49, 110, 158, 178
Symbols and symbolism, 11, 190, 192
Symons, Arthur, quoted, 137

Taylor, Edward, 141
Tears of Fancy, Watson, 97
Tempest, The, Shakespeare, 42, 82
Tennyson, Alfred Lord, 39, 60, 72, 78, 115, 144, 157–161
Terza rima, 74
Testament of Beauty, The, Bridges, 29, 115, 133, 177, 184
Theocritus, 116
Things of This World, Wilbur, 214
Thomas, Dylan, 200, 204–207
Thomson, Francis, 71, 153, 156
Thorpe, Thomas, 102–103
Threnos, Shelley, 77
Time meter, 23
Time units, classical, 24
Tithonus, Tennyson, 159
To Autumn, Keats, 78, 157
To Helen, Poe, 165
To His Coy Mistress, Marvell, 17, 142
To Lovers of Earth: Fair Warning, Cullen, 70
Tofte, Robert, 97
Tottel's Miscellany, 96
Tragedy, 3–4, 174
Traherne, Thomas, 141, 148
Trevelyan, G. M., quoted, 120
Triolet, 88
Triolet, Bridges, 88
Tristram, Robinson, 82
Troilus and Criseyde, Chaucer, 123
Tuft of Flowers, The, Frost, 64
Two Voices, The, Tennyson, 160

Under the Microscope, Swinburne, 110, 158
Upanishads, 165

Vanderbilt University, 193
Vaughan, Henry, 135, 140–141, 148–149
Venus and Adonis, Shakespeare, 76
Verse, elements of, 31–118
   technique of, 8–9
Victorian poets, 157–163
Vigna, Pietro della, 89
Village, The, Crabbe, 108, 146
Villanelle, 83, 86
Villon, François, 84
Virgil, 2, 21, 81, 91, 94, 117

Wales, 120, 207
Waller, Edmund, 26, 61–62
Walt Whitman's Prose, Shephard, 168
Waste Land, The, Eliot, 190–191, 194
Watkins, Vernon, 207–208
Watson, Thomas, 97–98
Webster, John, 191
West-Running Brook, Frost, 82
Whitman, Walt, 6, 27–28, 148, 159, 163–164, 167–169
White Devil, The, Webster, 191
Wife of Usher's Well, The, 57–58
Wilbur, Richard, 209, 214–216
Wilde, Oscar, 41, 60, 102, 157, 178, 194
Wild-goose Chase, The, Fletcher, 25
Will Shakespeare, Dane, 116
Williams, Charles, quoted, 176
Williams, William Carlos, 28
Windhover, The, Hopkins, 169–170
Winter Come, a Summer Gone, A, Moss, 213
Woolf, Virginia, quoted, 124
Words, magic of, 1–30
Wordsworth, William, 2, 6, 13, 79–80, 89, 98, 108–109, 148, 151–153, 157
World War I, 183–185
Wriothesley, Henry, Earl of Southampton, 102–103
Wyatt, Sir Thomas, 68, 72, 96–97
Wylie, Elinor, 156

Yeats, William Butler, 148, 178–181

Zepheria, 97–98

About the Author

Robert Hillyer is one of America's most honored and respected poets, winner of the Pulitzer Prize in poetry in 1934. His most recent volumes of verse include *The Death of Captain Nemo, The Relic and Other Poems,* and *Suburb by the Sea.* He is also the author of a book on the techniques of poetry for poets, *First Principles of Verse.* He has written several novels, and his poems and articles have been widely published. He is currently Professor of English Literature at the University of Delaware.